Lincoln Christian College

D1255859

COCKNEY PHONOLOGY

OSLO UNIVERSITY PRESS

Distribution Offices:

NORWAY:

KARL JOHANSGATE 47, OSLO

UNITED KINGDOM:

CANNON HOUSE, MACKLIN STREET

LONDON W. C. 2

COCKNEY PHONOLOGY

by

EVA SIVERTSEN

OSLO UNIVERSITY PRESS

OSLO STUDIES IN ENGLISH, NO. 8

Publications of the British Institute in the University of Oslo

General editors:
Professor Paul Christophersen
Professor Kristian Smidt

Printed on a grant from The Norwegian Research Council
for Science and the Humanities

Printed in Norway by
A.s. John Griegs Boktrykkeri
Bergen — 1960

427. 1
5. 6

BAKER & TAYLOR

97. 13

19 Jan 71

Acknowledgements

I wish to express my sincere gratitude to the following institutions, which, by their generous grants, have enabled me to carry out the research which has resulted in the present volume: the British Council, the Norwegian Advanced Teachers' College (*Norges Lærerhøgskole*), the Norwegian Research Council for Science and the Humanities (*Norges almenvitenskapelige forskningsråd*), and the University of Oslo.

I am grateful for valuable help and advice received from many colleagues, in particular from the staff of the Department of Phonetics of University College, London, and from Professor Paul Christophersen of the University of Oslo, who has read the manuscript and suggested many improvements as regards both content and form. These scholars are not, of course, responsible for any opinions expressed in this book.

I owe a debt of deep gratitude to the social settlement in Bethnal Green where I was allowed to live for a time, to take part in the club activities and thereby to get to know the Bethnal Greeners.

My warmest thanks are due to my informants, who graciously gave me so much of their time, who patiently helped me learn their language, and who opened their homes to me and showed me true Cockney hospitality and friendliness.

E. S.

37925

Table of Contents

viii

xiii

LIST OF FIGURES AND TABLES

1. Introduction

1.1. PURPOSE

This monograph has a double purpose:

(1) It is a description of the phonological system of Cockney, including a detailed phonetic statement of allophonic variations.

(2) It is an attempt to apply a certain line of approach in linguistic analysis to specific language material, with a discussion of the underlying principles.

The work grew out of an earlier, unpublished study,[1] where the emphasis was heavily on the phonetic side and on a comparison with the Received Pronunciation of Southern England. The material suggested some interesting phonological problems, and afforded an opportunity to apply a model of phonological analysis and description which had been provided by several modern American linguists.

Long theoretical digressions would have made the description of Cockney less readable. Nor should an understanding of the underlying theory have to be gleaned from scattered paragraphs throughout the book. I have therefore lifted the discussion of theoretical and methodological questions out and placed it as a separate chapter; in the description itself the theoretical framework is taken for granted.

The general phonological section does not pretend to be a new and original contribution to linguistic theory. It is rather a survey and evaluation of several points of view.

[1] University of Oslo thesis, 1951.

1.2. COCKNEY VS. RP

The analysis is *descriptive*, but not purely so: it is also *comparative*, in that a comparison is made, at every point, with the Received Pronunciation (RP) of Southern England.[1] Two publications by Daniel Jones are my authority for what constitutes RP: *An Outline of English Phonetics* and *An English Pronouncing Dictionary*. I have pointed out differences from RP both in allophonic manifestation and in distribution.

Among the distributional characteristics of Cockney I would like to underline the contrast between the syllable peaks /oh/ and /ow/ (§ 3.451), the neutralization of several syllable peaks before pre-junctural /l/ (§ 4.414), and the phonemic status of the glottal stop (§§ 4.14, 7.32). Apart from these systemic differences Cockney differs from RP in the distribution of phonemes within specific morphemes.

1.3. THE LANGUAGE

Cockney is a term which is used, rather vaguely, for speech forms found in the London area. There is no homogeneous speech form which might be so labelled: there are regional and local variants, and there are social and stylistic differences. I use the term in a somewhat restricted sense.

The material was collected only in a limited area in the East End of London, viz. Bethnal Green, a borough just east of the City, among the class of manual and unskilled labourers. My informants were transport workers, factory workers (men and women), housewives, and children.

Some forms of Cockney are supposed to be more 'genuine' than others. Julian Franklyn[2] distinguishes between the 'light' Cockney of the Cockney clerk and the 'deep' Cockney of the

---

[1] For a definition of this term, see D. Jones, *An English Pronouncing Dictionary* p. XV sq.

[2] *The Cockney*, e.g. pp. 234, 236, 241.

coster. I have made no special study of the strange sounds and
phrases which may be picked up from costermongers and street
criers in the East End of London. My material is the day-to-day
talk, the unaffected speech, of the inhabitants of Bethnal Green.
But even within this fairly uniform class there are considerable
differences.

None of the informants had had any education beyond the
elementary stage, and once they had left school they were only
occasionally in contact with people of another social background.
However, they were exposed to the continual influence exer-
cised by such institutions as the school, radio and television,
and the cinema. Every day people like my informants hear a
type of speech different from their own, spoken by people who
are considered as being, socially, their superiors. As for the
younger generation they receive, even at the elementary stage,
an education which deliberately tries to uproot dialectal peculiarities in their speech, to correct their pronunciation according
to a widely accepted norm, to polish and standardize them in
speech as well as in manners. This does not mean that they
adopt, wholesale and without any effort, any such standard
form of speech. But it does mean that their speech is changing.
Some people have a better ear for dialect differences than others.
Some consider it more important to approach a standard speech
form than others do. The result is a conflict not only between
two, but between a great number of different speech forms, such
as we find it in many large urban areas today. There is inter-
ference on a large scale, but of a type which is not easily subjected
to the kind of analysis proposed by Uriel Weinreich.[1] There
are erratic pronunciations, vacillations, uncertainty, lack of
consistency.

However, in this mass of sometimes apparently conflicting
material one can detect certain trends. One will notice that the
speaking situation, the interlocutor, the subject of conversation
are all of them important for the particular forms used, and this

[1] *Languages in Contact;* see particularly 1.1 and 1.2.

applies to vocabulary, grammar, phonology, and allophonic variants. One can vaguely perceive the outlines of several styles of speech, though one can by no means define them. There is thus some justification for distinctions such as the one made by Franklyn. My informants themselves distinguish between what is 'rough' or 'real' Cockney and what is 'posh'.

The subject of this study is the speech form or forms used when the speakers are most off their guard, when they are least conscious of how they speak, in so far as it is possible to make such an abstraction. The abstraction of such a hypothetical speech form may be arbitrary, or at least difficult: the analyst must exercise his own judgement to decide whether the speech is natural and unaffected or not. However, one has to assume that it is possible.

1.4. DATA

The data were collected in London over several periods from 1949 to 1956. Most of the observations were made on natural unrecorded speech, in conversations in the homes of the informants, in the street, and in clubs. Some details of allophonic variations were studied by letting the informants read word lists prepared for the purpose, but data obtained in this way were always checked against conversation material. Extensive tape recordings were made of both types of data, for later reference and checking.

The informants sometimes volunteered comments on various aspects of the dialect, and during the later stages of the investigation, when their rôle as regular informants was over, I elicited their opinion on several points. I was particularly interested in learning (1) which out of several allophonic variants was 'rough' and which was 'posh', and (2) whether they considered certain pairs of sounds or words as 'the same' or 'different'. Another type of information was provided by spelling mistakes in letters from one woman informant (EE) to the analyst. Such data, however, were used only as interesting illustrations of my own observations and conclusions.

The material is all my own. However, I have taken the opportunity to check earlier statements on and descriptions of Cockney, by laymen and phoneticians alike.[1] I have also used the clues provided by literature trying to suggest Cockney speech by means of unusual spellings.[2] I have made an effort to check whether the traditional, conventionalized view of what Cockney is applies to present-day speech.

As far as phonetics is concerned, this is mainly an impressionistic articulatory study of the traditional type, not an instrumental (articulatory or acoustical) one. Thus, the vocoid charts represent nothing but auditory impression projected on kinesthetic feeling. However, a few points have been made the subject of instrumental-acoustical analysis (§ 5).

1.5. INFORMANTS

Most of my informants were people who had some connection with a social settlement in Bethnal Green. The settlement is a centre for club activities, for all age groups and for both sexes. In such a setting it is relatively easy to compare the speech forms of various groups: children of pre-school age, a club for children from six to ten, a young teenage club, a senior youth club, a young mothers' club, a club for elderly women, and a mixed club for oldsters.

For intensive study some elderly housewives were picked out. I chose women rather than men because (1) a housewife has more time to spare during the day, and (2) a woman will feel more at ease in front of a woman analyst. Men felt much more embarrassed and could not quite let themselves go, at least when there were only a few people present; they remained too conscious of their manners and their speech. With women

[1] See references in 6.10.
[2] Cf. 6.22.

I could establish some common ground of interest, and I was accepted more willingly as one of them.

The following paragraphs contain some biographical notes on the main informants.

EE, a housewife, was born around 1890. Her parents' families came from Hertfordshire, but they themselves were born in London. EE herself was born in St. Luke's parish, London E.C. 2, where she lived till she was ten years old. After one year in Tottenham the family moved to Bethnal Green, where EE had lived ever since, in or near Brick Lane. Her father, originally employed in the printing trade, later worked as a house repairman; he died when EE was a child, and the family had to 'rough it' till the children were old enough to earn their own living. EE did not even complete the ordinary elementary school training, as she was kept out of school for one year. She left school at fourteen, and worked as a feather-curler till she got married; she had later gone back to the same trade for shorter periods, but otherwise her main occupation had been a housewife's. Her husband learned the frame-guilding trade, and was later a packer in various factories. He had frequently been out of work, and money had been scarce in the family. Among her children, the younger son had had better training and wider experience than the other members of the family; he was now a policeman; however, his influence on the speech form of his mother seemed to have been negligible.

EE was my main informant. Her family — husband, children, and grandchildren — provided valuable data for a comparison between the sexes and between three generations.

MM was born in 1892 in a house near the corner of Bethnal Green Road and Brick Lane, and had lived in the same district all her life. Her parents were both of Irish origin. She had been married twice; her second husband did linoleum and carpet laying for the Ministry of Works. She had several children and grandchildren. In addition to her housework she had had work outside her home all her life until 1953, in the trade of upholstery buttoning and in tea factories. By her neighbours she was considered a 'real, rough Cockney girl', in speech and manners. MM was, after EE, my main informant.

EC was born in 1874 just off Shoreditch, and she had lived near Bethnal Green Road ever since. Her father was a dock worker, and her husband, who was dead, had been in the cabinet-making trade. She had several children and grandchildren, but lived alone. She left school at fourteen years of age, and was apprenticed to a feather-curling firm. After she got married she made fancy cardboard boxes for a firm at home. By her neighbours she was considered an authority on life in Bethnal Green in 'the good old days', before the slum clearance at the turn of the century.

AP, a sister of EC, born in 1876, was also a widow. Her husband had worked as a corker at a wineseller's. She had children, but lived alone. She left school at fourteen, and like her sister she worked as a feather-curler till she got married. Since then she had lived in the same flat, just off Shoreditch, never going out to work except for a very brief period. She knew all the old Cockney songs, and was always ready to entertain with them.

None of these four informants had travelled. They might go as far as Southend for a holiday, but never farther. They were all regular members of one of the clubs at the social settlement, and this club seemed to be their main interest in life outside their family. None of them went to the cinema or to the pub any more, though they might have done so in their younger days. But the wireless was generally kept going all day.

1.6. TERMINOLOGY, SYMBOLS, TRANSCRIPTION

The terminological framework for the *phonetic* description of sounds is that of the International Phonetic Association (IPA),[1] as applied, for example, to RP by D. Jones in various publications.

[1] *The Principles of the International Phonetic Association*, 1949.

The terms vocoids and contoids, as distinct from vowels and consonants, are used in the sense given to them by K. L. Pike:[1] vocoids and contoids are phonetic units, vowels and consonants are functional units. Pike has also given us the terms phonemic norm[2] and manifestation.[3]

The terms needed for the *phonological* description, such as macrosegment, microsegment, syllable, syllable peak, syllable margin, onset, coda, interlude, peak nucleus, peak satellite, vowel, consonant, semiconsonant, juncture, intonation, intonation centre, terminal contour, pitch level, are used in the sense given to them by Charles F. Hockett.[4]

The term phoneme is taken in the sense 'as most usually used in American linguistics',[5] i.e. including the so-called suprasegmental phonemes as well as the segmental ones, and as used by Hockett himself in *A Course in Modern Linguistics*.[6] Seen

---

[1] *Phonetics* p. 78, *Phonemics* p. 13 sq.

[2] *Phonemics* p. 62a.

[3] *Language*, especially §§ 3.5 (2), 3.52, 8.4.

[4] *A Manual of Phonology* and *A Course in Modern Linguistics*. There is some confusion in the use of the terms 'nucleus' and 'peak'. Even Hockett occasionally uses the term 'nucleus' in the sense of our 'peak' (e.g. *A Course in Modern Linguistics* pp. 339, 348 sq.), and this is the term used by Gleason (*An Introduction to Descriptive Linguistics* p. 28) and Pike (*Phonemics* pp. 62b, 149; *Language* §§ 8.65, 9.223). Personally I prefer the term 'nucleus' as more in accordance with the terminology of IC analysis. An alternative would be to relabel our terms in the following way:

syllable peak	→ syllable nucleus
syllable margin	→ syllable margin
peak nucleus	→ nuclear peak (or nuclear nucleus)
peak satellite	→ nuclear satellite

However, I do not want to add to the confusion by changing Hockett's terminology, since I follow him in other respects. I have therefore, for the sake of consistency, adopted Hockett's terminology throughout.

[5] C. F. Hockett, *A Manual of Phonology* p. 74.

[6] See e.g. *op.cit.* p. 112: 'A phoneme is defined, not as a sound produced in such-and-such a manner, but as a point of reference in an interlocking network of contrasts.' See also pp. 24 and 26.

from another point of view, the phonemes may be considered
as the ultimate non-simultaneous phonological constituents of
a language.[1] In this sense Malone is right when, deploring the
terms segmental and supra-segmental phonemes, he asserts that
'all phonemes are segmental'.[2]

In formulaic statements certain abbreviations are used, the
most important of which are: V = vowel, C = consonant,
S = semiconsonant, P = plosive (or stop), F = fricative,
N = nasal. Other occasional abbreviations are explained or can
be understood from the context. RP = the Received Pronunciation of Southern England (cf. 1.2). IPA = the International
Phonetic Association.

For the phonetic transcription I follow the usage of the IPA
as nearly as possible. The symbols do not always have exactly
the same value as for the transcription of RP; thus, [ʌ] is used
as a symbol for the stressed vowel of *but*, though its phonetic
value in Cockney differs considerably from that of RP. The
table in 3.03 shows the phonetic symbols used for the phonemic
norm of the syllable peaks. A definition of the exact value of
every letter symbol should be sought under the phoneme one
of whose allophones it represents.

The following diacritical marks and extra symbols are used:

ˌ	below	syllabic
̆	above	non-syllabic
·	after	long
˳	below	voiceless
ˬ	below	voiced
̃	above	nasalized

---

[1] On ultimate phonological constituents, see C. F. Hockett, *A Manual
of Phonology* p. 126 sqq. Hockett uses the term in another sense: not
being concerned with simultaneity, he analyses vowels and consonants
into distinctive features as the ultimate phonological constituents.

[2] 'The Phonemes of Current English', 1959 edition p. 240. But cf.
also 7.41 of the present study.

··	above	centralized
_	below	retracted
.	below	close
،	below	open
˗	below	dental
'	upper right-hand corner	glottalized
ǀ	before	(phonetic) primary stress
،	before	(phonetic) secondary stress
′	above	(phonemic) primary stress
`	above	(phonemic) secondary stress
+		internal juncture
↓ ↑ ǀ		terminal contours
#		terminal contour (unspecified)

I have tried to avoid overloading the transcription with diacritical marks. I have simplified and stylized the transcription, and adopted a standard symbol, or diagraph, for each allophonic type. I have generally disregarded, in my transcription, many observable features, such as aspiration, glottalization, and devoicing of consonants. Such allophonic variations are described in the text. The more unpredictable allophonic variants, such as the occurrence of the glottal stop, [ʔ], as an allophone of /t/, or of [ɤ̆] as an allophone of /l/, are always marked, though.

Two types of transcription are used, one phonetic, included in square brackets, [ ], and one phonemic, included between slanting lines, / /. The symbols used in the phonemic type of transcription do not have the usual IPA value: they are symbols for functional units rather than for phonetic segments. For reasons of economy, ease of printing, and legibility, most utterances quoted are given only in phonemic transcription.

2. Phonological System

2.1. FRAMEWORK OF DESCRIPTION

I have accepted the phonological analysis worked out by C. F. Hockett in his *Manual of Phonology* and his *Course in Modern Linguistics* as a convenient framework for my description. This applies, for example, to the units of macrosegment and microsegment, to the distinction between syllable peaks and syllable margins, between peak nuclei and peak satellites, and between onsets, codas, and interludes, to the setting up of one internal juncture and three contrastive stresses, and to the analysis of intonation as a system of four pitch levels and three terminal contours (or external junctures).

2.2. NUMBER AND TYPES OF PHONEMES

The following phonological units are postulated for Cockney:
There are six vowel phonemes (/i e a o u ə/), twenty-two consonant phonemes (/p t k b d g f θ s ʃ v ð z ʒ m n ŋ l r h j w/), three types of stress (primary stress /ˊ/, secondary stress /ˋ/, and absence of stress), one internal juncture (/+/), three terminal contours (/↓ ↑ |/), and four pitch levels (/¹ ² ³ ⁴/).

2.3. MACROSEGMENTS AND MICROSEGMENTS

The utterance chunk between two terminal contours is called a *macrosegment*. A macrosegment may consist of one or more microsegments plus an intonation:

/jés↓/ *Yes.* /ajl+télə↓/ *I'll tell her.*
/aj+félt+sə́w+kwíh↑ sə́w+bád↑ aj+wówkt+stréjt+inð́éh+
ənléjd+onð́ə+béd↓/ *I felt so queer, so bad, I walked
straight in there and laid on the bed.*

The last utterance quoted consists of three macrosegments.

The section of an utterance occurring between two internal
junctures, or between an internal juncture and a terminal contour,
or between two terminal contours when there is no internal
juncture within the macrosegment, is called a *microsegment*.
A microsegment may consist of one or more syllables[1] plus a
stress pattern:

/déj↓/ *day,* /tədéj↓/ *today,* /káhbənèjtid+sə́wdə↓/ *carbonated soda.*

The last utterance quoted consists of two microsegments.

A microsegment may contain no stresses, e.g. /ij/ and /tuð́ə/
in

/ij+séz+tuð́ə+blə́wk|/ *he says to the bloke,*

or one or more secondary stresses, e.g. the first two microsegments in

/sə̀waj+sèd+jés↓/ *so I said yes,*

or one or more primary stresses, with or without any secondary
stresses:[2]

---

[1] There is no example in my data of a microsegment consisting of
less than a syllable, a type mentioned by Hockett: *'s cool* would, if it
occurred in Cockney, probably be [ṣ'kʊ·] /əskúl/, i.e. two syllables, and
Bea's going would be /bíjz+gə́win/, where /bíjz/ is homophonous with
the genitive *Bea's* (*A Course in Modern Linguistics* pp. 57 and 85; cf.
also *A Manual of Phonology* p. 62 sq.).

[2] According to Gleason (*An Introduction to Descriptive Linguistics*
4.12) and Hockett (*A Manual of Phonology* p. 67) a microsegment may
contain only one primary stress. Microsegments with more than one
primary stress are rare in my data. However, if we do not accept the
possibility of such microsegments it is difficult to account for the non-
velarized allophone of /l/ in the last of the utterances quoted and in

/wénij+gót+kówt↑/ *when he got caught,* /éniwèj↓/ *anyway,*
/ʃij+áz+əbjúwtifəláwm↓/ *she has a beautiful home.*

2.4. SYLLABLE TYPES

Any syllable contains a *peak*, which may be simple or complex.
A simple peak consists of one of the six vowels. A complex
peak consists of one of the six vowels as peak nucleus plus one
of the peak satellites /h j w/.

In addition, a syllable may contain one or two *margins*. A
syllable margin consists of one or more of the twenty-two
consonants. A pre-nuclear margin is called an *onset;* a post-
nuclear margin is called a *coda.* The occurrence of consonants
in onsets and codas is subject to certain restrictions (4.01 sq.).

If P represents a syllable peak and M a syllable margin
the following syllable types occur: P, MP, PM, MPM. Thus:

P: /áj/ *I;*
MP: /máj/ *my,* /dráj/ *dry;*
PM: /ájs/ *ice,* /ás/ *ass,* /áhsk/ *ask;*
MPM: /májs/ *mice,* /fráŋk/ *frank.*

Simple and complex peaks do not occur with equal freedom.
The minimum macrosegment is a *complex* peak (plus a stress
pattern and an intonation), and before a juncture or a phonetic
syllable cut (2.5) only the following syllables occur in stressed
position (P_s indicates a simple peak, P_c a complex one): $-P_c$,
$-P_cM$, $-P_sM$. They may be preceded by an onset:

/ówlás↓/ *all us,* and for the presence of /r/ in utterances like /fáhrəwéj↓/
far away, /bət+ðéhrəgéjn↓/ *but there again.* Postulating a juncture after
/l/ and /r/ in such cases would be in defiance of phonetic facts — /l/ and
/r/ are true phonetic interludes, belonging neither to the preceding nor
to the following syllable — and it would be in conflict with a distributional fact which is otherwise clearly in evidence: the non-velarized
allophone of /l/ ('clear l') and the phoneme /r/ never occur before juncture (4.01, 4.4122, 4.4221). In *A Course in Modern Linguistics* Hockett
admits more than one primary stress in a microsegment provided they
do not occur on adjacent syllables.

−P$_c$: /ə́w/ *oh,* /lə́w/ *low;*
−P$_c$M: /ə́wk/ *oak,* /brə́wk/ *broke;*
−P$_s$M: /ə́s/ *us,* /bə́s/ *bus.*

Stressed −P$_s$ does not occur before juncture or syllable cut. In unstressed syllables both simple and complex peaks occur, with or without onsets and codas:

P$_s$: /ə+néjm/ (or, more usual, /ənéjm/) *a name,* /ə/ in /bétə/ *better;*

MP$_s$: /ðə+néjm/ (or /ðənéjm/) *the name,* /də/ in /wíndə/ *window;*

P$_s$M: /ən+éjm/ *an aim,* /ək/ in /stə́mək/ *stomach;*

MP$_s$M: /mis+ə́nt/ (or /mis+hə́nt/) *Miss Hunt,* /liʃ/ in /íŋgliʃ/ *English;*

P$_c$: /aj+díd/ *I did,* /ij/ in /lə́kij/ *lucky;*

MP$_c$: /ðij+áws/ *the house,* /dij/ in /sə́ndij/ *Sunday;*

P$_c$M: /ijz+áwt/ (or /ijzáwt/) *he is out,* /ijz/ in /lə́kijz/ *Luckies;*

MP$_c$M: /fajn+áwt/ (or /fajnáwt/) *find out,* /tajmz/ in /sə́mtajmz/ *sometimes.*[1]

However, among the simple peaks only /i u ə/ occur in syllable-final position before juncture or phonetic syllable cut.[2]

2.5. SYLLABLE CUT[3]

2.50. In some of the utterances quoted above the syllable in question is part of a microsegment consisting of more than

[1] Several of the utterances quoted have variants with a secondary stress instead of no stress.

[2] For a statement of the distribution of syllable peaks, in stressed and unstressed position, finally and non-finally in the syllable and in the utterance, see Kemp Malone, 'The Phonemes of Current English'. Malone's analysis differs considerably from mine, and the dialects to which it applies are different from Cockney.

[3] For notes on the syllable division in American English, see Kemp Malone, 'The Phonemes of Current English'; M. Swadesh, 'On the Analysis of English Syllabics'; G. L. Trager and B. Bloch, 'The Syllabic Phonemes of English'.

one syllable. In such cases the syllable cut is only a sub-phonemic feature of the utterance; as a manifestation of juncture (2.6) the position of the syllable division is phonemically relevant, but within a microsegment it is predictable from the stress pattern, from the nature of the interlude (whether it is a zero interlude or an interlude consisting of one or more consonants), and from the nature of the interlude consonants in question, and of the preceding syllable peak. The conditioning factors seem to be the same as in RP, and they are only briefly summarized here. On the following pages, V represents a vowel, S one of the semiconsonants /h j w/, and C any other consonant; the syllable cut is marked by a hyphen, in an otherwise phonemic transcription. A really phonetic transcription is enclosed in square brackets, and the syllable cut may be shown by the position of the stress marks. In the VSC formulae ' represents any stress, secondary or primary.

2.51. In –VV–[1] the syllable cut is always between the vowels, irrespective of the stress conditions, since there is never more than one vowel in a syllable:

/piánə/ pi-ánə *piano*, /əfíliejtid/ əfíli-ejtid *affiliated*, /áhgjuin/ áhgju-in *arguing*.

2.52. In –VSV– there might theoretically in many cases be two ways of making the syllable cut, since those consonants that serve as peak satellites may also be onset consonants.

[1] According to Hockett (*A Manual of Phonology* p. 63) there is a zero interlude in English only after a complex syllable peak, as in *layer*. We conclude that there is always a juncture between simple peaks. Such a distributional statement does not cover the Cockney data, nor is it valid for RP. There is at least a potential contrast between /stə́diin/ *studying* (*hard*) and /stə́di+in/ *study in* (*class*), /váljuə/ *valuer* and /válju+ə/ *value a* (...) (such pairs *may* also be homophonous, without any juncture), and there seems to be no phonetic justification for postulating a juncture in utterances like /piánə/ *piano*, /lə́kiə/ *luckier*, /ikspíhriəns/ *experience*, /ínfluəns/ *influence*, /lúis/ *Lewis*, /síj+tuit/ *see to it*.

However, the ambiguity is limited because of the following distributional facts.

(1) /h/ occurs as an onset consonant only after juncture before a stressed vowel. Therefore junctureless VhV is always Vh–V, whatever the stress pattern:

/sóhəh/ sóh-əh *saw her*, /híhit/ híh-it *here it (is)*, /fohéniwən/ foh-éniwən *for anyone*.[1]

(2) /e a o/ never occur in syllable-final position in my data. I tentatively consider this a systemic limitation in their distribution, and eSV, aSV, oSV are always eS–V, aS–V, oS–V, whatever the stress pattern:

/séjit/ séj-it *say it*, /ðejáv/ ðej-áv *they have*, /ðejəv/ ðej-əv *they have (never)*, /páwə/ páw-ə *power*, /ajáhst/ aj-áhst *I asked*, /ajəl/ aj-əl *I'll (do it)*, /indʒójin/ indʒój-in *enjoying*.

(3) Not all possible VS combinations occur as syllable peaks. The following combinations do not occur: */iw ew uj əj/. Therefore iwV, ujV, əjV are always i-wV, u-jV, ə-jV (*e-wV does not occur):

/ʃiwóz/ ʃi-wóz *she was*, /wiwəz/ wi-wəz *we was (kids)*, /tujúw/ tu-júw *to you*, /duju/ du-ju *do you (know)*, /əjə́h/ ə-jə́h *a year*, /fəjə/ fə-jə *for your (tea)*.

Consequently the only ambiguous sequences might be ijV, uwV, əwV. When the first syllable is stressed the syllable cut is after S, since no vowel occurs stressed in syllable-final position:

/bíjin/ bíj-in *being*, /dúwin/ dúw-in *doing*, /gə́win/ gə́w-in *going*.[2]

When the first syllable has no stress ij-V and i-jV, uw-V and

---

[1] There are variant forms of most of these and the following utterances. Thus, *saw her* may also be /sóh+əh/ ['sɔ·ʔɜ·] or /sóhrəh/; *for anyone* may be /foh+éniwən/ [fɔ·'ʔenɪwən], /fohréniwən/ or /fəréniwən/.

[2] There is no example of *V́SV́. V́S+V́, with internal juncture, would probably occur instead: /gə́w+ín/ go *in*, /íj+íz/ *he is*.

u-wV, əw-V and ə-wV are all possible, since /i u ə/ occur in
syllable-final unstressed position. I shall postulate the occurrence
of an internal juncture in the case of ij-V, uw-V, and əw-V:

/ʃijúwstə/ ʃi-júwstə *she used to* vs. /ðij+íŋgliʃ/ ðij-íŋgliʃ
the English, /bérij+im/ bérij-im *bury him;*
/tuwín/ tu-wín *to win* vs. /tuw+íjt/ tuw-íjt *to eat;*
/juwəz/ ju-wəz *you was* (*doing*) vs. /juw+əl/ [juˑɫ] *you will*
(*never*), /tuw+əh/ tuw-əh (*say*) *to her;* /ðəwóh/ ðə-wóh *the
war* vs. /gəw+áhftrim/ gəw-áhftrim *go after him;* /ðəwəz/
ðə-wəz *there was* (*never*) vs. /səw+əkóws/ səw-əkóws *so of
course.*

The unstressed sequences ij+V and uw+V are rare. There are
more frequent alternants in iV and uV:

/bériim/ *bury him*, /tuəh/ (*say*) *to her;*
or with a secondary stress on /i u/:

/ìjad+fóh/ *he had four*, /jùwəl/ *you will* (*never*).

Secondary stress is also common on the first syllable of əwV:

/sə̀wəkóws/ *so of course.*

2.53. In –VSSV– the syllable cut is between the semiconsonants, whatever the stress pattern:

/fóhjə/ fóh-jə *for you*, /ðáts+wəhji+gə́w/ wəh-ji *that is
where you go*, /síjjə/ síj-jə *see you*, /ajwəz/ aj-wəz *I was*
(*never*), /ówwəz/ ów-wəz *always*, /ʃə́wjə/ ʃə́w-jə *show you*,
/juwwəz/ juw-wəz *you was* (*ill*).

The reason for this regularity is that there is no SS combination
pre- or post-vocalically. The RP pre-vocalic sequence /hj-/ has
no parallel in Cockney; if we were to find it it would be only
after juncture: –V+hjV–.

2.54. In –VCV– the syllable cut is after, or in the last part
of, C, particularly when the first syllable is stressed (VC-V):

/lívin/ *living,* /wédin/ *wedding,* /mánə/ *manner;*
though /l r/ may be more truly phonetic interludes, being closely
linked to both syllables (VlV and VrV):

/sílij/ *silly,* /bórə/ *borrow.*

When the first syllable is unstressed the syllable cut is before,
or in the first part of, C (V-CV):

/səpɔ́wz/ *suppose,* /misélf/ *myself,* /bátəsij/ bát-ə-sij *Batter-
sea,* /lɔ́ndənə/ lɔ́n-də-nə *Londoner;*

though again /l r/ are true phonetic interludes:

/ítəlij/ *Italy,* /séntʃərij/ *century.*

In –VSCV– the syllable cut is between the semiconsonant
and the consonant, whatever the stress pattern (VS-CV):

/ríhlij/ *really,* /míʃənèhrij/ *missionary,* /gláhsiz/ *glasses,*
/péjpə/ *paper,* /míjnit/ *mean it,* /wówkinə+rɔ́w/ *walk in a
row,* /ówgejt/ *Aldgate,* /pɔ́wlən/ *Poland,* /kówzits+nót/
ków-zits-nót *'cause it is not.*

The syllable cut in –VCSV– is the same as in –VCCV– (2.55),
since S functions as a normal onset consonant in this context,
Any other type of syllable cut in VCV and VSCV sequences
can be accounted for by the presence of juncture. In VC+V
the syllable cut is more clearly *after* the consonant, and there
is more of a break, which may be marked by a glottal stop:

/lív+in/ (a variant form of /lívin/) *live in,*
/nót+intəfíh/ *not interfere,* /ɔ́p+əgèjnst/ *up against;*

just as it is after the consonant in VSC+V:

/áhd+ɔ́p/ *hard up,* /míjn+it/ (a variant form of /míjnit/)
mean it, /fájt+oh+dáj/ *fight or die,* /bròwt+ɔ́p/ *brought
up,* /gəwz+áwt/ *goes out.*

2.55. In –VCCV– the syllable cut is conditioned by the nature
of the consonants. Generally it is clearly placed between the
two consonants (VC-CV):

/dóktə/ *doctor,* /əttájmz/ *at times,* /brékfəst/ *breakfast,*
/ðatsów/ *that is all,* /kóknij/ *Cockney,* /líbrəl/ *liberal,*
/bískit/ *biscuit,* /ázbən/ *husband,* /lándən/ *London,*
/bíldin/ *building,* /səmtájmz/ *sometimes,* /gívzəs/ *gives us,*
/dífrənt/ *different,* /frénlij/ *friendly.*

However, when the first vowel is unstressed and the consonant
combination also occurs as a common complex onset, the syllable cut is before, or in the middle of, the first consonant
(V-CCV):

/ðəblówk/ *the bloke,* /əgríj/ *agree,* /mistéjk/ *mistake,*
/práktiklij/ prák-ti-klij *practically,* /əndəstán/ ən-də-stán
understand.

In –VSCCV– the syllable cut is before, or in the middle of,
the first consonant when CC also occurs as a complex onset
(VS-CCV):

/tíjtʃə/ *teacher,* /líjdʒə/ *lead you,* /sájprəs/ *Cyprus,*
/áhskim/ *ask him,* /pəlíjsmən/ pə-líj-smən *policeman.*

Otherwise the syllable cut is between the two consonants
(VSC-CV):

/áwttu/ *out to,* /spájtfəl/ *spiteful,* /áhftə/ *after,*
/péjvmənt/ *pavement,* /fáijndit/ *find it,* /dáhnsin/ *dancing,*
/spójlzit/ *spoils it,* /áwnlij/ *only.*

In –VCSV– the syllable cut is as in –VCCV–, i.e. VC-SV:
/létjuw/ *let you,* /mónjumənt/ món-ju-mənt *monument,*
/itáljən/ i-tál-jən *Italian,* /dídwij/ *did we,* /sámweh/ *somewhere;*

and in –VSCSV– it is as in –VSCCV–, where CC is a possible
complex onset, i.e. VS-CSV:

/téjkjuw/ *take you,* /áhgjumənt/ áh-gju-mənt *argument.*

Any other type of syllable cut in VCCV and VSCCV can be
accounted for by the presence of juncture:

/nájs+tájm/ *nice time*, /brík+léjn/ *Brick Lane*, /ðəbígis+kúw/ *the biggest coup*, /sənt+íldəz/ *St. Hilda's*, /ðats+ów/ *that is all*.[1]

2.56. In longer interludes the syllable cut is determined by the complexity of the preceding syllable peak and by the possibility of dividing the interlude into coda + onset,[2] according to the same principles as in V(S)CCV. In general, the syllable cut comes earlier after a complex peak than after a simple one. It is after, or in the last part of, the second consonant (VCC-CV) in

/píktʃə/ *picture*, /fáktrij/ *factory*, /krístʃən/ *Christian*, /séntʃərij/ *century*, /distíŋkʃən/ *distinction*, /kə́ntrij/ *country*, /ínstəns/ *instance*, /tʃíldrən/ *children*,

---

[1] I assume that the presence of juncture may explain the syllable cut described in the first half of the following statement by Malone ('The Phonemes of Current English', 1940 edition p. 148): 'The syllabic division in some of these words is based on the morphemic analysis; in others, it is based simply and solely on the rules that govern the composition of initial standing sequences in English.'

Malone's syllabification differs from mine in one respect: he divides VCrV, VClV, VCjV, and VCwV after the first vowel: e-flʌks *efflux*, mæ-krɒn *macron*, i-sjuu *issue*, e-kwiti *equity* (the transcription is Malone's). In Cockney the syllable cut would be after the first consonant.

The above discussion is based on the 1940 edition of Malone's article. However, no major changes seem to have been made on this point in the 1959 article.

[2] Cf. Hockett, *A Manual of Phonology* p. 64, on the syllable cut in complex interludes in English: 'In interludes where only one division of the kind described above [i.e. into two successive parts, the first of which occurs also as a coda, the second of which occurs also as an onset] is possible, the phonetic point of syllable division is quite clear ... Where multiple division is possible, the phonetic point of syllable division is obscure or variable.'

I suggest that it may be possible to find a most favoured way of making the syllable cut, though it may be 'variable'. The syllable division may be 'obscure' in the sense that the consonant sequence in such cases is more truly a phonetic interlude, closely linked both to the preceding and to the following syllable peak, and there is not such a clearly marked rhythmic break at the syllable cut, which may seem to be in the middle of a consonant.

whereas it is before, or in the first part of, the second consonant (VSC-CCV) in

/áhftrim/ *after him,* /éjntʃə/ *ain't you,* /kéjmbridʒ/ *Cambridge,* /sə́wldʒə/ *soldier.*

After unstressed vowels the syllable cut may fall earlier, provided the following consonants form a possible syllable onset:

/rédʒistrij/ réd-ʒi-strij *registry,* /ikspléjn/ ik-spléjn *explain.*

Some examples of syllable cut in longer interludes:

/wóntstuw/ *wants to*: after or in the middle of /s/;
/əpə́wlstrin/ *upholstering*: before or in the beginning of /s/.

Any other type of syllable cut can be accounted for by the presence of juncture:

/fén+tʃəhtʃ/ *Fenchurch (Street),* /ðát+swíjtinəf/ *that sweet enough?*

Interludes consisting of more than four consonants are rare, if they ever do occur.

2.6. JUNCTURE

There is a phoneme of internal juncture, /+/, the occurrence of which serves to distinguish utterances:

/sít+in/ *sit in* (as in *sit in a chair*) vs. /sítin/ *sitting,*[1]
/ən+éjm/ *an aim* vs. /ənéjm/ (or /ə+néjm/) *a name,*

---

[1] These two utterances do not necessarily contrast: *sit in* may be manifested by another variant, /sítin/, which is homophonous with *sitting.* However, where the two utterances *are* distinguished they are differentiated in the manner indicated above. The same argument applies to many other occurrences of juncture: it is one of the means by which a potential contrast between certain utterances is manifested.

It is possible that a rapid colloquial style has fewer occurrences of internal juncture than a slow, careful style. The fewer the junctures, the more the listener has to rely on the (linguistic and extra-linguistic) context for a proper understanding of what he hears.

/plə́m+ṕaj/ *plum pie* vs. /plə́mp+́aj/ *plump eye,*
/gréj+táj/ *grey tie* vs. /gréjt+́aj/ *great eye.*

Internal juncture is manifested by the potential for a slight pause, by a phonetic syllable cut, and by the particular allophones of the phonemes on each side. The juncture may also be manifested by an extra segment, a glottal stop, before stressed vowels:

/əmíljən+éh/ [ə'mɪljən'ʔe·ɔ̌] *a millionaire.*

The following are the main allophonic variations which are conditioned by the presence of juncture.

The complex syllable peaks are generally longer and more glided before juncture (3.052, 3.053), and the consonants, too, are longer in this position than before C+. Phonemically voiced consonants may be phonetically fully or partly voiceless before and after /+/ (4.051). The stops may be glottalized before juncture (4.123), but are rarely aspirated there, whereas they are generally strongly aspirated or affricated after /+/ when a stressed syllable peak follows (4.122). The presence of a strongly affricated /t/ after an unstressed syllable before an unstressed vowel is indicative of the presence of a juncture before /t/. /t/ is never manifested by the voiced flap, [ṭ], before or after juncture, and never by [ʔ] after juncture (4.15). The non-velarized lateral contoid allophone of /l/, 'clear l', never occurs before juncture (4.4122). /h/ before /+/ is a voiced vocoid (3.03), and after /+/ it is a voiceless contoid (4.431); this is the distinction between /h/ as a peak satellite and as an onset consonant. A similar distinction between a pre-junctural peak satellite variant and a post-nuclear onset consonant variant applies to /j/ and /w/ (3.03, 4.441, 4.51). The special consonant allophones found in the neighbourhood of certain other consonants do not occur when a juncture intervenes. Thus, the voiceless allophones of /l r j w/ which are usual after voiceless consonants (4.051) are not found after C+, and the dental contoid manifesting the phonemic sequence of a back (alveolar) apical and the front (dental) apical fricative /ð/ ([ṭ] = /tð/, [ṇ] = /nð/, etc., 4.21) does not occur if a juncture interrupts the sequence (/t+ð/, /n+ð/, etc.).[1]

There are also certain restrictions on the occurrence of phonemes dependent on juncture. Stressed simple syllable peaks do not occur before juncture, and there are other limitations in the distribution of unstressed peaks in this position (2.4, 3.01). Only a limited number of complex syllable peaks occur before /1+/ (and 1C, cf. 4.414). /ʒ r/ do not occur post-vocalically before /+/, nor are /h j w/ ever coda consonants, and /ʒ ŋ/ are never found after /+/ (4.01). There is no combination of phonemically voiced and voiceless consonants before or after juncture (4.02).

Internal juncture is often utilized for marking more clearly the morphological-syntactical composition of an utterance:

/kóws+its/ 'course it is (true) vs. /kówsits/ corsets,
/dríjm+ə(v)/ dream of vs. /dríjmə/ dreamer, /stə́di+in/
study in vs. /stə́diin/ studying.

However, when there is no need for such a distinction, pairs of utterances like those quoted above may be homophonous, without any juncture. Internal juncture may even occur in the middle of a morpheme, leaving the morpheme boundary unmarked:

/sən+tíldəz/ [sən'tˢï̆ždəz] (or /səntíldəz/ [sən'tʰï̆ždəz] St.
Hilda's, /i+tíz/ (or /itíz/) it is.

2.7. STRESS

There is a contrast of three degrees of stress: primary stress /ʹ/ vs. secondary stress /ˈ/ vs. absence of stress (left unmarked).

[1] Cf. the description given by D. Jones (An Outline of English Phonetics §§ 1089–97) of the characteristics of the sounds on both sides of the syllable cut, particularly in those cases where he considers it necessary to mark, in his transcription, the point of syllable division by means of a hyphen, in order to render the pronunciation unambiguous. In most of these cases I would postulate a juncture.

Illustrations of the various stress contrasts are as follows.

/´/ vs. no stress:

/bíləw/ *billow*[1] vs. /biláw/ *below*, /bígin/ *Biggin* (geographical name) vs. /bigín/ *begin*, /púlin/ *pulling* vs. /pulín/ *pull in*, /mís+print/ *misprint* vs. /mis+prínt/ *Miss Print*, /lándən/ *London* vs. /əndán/ *and done*.

/´/ vs. /ˋ/:

/blák+bəhd/ *black bird* vs. /blák+bəhd/ *blackbird*, /tráhn(+)spòwt/ *transport* (noun) vs. /tràhn(+)spówt/ *transport* (verb).

/ˋ/ vs. no stress:

/əndán/ [ˌʌn'dʌn] *undone* vs. /əndán/ [ən'dʌn] *and done*,[2] /sílvərìŋ/ *silver ring* (not a golden one) vs. /símərin/ *simmering*, /stádij+ìn/ (or /stádiìn/) (*a place to*) *study in* vs. /stádij+in/ (or /stádiin/) *studying*.[3]

In 7.42 I shall discuss some of the problems raised in postulating three, neither more nor less, stresses for English in general and Cockney in particular.

There are certain limitations on the occurrence of syllable peaks in unstressed syllables (2.4).

2.8. INTONATION

I have not made any special study of the intonation system of Cockney. However, C. F. Hockett's analysis in terms of four pitch levels (PL) and three terminal contours (TC)[4] seems to apply to my data.

---

[1] Or /bílə/, which is a more common variant (cf. 3.642).

[2] *Undone* has another allomorph, /əndán/ [ən'dʌn], which is homophonous with *and done*.

[3] *Study in* also has a morphemic alternant without /ˋ/, in which case it is homophonous with *studying*.

[4] *A Manual of Phonology* pp. 45–49 and *A Course in Modern Linguistics* pp. 33–46. Similar analyses are given by H. A. Gleason (*An Introduction to Descriptive Linguistics* 4.12–4.18) and H. L. Smith (*Linguistic Science and the Teaching of English*).

No absolute pitch values can be assigned to each of the pitch levels. I suspect that in terms of cycles per second on the frequency scale there is considerable overlap between the levels, even with a single speaker speaking in one style. The levels represent *relative* values only, within the framework of one utterance or conversational chunk. The levels are numbered from 1 (the lowest level) to 4 (the highest level).

The terminal contours are defined by Hockett[1] in the following way: 'One of the TCs [i.e. / | /] is neutral, involving simply articulatory pause (which can be extremely short), without any rise or fall in pitch ... A second [i.e. /↓/] involves normally a lowering of pitch from the last PL in the macrosegment, accompanied by a relaxation of force of articulation — a sort of 'dying-away' effect ... The third [i.e. /↑/] involves a rise of pitch from the last PL; the amount of rise varies a good deal without contrast, and is accompanied, not by relaxation in force of articulation, but either by relatively steady force or, perhaps, by a slight increase.'

In addition, the terminal contours are manifested by special allophonic variants of the phonemes occurring on either side. These are the same as those which are conditioned by internal juncture (2.6), except that the stops may be strongly affricated or aspirated before a terminal contour, which they are generally not before /+/. The position immediately before TC seems to be of particular importance for the length and amount of diphthongization of syllable peaks; it is a rhythmically prominent position (3.052, 3.053).

Since terminal contours share certain features with the internal juncture, /+/, it might be preferable to call them 'external junctures'. The term 'juncture', without any qualifying adjective, is used in this study in the sense of 'internal juncture or terminal contour', and the symbol /#/ is adopted as a cover symbol for / ↓ ↑ | /.

---

[1] *A Manual of Phonology* p. 45 sq. Similar definitions are found in Hockett's *Course in Modern Linguistics* p. 37 and in Gleason's *Introduction to Descriptive Linguistics* p. 46.

Just as the distribution of segmental phonemes (vowels and consonants) are statable in terms of a higher phonological unit, the syllable, so the distribution of the intonation phonemes (PL's and TC's) may be stated in terms of the macrosegment. The macrosegment corresponds to the utterance chunk covered by Armstrong and Ward's 'tune'.[1]

According to Hockett's analysis an 'intonation', i.e. the intonation pattern covering a macrosegment, consists of a TC and at least two PL's: one PL at the centre of the intonation and one at the end. The centre is the most prominent syllable of the macrosegment, and it has always primary stress. If there are any syllables before the centre there is also a third PL, at the beginning of the macrosegment. Occasionally there is a fourth PL somewhere between the beginning and the centre. Examples with two PL's:

/³ónistlij¹↓/ *Honestly.* /²síj²↑/ *See?* /³jés¹↓/ *Yes —*

Three PL's:

/³ów+²jés¹↓/ *Oh yes.* /³juw+¹nów¹↑/ *You know —*
/²ízit+²édítə³↑/ *Is it 'editor'?* (i.e., Is that what you call it?).
/²əw+³áh+ðej²↑/ *Oh, are they?* (said with raised eyebrows).
/³wótsəh+²néjm²| ³níjnə¹↓/ *What is her name — Nina.*
/²julív+ət+sənt+³íldəz²| ³dówntju¹↓/ *You live at St.Hilda's, don't you?*

Four PL's:

/²ðejə+nìhli+³ów+³lóndənəz¹↑/ *They are nearly all Londoners.*
/²juw+³nów+wotə+¹kówt+mìʃənehri+ìz²↑/ *You know what a court missionary is?*

In this type of analysis there is no implication that the pitch remains, phonetically speaking, the same from one occurrence of a pitch phoneme up to the next. But the pitch pattern between the PL's can be predicted. In the following paragraphs I shall

[1] L. E. Armstrong and I. C. Ward, *A Handbook of English Intonation.*

indicate some of the conventions which apply to Cockney (and to RP, but not necessarily to the dialects Hockett has in mind). 'PL' represents any occurrence of a pitch level phoneme.

(1) In an intonation of three or more PL's, if the PL at the beginning occurs on a syllable without primary stress and is lower than the second PL, there is a gradual rise between them:

/¹aj+névə+wént+təskúwlət+³ów¹↓/ *I never went to school at all.*

If the first PL is higher than the second, there may be a gradual fall between them, or the pitch may remain essentially level, without any difference in meaning:

/³wəzit+¹jéstədij²↑/ *Was it yesterday?*

(2) Between two PL's (exclusive of the last PL of an intonation) both of which occur on a syllable with primary stress there is a gradual fall; if there are syllables with primary stress between the PL's the fall takes the form of a gradual stepping-down from one stressed syllable to the next. There is this kind of fall between the first and the second PL in

/³wénij+gót+¹kówt¹↑/ *When he got caught,*

and between the second and the third PL in

/¹ðej+ə³vérij+vérij+gúd+²píjpəl¹↓/ *They are very, very good people;*
/¹aj+³névə+wént+təskúwlət+⁴ów¹↓/ *I never went to school at all.*

In the latter utterance, which is a variant form of the one quoted above, there is a gradual stepping-down from *never* to *at*, followed by a sharp rise, or rather a step up, to PL 4 at the beginning of *all*.

(3) Between the last two PL's of an intonation, i.e. between the centre and the end, the following patterns prevail. When the centre PL is higher than the end PL the fall, or the main part of the fall, takes place on the centre syllable. If the macro-

segment is followed by one of the TC's /↓/ or / | |/, the pitch remains low throughout the rest of the macrosegment:

/²ajwəz+³gówn+làjk¹↓/ *I was gone like,*
/³dʒúwn+wəzíh¹↓/ *June was here.*

If the following TC is /↑/, the rise, which is a characteristic of this TC, takes place from the last syllable with primary stress:

/²wènjuw+³fə́hs+gə́w¹↑/ *When you first go,*
/¹aj+də̀wnəw+³wót+²kə́ntrij+ʃikə́m+from¹↑/ *I do not know what country she come from;*

or from the syllable following the centre if there is no primary stress after the centre:

/²wel³éniwèj¹↑/ *Well, anyway* —
/²sə́mwə+níh+màjl³éndajθìŋk¹↑/ *Somewhere near Mile End, I think.*

If the centre syllable is also the last syllable of the macrosegment, the fall and the rise take place within the same syllable:

/²wèlit+³íz¹↑/ *Well, it is,*
/²wèlajfèlt+³sə́w+²kwíh¹↑/ *Well, I felt so queer.*

When the centre PL is lower than the end PL, the rise takes place from the centre syllable on. Any syllables with primary stress between the centre and the end may somewhat delay the completion of the rise:

/³də́wnt+mémrim+¹tówkin+təmij²↑/ *Do not remember him talking to me,*
/²sə̀wij+³túk+ə¹nə́ðə+wə́n+sìj²↑/ *So he took another one, see.*

Hockett has postulated a maximum of four occurrences of PL in any intonation; most intonations have only two or three PL's. In my data intonations with four PL's are very common, and I consider it not unlikely that we may occasionally have to postulate five PL occurrences in one macrosegment. One particu-

lar difficulty is the 'fall-rise':[1] if the extent of the final rise is
found to be contrastive,[2] e.g. if 3 1 ↑ with a long rise has a different meaning from 3 1 ↑ with a short rise, we may have to re-
interpret these intonations and to set up an extra PL between
the centre and the end; 3 1 ↑ with a long rise may perhaps be
/3 1 2 ↑/, while 3 1 ↑ with a short rise is /3 1 1 ↑/.

The combination of the centre PL and the end PL plus the
TC seems to carry the greatest amount of information relative
to the particular 'meaning' of the intonation.

As an example of my analysis I give below two short passages
transcribed in terms of the system of description set out above.
The informants are EE and EC.

/³óh²| ³fóh+³ðís+wóh¹↓   ³ðís+wóh¹| ¹wózən+it²↑   ³nə́w+
Oh,   *'fore this war.*   *This war,*   *wasn't it?*   *No,*

it+wózənt¹↑   ²àjəm+gètən+mìkst+³ə́p¹↓   ²it+wəz+ðij+⁴ə́ðə+
it was not.   *I am getting mixed up.*   *It was the other*

wóh¹↓   ²jèhsit+⁴mə́stəv+bìjn+bifòh¹| ²it+⁴wóz¹| ²bifòh+
war.   *Yes, it must have been before —*   *It was*   *before*

⁴ðís+wòh¹↓   ⁴kówsit+²wóz¹↓/
this war.   *'Course it was.* (EE)

/²its+³bjúwtifələ́p+in+ájgit+vílidʒ¹↓   ²if+³júw+gəw+ə́p+
It is beautiful up in Highgate Village.   *If you go up*

ðéhronə   ²if+³júw+gəw+ə́p+ðéhronə+fájn+¹déj¹↑   ²ən+
there on a …[3] *If you go up there on a fine day,*   *and*

³stándon+hájgit+²híl¹↑   ¹jùwkən+sìj+sən³pówz¹↓   ²ʃə́wz+
stand on Highgate Hill,   *you can see St. Paul's.*   *Shows*

aw³ráj+juàh¹↓/
how high you are. (EC)

---

[1] Or 'tune II with emphasis'; see L. E. Armstrong and I. C. Ward,
op.cit. p. 56 sqq.

[2] Hockett does not think it is; cf. *A Manual of Phonology* p. 46.

[3] Interrupted intonation.

In the rest of the transcriptions given in this study the pitch levels are left unmarked, since I consider my conclusions in this field tentative only. But the terminal contours are indicated wherever their presence is of importance to the point under discussion.

2.9. NON-SYSTEMIC CHARACTERISTICS

Certain features which have generally been considered characteristic of the London dialect, by linguists and laymen alike, do not lend themselves easily to a systemic analysis. They have to do, among other things, with what we might vaguely call voice quality and with manner of delivery. It suffices to quote two authors on the subject.

W. Matthews discusses[1] 'the slackness of Cockney speech' and says, 'Cockneys avoid movement of the lips and jaw as far as possible, preserving a roughly half-open position of the lips. This habit causes a slight but very noticeable nasalisation and leads to a slight rounding of vowel sounds which need a full opening of the lips for their correct articulation. As a further tendency of the dialect is to centralise back vowels and diphthongs, many sounds which are widely separated in standard speech become closer to one another in Cockney ... The general effect of these tendencies is to make the dialect rather confused and flabby, an effect which is increased by the habit of many Londoners, particularly women, to drag out an accented syllable. ... to many outsiders [the dialect] appears whining and flaccid. This judgment is probably true of the speech of many Cockney women, but other Cockneys, costermongers in particular, overcome the defect by a loud utterance which transforms the dialect into a speech which is vigorous and confident, although ugly and raucous.' He further states[2] that 'In vowel sounds, the dominant feature of Cockney is its use of diphthongs in words

[1] *Cockney Past and Present* p. 77.
[2] *Op.cit.* p. 78.

which in standard English are pronounced with monophthongs, and its use of monophthongs where standard English employs diphthongs.'

J. Franklyn states[1] that 'Cockneys clench the teeth, part the lips slightly — not much more than an eighth of an inch — draw them back taut against the gums and, without relaxing any of the muscles employed in this contortion, articulate (in as far as they do articulate) every word perfectly (in as far as it is perfect)', and this basic position is supposed to be the reason for most of the particular sound variants used in Cockney. But 'certain sounds demand a relaxation. At these rare moments the lower jaw should be thrust forward slightly, and the lips protruded.'

I consider Franklyn's description somewhat fanciful. Besides, it seems to imply that Cockney is a kind of distortion of normal speech. However, both authors have pointed out certain features in the basis of articulation for Cockney to which we can subscribe, without agreeing in every detail. In the following paragraphs I shall give a brief survey of these features.

A number of syllable peaks which in RP are phonetically rather far apart are closer to each other in Cockney. A chart of all the syllable peaks shows certain clusterings, for example in the front half-close to open area and in the back area; cf. the relatively great similarity between the phonemic norms of /eh/, /a/, and /aw/ (3.22, 3.31, 3.34) and between /ow/ and pre-junctural /ol/, /owl/, and /əwl/ (3.41, 3.44, 3.63); cf. also the general similarity among many syllable peaks before pre-junctural /l/, even when they are phonemically distinct (3.051). This may be the reason why both the authors quoted have the impression that Cockneys avoid, as far as possible, any unnecessary movements of the articulating organs.

The tendency 'to drag out an accented syllable' is very marked, and is discussed at some length in 3.052. Closely associated with this feature is the fact that syllable peaks whose phonemic norms are monophthongal may be glided, and that

[1] *The Cockney* p. 242.

peaks whose phonemic norms are glided may be monophthongs (3.053, 3.054). There is thus no clear-cut phonetic distinction between short vowels, long vowels, and diphthongs (3.04).

The difference which Matthews seems to have found between men and women may have something to do with the wider use of the glottal stop among men, or among speakers of the 'rougher' type generally (4.15). The clipped effect given to speech by the frequent use of [ʔ] is of course the exact opposite of 'whining' and 'drawling'.

However, a characteristic feature of the dialect is the use of the glottal stop not only as a separate segment (4.14), but also as a secondary articulation in other segments.[1] There is often, if not a complete closure, at least a constriction in the larynx immediately before or during the closure of voiceless stops. This phenomenon has been observed in post-peak position only. It is not marked in the transcription.

Another characteristic is nasalization. What I have in mind is not only the phonologically relevant nasalization, according to which a nasal consonant phoneme is manifested in the nasality of the previous segment, but a weaker type of nasality which, with many speakers, permeates their speech delivery generally (4.32).

[1] Cf. 'the reinforcing glottal stop' in RP described by B. S. Andrésen in 'The Glottal Stop in the Received Pronunciation of English' and by J. D. O'Connor in 'RP and the Reinforcing Glottal Stop'.

3. Syllable Peaks

3.0. GENERAL SURVEY

3.01. Number and Distribution of Vowels

There are six vowel phonemes, /i e a o u ə/. They occur singly
as syllable peaks:

/pít/ *pit*, /pét/ *pet*, /pát/ *pat*, /pót/ *pot*, /pút/ *put*, /pát/ *putt*;

and as nuclei of complex peaks, with the satellites /h j w/:

/píh/ *peer*, /péh/ *pair*, /páh/ *pa*, /póh/ *paw, pour*, /púh/
poor, /páh/ *purr*; /bíhz/ *beers*, /béhz/ *bears*, /báhz/ *bars*,
/bóhz/ *bores*, /búhz/ *boors*, /báhz/ *burrs*; /bíj/ *bee*, /béj/
bay, /báj/ *buy*, /bój/ *boy*; /líjn/ *lean*, /léjn/ *lane*, /lájn/ *line*,
/lójn/ *loin*; /báw/ *bow*, /bów/ *ball*, /búw/ *boo*, /báw/ *bow*;
/báwt/ *bout*, /bówt/ *bought*, /búwt/ *boot*, /báwt/ *boat*.

Only four vowels occur with each of the satellites /j/ and /w/:
/i e a o/ with /j/, and /a o u ə/ with /w/. Thus, the following
combinations are missing: high back or central nucleus plus
high front satellite, and high or mid front nucleus plus high
back satellite.

No vowel occurs stressed in syllable-final position, and only
/i u ə/ occur unstressed in this position (2.4).

3.02. Classification of Vowels

The vowels can be defined as follows: /i/ is high front, /e/
is mid front, /a/ is low front, /o/ is low back, /u/ is high back,
/ə/ is central:

$$
\begin{array}{ll}
\text{i} & \text{u} \\
\text{e} & \text{ə} \\
\text{a} & \text{o}
\end{array}
$$

As to the peak satellites, /h/ is a back dorsal sonorant, /j/ is a front dorsal sonorant, and /w/ is a labial sonorant.[1]

3.03. Phonemic Norm of Syllable Peaks

In the following peak chart the main allophonic variants of vowels and semiconsonants as part of the syllable peaks are indicated roughly. For the value of the phonetic symbols as used here, see 1.6 and the detailed discussion of the individual syllable peaks.

V	Vh	Vj	Vw
/i/ [ɪ] *pit*	/ih/ [ɪ̆ə] *beer*	/ij/ [ə̆i] *bee*	
/e/ [e] *pet*	/eh/ [eə̆] *bear*	/ej/ [æɪ̆] *pay*	
/a/ [ɛ] *pat*	/ah/ [ɑ·] *bar*	/aj/ [ɑɪ̆] *pie*	/aw/ [ɛə̆] *now*
/o/ [ɔ] *pot*	/oh/ [ɔə̆] *bore*	/oj/ [ɔɪ̆] *boy*	/ow/ [ǫʊ̆] *bought*
/u/ [ʊ] *put*	/uh/ [ʊə̆] *tour*		/uw/ [ə̆ü] *boot*
/ə/ [ʌ] *but*	/əh/ [ɜ·] *fur*		/əw/ [œʊ̆] *no*

If one considers the vowel variants occurring in CVC$_x$ (where C$_x$ is any coda consonant other than /l/) as norm, some general statements can be made about the allophonic variants of the complex peaks:

Vh: /h/ is a voiced non-syllabic vocoid glide towards mid central tongue position and neutral lip position, or, in /ah oh əh/, alternatively a non-syllabic continuation of the previous segment. V is represented by allophones which are closer than the norm in /ih oh əh/, more open and back than the norm in /ah/, and the same as the norm in /eh uh/.

Vj: /j/ is a voiced non-syllabic vocoid glide towards high front

[1] Cf. 4.04. For a discussion of distinctive features, with an indication of other interpretations, see 7.23.

tongue position and spread or neutral lip position, or, in /ij/, alternatively a non-syllabic continuation of the previous segment. V is represented by allophones which are more open and back than the norm in /ej aj/ (and in /ij/ when the latter is clearly glided), and slightly closer than the norm in /ij oj/ (in /ij/ only when the latter is not glided).

Vw: /w/ is a voiced non-syllabic vocoid glide towards high back tongue position, with progressive rounding of the lips in /ow uw əw/ and in one variant of /aw/, or, in /uw/, alternatively a non-syllabic continuation of the previous segment. V is represented by allophones which are closer than the norm (in /uw/ only when the latter is not glided; when /uw/ is clearly glided the /u/ allophone is more open than the norm).

I have called /h j w/ *non-syllabic* vocoid glides. This implies that the diphthongs are all of the *falling* type.[1] This is true for most of the glided complex peaks, but not for /ij uw/. One should thus rather say that /h j w/ are vocoid glides forming one syllable with the preceding vowel.

Figures 1–4 indicate the main vowel allophones occurring in the contexts CVC_x, CVh, CVj, CVw, and Fig. 5 shows the phonemic norm of all the syllable peaks.

3.04. Short Vowels vs. Long Vowels vs. Diphthongs?

The syllable peaks of RP have traditionally been subdivided into short vowels, long vowels, and diphthongs.[2] More recently some doubt has been cast upon the validity of the distinction between long and short vowels,[3] and experiments suggest that out of the two factors which combine to distinguish the peaks

---

[1] Cf. D. Jones, *An Outline of English Phonetics* § 223.

[2] See e.g. D. Jones, *op.cit.* §§ 240–2, 378, 863.

[3] See e.g. D. Jones, *An Outline of English Phonetics* §§ 874–9; D. Jones, *The Pronunciation of English* §§ 429–30; I. C. Ward, *The Phonetics of English* § 361 (vi).

For a discussion of the justification of a distinction between long and short vowels in American English, based upon instrumental studies, see R-M. S. Heffner *et al.*, 'Notes on the Length of Vowels'.

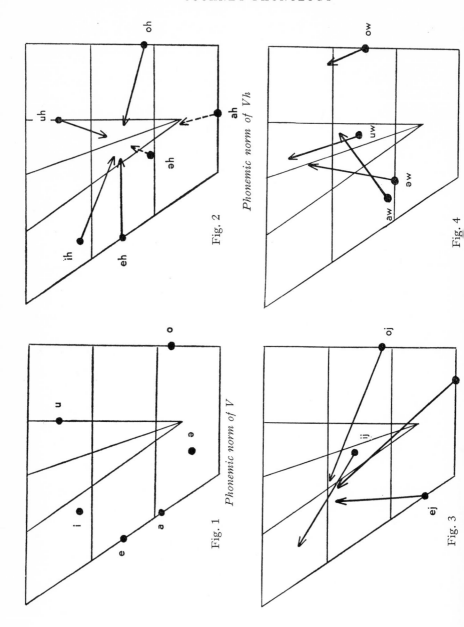

Fig. 2

Phonemic norm of Vh

Fig. 4

Fig. 1

Phonemic norm of V

Fig. 3

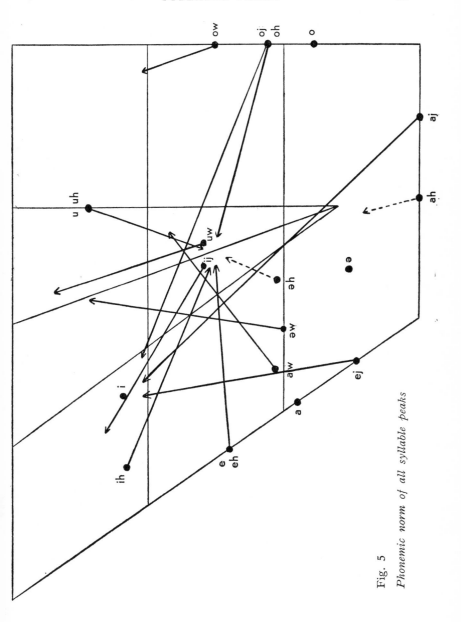

Fig. 5

Phonemic norm of all syllable peaks

of *seat* and *sit, caught* and *cot, wooed* and *wood*, viz. quality and quantity, the former is the more important.[1]

It is not convenient to set up a similar tripartite system for Cockney, for reasons of distribution (distributional criteria lead to a two-way rather than a three-way classification: 7.2121) any more than on purely phonetic grounds (the so-called long vowels may be strongly diphthongized, and the so-called diphthongs may be monophthongal: 3.053, 3.054).

On the other hand, there may be some justification for calling the peaks of *pit, pet, pat, pot, put, but* short, in contradistinction to all the other peaks: though /i e a o u ə/ may have rather long variants under certain statable conditions (3.052), they are always shorter than the other peaks before an interlude, for example in words like *swimming, penny, manner, bombing, woman, funny*. Besides, the position of the non-phonemic syllable cut in an interlude depends on whether the preceding syllable peak is simple (/i e a o u ə/) or complex (/ih ij eh ej/, etc.). After a simple peak a single-consonant interlude is ambisyllabic or belongs to the preceding syllable, for example in /sítin/ *sitting*, /sílij/ *silly*; after a complex peak it belongs to the following syllable, for example in /síjtin/ *seating*, /ríhlij/ *really*. In an interlude consisting of several consonants the syllable division falls later after a simple peak than after a complex one: between /p/ and /t/ in /séprit/ *separate*, but before /k/ in /séjkrid/ *sacred*; between /d/ and /ʒ/ in /lédʒə/ *ledger*, but before /d/ in /méjdʒə/ *major*; between /s/ and /t/ in /místə/ *mister*, but before /s/ in /máhstə/ *master*; in the middle of /t/ in /hístrij/ *history*, but rather before /t/ or in the middle of /s/ in /péjstrij/ *pastry*.[2]

However, because length is not a feature consistently asso-

[1] A. C. Gimson, 'Implications of the Phonemic/Chronemic Grouping of English Vowels'.

[2] There are two exceptions to the above rule of (non-phonemic) syllable division: after /a/ a complex interlude may have the same syllable division as after complex peaks (3.312), and after /əh/ the syllable division is sometimes as after simple peaks (3.62). On non-phonemic syllable cut in general, see 2.5.

ciated with complex peaks in contradistinction to simple ones in all contexts, its presence or absence is not considered a distinctive feature in Cockney.

3.05. Allophonic Variations

3.050

There are certain allophonic variations which are common to many or all syllable peaks. They may be conditioned by contiguous consonants, so that for instance the front peaks have more retracted variants before or after velar consonants, and the peaks may be more open before /r/. After the phonetically labialized consonants /w ʃ ʒ/ there are labialized variants, and after /w/ front vowels may be more back and back vowels may be closer. Similar variants are found in RP. In the following paragraphs I shall discuss some variations which may be more marked in Cockney than in RP.

3.051. *Before /l/*

The last part of the Vj peaks is more open than the norm before pre-vocalic /l/:[1] the glide does not reach the target position in /séjlə/ *sailor*, /nájlən/ *nylon*, /bójlə/ *boiler* (3.232, 3.332, 3.63). The peak nucleus itself may be slightly more open and back than the norm in this position. This is particularly noticeable in /əw/: /bə́wlə/ *bowler* (3.63).

These variations are insignificant compared with the ones occurring before /l/ in pre-consonantal and pre-junctural position, whether /l/ is manifested by a lateral or a vocoid allophone.[2] There are similar variations in RP, though they are less striking there.[3]

Generally speaking, the syllable peaks are represented by more open and back variants before /lC/, /l+/, and /l#/. This

---

[1] 'Clear l': cf. 4.4122.
[2] 'Dark l' or a back vocoid: cf. 4.4122, 4.413.
[3] Cf., for RP, D. Jones, *Outline* §§ 274, 404.

is particularly noticeable in the peaks /i e a aw o ow u uw ə əh əw/ (3.11, 3.211, 3.311, 3.344, 3.41, 3.44, 3.51, 3.53, 3.611, 3.612, 3.62, 3.63):

/fíl/ [fïɤ̌] *fill*, /fél/ [fëɤ̌/ *fell*, /pál/ [pæɤ̌] *pal*, /fáwl/ [fa̰ŏ] *foul*,[1] /dól/ [dɒŏ] *doll*, /fówl/ [fɔŏ] *fall*,[1] /fúl/ [fʊ̤ŭ] *full*, /fúwl/ [fʊ·ŭ] *fool*,[1] /də́l/ [dʌɤ̌] *dull*, /ówfəl/ ['ʊ̆fɤ] *awful*,[2] /gə́hl/ [gɜɤ̌] *girl*, /rə́wl/ [rɔ̰ŏ] *roll*.

When /l/ is manifested by a vocoid the vocoid glide of a preceding Vj peak is reduced and does not reach its target position (3.234, 3.334, 3.43):

/dʒéjl/ [dʒæ̈ɔ̌ɤ̌] *gaol*,[1] /pájl/ [pɑ̰ɔ̌ɤ̌] *pile*, /bójl/ [bɔ̰ɔ̌ɤ̌] *boil*.

The Vw peaks, and often also /aj/, in this position are monophthongs, and the sequence syllable peak + /l/ is manifested by a one-directional vocoid glide (3.334, 3.344, 3.44, 3.63):

/pájl/ [pɑ̰ɤ̌] *pile*, /fáwl/ [fa̰ŏ] *foul*,[1] /fówl/ [fɔŏ] *fall*,[1] /rə́wl/ [rɔ̰ŏ] *roll*.

Fig. 6 shows the vocoid glides which are the most common manifestations of the sequence syllable peak plus /l/ in preconsonantal and pre-junctural position. The chart should be compared with Fig. 5, which presents the phonemic norm of the peaks. It will be seen that there is some overlapping between the variants of different peaks in the two contexts (cf. 7.2213).

3.052. Length

Length variations are more marked in Cockney than in RP. The extraordinary length given to syllable peaks under conditions favourable to lengthening[3] is very characteristic, and

---

[1] /ejl awl owl uwl/ do not usually occur before a consonant or a juncture. Cf. 3.241, 3.351, 3.452, 3.541.

[2] Unstressed /əl/ is commonly manifested by a single syllabic segment, [ɤ].

[3] These conditions seem to be the same in RP and in Cockney, though they may have been stated in other terms by those who have described RP. Cf. D. Jones, *Outline* §§ 862–73; I. C. Ward, *The Phonetics of English* § 293.

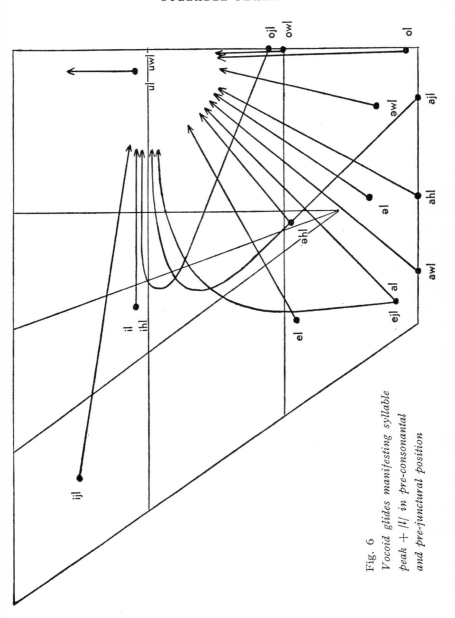

Fig. 6
*Vocoid glides manifesting syllable
peak + /l/ in pre-consonantal
and pre-junctural position*

may give the impression of drawling or whining. The greater length affects particularly the first part of a complex peak, so that such a peak may consist of a somewhat sustained segment plus a glide. One might transcribe /aj/ [ɑ·ɪ̈], /aw/ [ɛ·ə̈], etc. Those peaks that occur stressed before juncture, i.e. the complex peaks, are longer in this position than otherwise. Thus, the peak of the first member of the following word pairs is longer than the peak of the second member:

/bíh/ *beer*, /bíhd/ *beard*; /skéh/ *scare*, /skéhd/ *scared*; /méj/ *May*, /méjd/ *made*; /báj/ *buy*, /bájt/ *bite*; /bój/ *boy*, /bójz/ *boys*; /(h)áw/ *how*, /(h)áws/ *house*.

Before a coda, i.e. in closed syllables, any peak is longer before a voiced consonant than before a voiceless one. Thus, the peak of the first member of the following word pairs is longer than the peak of the second member:

/béd/ *bed*, /bét/ *bet*; /bág/ *bag*, /bák/ *back*; /bə́z/ *buzz*, /bə́s/ *bus*; /fíhz/ *fears*, /fíhs/ *fierce*; /skéhz/ *scares*, /skéhs/ *scarce*; /máhdʒ/ *marge(rine)*, /máhtʃ/ *march*; /réjz/ *raise*, /réjs/ *race*; /rájd/ *ride*, /rájt/ *right*; /rúwd/ *rude*, /rúwt/ *root*.

The peak is longer before a coda than before an interlude. Thus, the peak of the first member of the following word pairs is longer than the stressed peak of the second member, and this is the case whether the words occur before a terminal contour or not (see below):

/fíʃ/ *fish*, /fíʃin/ *fishing*; /béd/ *bed*, /bédin/ *bedding*; /mán/ *man*, /mánə/ *manner*; /rób/ *rob*, /róbin/ *robin*; /sə́m/ *some*, /sə́mə/ *summer*; /kéhz/ *cares*, /kéhləs/ *careless*; /káhm/ *calm*, /báhmij/ *balmy*; /réjs/ *race*, /réjsin/ *racing*; /lájn/ *line*, /lájnin/ *lining*; /ʃúwt/ *shoot*, /ʃúwtin/ *shooting*.

The influence of intonation and stress on the length of syllable peaks is even more important. The syllable peak is particularly long in the last syllable of a macrosegment, i.e. immediately before the terminal contour, whether this syllable has primary stress:

/wèlit+íz↑/ ['ɪ·z] *Well, it is,* /ðej+kówt+ðat+mán‖/ ['mɛ·n] *They caught that man,* /its+ðéhz↓/ ['ðe·ɜ̃z] *It is theirs,* /nót+míj↓/ ['mɜ̃i·] *Not me,* /ów+ðətájm↓/ ['tˢɑ·ɪ̃m] *All the time;*

or not:

/ðej+pínʃtim↑/ [ɪ·m] *They pinched him,* /téjk+jutuw+ áwnzditʃ↑/ ['ɛ̃nzdɪ·tʃ] *take you to Houndsditch,* /ávə+ bískit+ʃijsèd↓/ [ˌse·d] *Have a biscuit, she said,* /áj+ dəwnt+kèh↑/ [ˌke·ɜ̃] *I do not care,* /énijwèj↓/ ['eniˌwæ·ɪ̃] *Anyway,* /ðəwúdbàjnz↓/ [ðə'wʊdˌbɑ·ɪ̃nz] *the Woodbines.*

The peak of the syllable which is the centre of the intonation is also fairly long even if it is not the last syllable of the macro-segment, as in the first syllable of *Houndsditch* and *anyway* above. The syllable peak of a monosyllabic macrosegment is particularly long:

/íh| ɹaj+wóntʃə↓/ ['ɪ·ð] *Here, I want you,* /jés↓/ ['je·s] *Yes.*

3.053. *Diphthongization*

Some syllable peaks which are, or are said to be, monophthongs in RP have glided variants in Cockney. This applies particularly to /ij uw/, but also to /e a o ah oh əh ow/. The nature of the glide will be discussed later (3.13, 3.212, 3.313, 3.32, 3.41, 3.42, 3.44, 3.53, 3.62).

The degree of diphthongization is determined by the same factors as the length of the peaks. Thus, the diphthongization is stronger in stressed position before juncture than before codas; it is stronger in the first member of the following word pairs:

/bíj/ *bee,* /bíjdz/ *beads;* /túw/ *two,* /tʃúwz/ *choose.*

The diphthongization is also stronger before a voiced coda than before a voiceless one; it is stronger in the first member of the following word pairs:

/béd/ *bed*, /bét/ *bet*; /bág/ *bag*, /bák/ *back*; /káhd/ *card*, /káht/ *cart*; /fíjd/ *feed*, /fíjt/ *feet*; /lúwz/ *lose*, /lúws/ *loose*.

Intonation and stress condition the degree of diphthongization even more markedly. The syllable peak is particularly strongly glided in the last syllable of a macrosegment, i.e. immediately before the terminal contour, whether this syllable has primary stress:

/ádə+kə́pə+tíj+in+béd↑/ ['beⁱd] *Had a cup of tea in bed*, /ðejə+nót+bád↑/ ['bɛᵉd] *They are not bad*, /its+fáh↓/ ['făə] *It is far*, /béθnəl+gríjn↓/ ['grə̆in] *Bethnal Green*, /sə̀w+əv+kóws↓/ ['ko̧ŭs] *So of course*, /míj+túw↓/ ['tˢə̆ü] *Me too*;

or not:

/də́wn+bi+sílij↓/ ['sɪlə̆i] *Do not be sillly!* /wəl+tédiz+got+ əmùwv| éniwèj↓/ [ˌmə̆üv] *Well, Teddy's got to move, anyway.*

The peak of the syllable which is the centre of the intonation may also be strongly glided even if it is not the last syllable of the macrosegment:

/wótə+tʃíjk+ijz+gòt↓/ ['tʃə̆ik] *What a cheek he has got*, /tédiz+múwvin↓/ ['mə̆üvɪn] *Teddy is moving*;

and even a stressed syllable which is neither the centre of the intonation nor the end of the macrosegment may be markedly glided:

/ðij+éd+dóktə↓/ ['eⁱd] *the head doctor*, /míj+túw↓/ ['mə̆i] *Me too.*

However, the diphthongization is generally stronger in the last syllable before a terminal contour than medially in the macrosegment. One should compare the two occurrences of /ij/ in each of the following utterances:

/bəlíjv+míj↓/ [bḷ'ĭiv'mə̆i] *Believe me,* /it+məs+bi+ə́ndrəd+
jə́hz+íjzij↓/ ['ĭizə̆i] *It must be hundred years easy;*

and diphthongization is most likely to be found, and it is particularly strong, in monosyllabic macrosegments:

/síj↑/ ['sə̆i] *See?*

3.054. Monophthongization

Some peaks which have vocoid glides as phonemic norms have monophthongal variants, or variants with very short offglides only. This applies particularly to /ej aj oj aw/, but also to /əw/ (3.232, 3.332, 3.342, 3.43, 3.63).
Monophthongs occur in those contexts where glided variants of the peaks discussed in 3.053 would *not* occur.

The end-point of these closing diphthongs is closer before voiced coda consonants than before voiceless ones; it is closer in the first member of the following word pairs than in the second one:

/méjd/ *made,* /méjt/ *mate;* /rájz/ *rise,* /rájs/ *rice;*
/bójz/ *boys,* /vójs/ *voice;* /káwz/ *cows,* /máws/ *mouse;*

and it is still more open before a terminal contour:

/méj↓/ *May,* /ráj↓/ *rye,* /bój↓/ *boy,* /káw↓/ *cow.*

It is more open before interludes than before codas. In this position monophthongs or variants whose glides are hardly perceptible may occur:

/séjlə/ *sailor,* /éjnàj/ *ain't I,* /nájlən/ *nylon,* /dájnin+rùwm/ *dining-room,* /bójlə/ *boiler,* /dáwnin+strìjt/ *Downing Street.*

Monophthongs are particularly common before the interlude /l/, and even more so before zero interlude, i.e. before a vowel:

/tájəd/ *tired,* /implójə/ *employer,* /fláwə/ *flower,* /sə́win+məʃìjn/ *sewing-machine.*

Monophthongs may occur in unstressed position, thus in /aj/ and /əw/ in:

/aj+síj↓/ *I see*, /nəwvémbə↓/ *November*.

Monophthongal variants may also occur under primary stress, provided it is not in the last syllable of the macrosegment:

/májlən+bítə↓/ ['mɑ·lən'bɪtˢə] *mild and bitter*,
/its+nájsəvəm↓/ [ɪts'nɑ·səvəm] *It is nice of them*,
/kəm+dáwn+náw↑/ [kəm'dᶻɛ·n'nɛ̰̈] *come down now*.

3.055. Vh Peaks

In those Vh syllable peaks whose phonemic norm is a centring diphthong, viz. /ih eh uh/ and, to a less extent, /oh/, there are allophonic variations in the last part of the glide, quite parallel to those found in the unstressed peak /ə/ (3.612).

Before a pause, i.e. particularly in the last syllable of macrosegments ending in the terminal contours /↓/ or /↑/, the glide ends with a more open and back tongue position than in non-final position, where the tongue position for the end-point of the glide is central, between half-close and half-open. Thus, the glide ends with a more open tongue position in

/bíh↓/ *beer*, /béh↓/ *bear*, /dróh↓/ *draw*, /túh↓/ *tour*

than in

/bíhd↓/ *beard*, /níhlij↓/ *nearly*, /əféhz↓/ *affairs*,
/éhrəplèjn↓/ *aeroplane*, /dróhz↓/ *draws*, /túhrist↓/ *tourist*.

3.1. /i/ PEAKS

3.11. Simple Peak /i/

The phonemic norm of the simple peak /i/, as we find it in sít [sɪt] *sit*, does not differ noticeably from RP.[1] Thus, it is an

---

[1] All comparisons with RP sounds are based on the description given by D. Jones, *An Outline of English Phonetics*.

unrounded, between front and central, between close and half-close vocoid.

There are allophonic variants conditioned by the contiguous consonants. The vocoid may be tenser, possibly also closer, before voiced consonants, especially before /d/: /bíd/ *bid*, /ádid/ *added*. After the palatalized consonants /ʃ ʒ/ it is somewhat closer, and often labialized: /idʒípʃiən/ *Egyptian*, /tʃílij/ *chilly*; whereas it may be centralized and labialized after /pr/: /prítij/ *pretty*.

Before pre-consonantal and pre-junctural /l/, /i/ is markedly centralized and often labialized, and the sequence /il/ may be a half-close, central to back vocoid glide, with or without labialization, [ïɤ]: /fíl/ [fïɤ] *fill*, /mílk/ [mïɤk] *milk*. Occasionally, the group /il/ before a consonant may be manifested by a simple back vocoid, with or without labialization and without any perceptible glide: /tʃíldrən/ ['tʃɤdrən] or ['tʃïɤdrən] *children*, /wílfrəd/ ['wɤfrəd] or ['wïɤfrəd] *Wilfred*. This variant has only been found after the labialized consonant onsets /tʃ/ and /w/.[1]

One can observe, with D. Jones,[2] many degrees of closeness in the vowel, depending on stress conditions: the weaker the stress, the more open the vowel. /i/ is closer in *is* than in *if* and *it* in /aj+wə́ndərifit+íz↓/ *I wonder if it is.*

/i/ is subject to the same variations in length as the other vowels (3.052).

3.12. Complex Peak /ih/

The phonemic norm of the complex peak /ih/, as we find it in /bíh/ [bɪə] *beer*, differs from that of RP by having a tenser and more fronted starting-point, possibly also closer.[3] Thus, /ih/ is a vocoid glide where the starting-point is between front

---

[1] Whereas the stressed syllabic vocoid for which we have chosen the symbol [ɤ] is thus to be interpreted as /il/, unstressed syllabic [ɤ] is /əl/, and non-syllabic [ɤ̆] is /l/. Cf. 3.612, 4.414.

[2] *Outline* § 262.

[3] Cf. D. Jones, *Outline* § 441.

and central, between close and half-close, with spread lips; the end is central, between half-close and half-open, with neutral lips.[1] There are allophonic variations in tongue position, less in the starting-point than in the end. The beginning may be less fronted in unstressed position: /wihrów+rájt↓/ *we are all right.* The end of the glide varies in the same way as in other Vh syllable peaks (3.055): in pre-pausal position the tongue glides to a rather open and back position — half-open or half-open to open, and back central: /bíh↓/ *beer,* /ajdíh↓/ *idea.* In non-final position the glide ends with a half-close to half-open, central tongue position: /bíhd↓/ *beard,* /níhlij↓/ *nearly.*

/ih/ does not normally occur before pre-junctural and pre-consonantal /l/ in colloquial style (3.141). When it does so occur /ihl/ may be a half-close, central to back vocoid glide, [ï·ɤ̆], differing from /il/ [ïɤ̆] in that the initial element is longer: /ríhl/ [rï·ɤ̆] *real.*

/ih/ is subject to the same variations in length as the other syllable peaks (3.052). The greater length affects particularly the initial element of the glide, which is sustained. One might transcribe /bíh/ [bɪ·ə̆] *beer* vs. /fíhs/ [fɪə̆s] *fierce.* Monophthongal variants (3.054) have not been observed, except perhaps in unstressed position.

3.13. Complex Peak /ij/

The phonemic norm of the complex syllable peak /ij/, as we find it in /síj/ [sə̆i] *see,* differs from RP in being strongly diphthongized.[2] The tongue glides upwards and forwards, but the starting-point may vary: it may be central and half-close to half-open, or it may be more frontish and half-close: [ə̆i] or [ïi]. Diphthongization is always accompanied by greater length.

---

[1] I. C. Ward, *The Phonetics of English* § 216, has apparently observed a disyllabic group [i·jə]. It might perhaps be possible to interpret it as /ijə/, i.e. as a sequence of the syllable peaks /ij/ and /ə/.

[2] Cf. D. Jones, *Outline* § 251; D. Jones, *Pronunciation* § 71 sq.; I. C. Ward, *The Phonetics of English* § 119 sq.

The degree of diphthongization is conditioned by the same factors as in other syllable peaks (3.053). In unstressed syllables non-finally in the macrosegment /ij/ is not perceptibly glided: /nə́w+wotij+míjnz↑/ ['nœŭ wɔṭi• 'mə̆inz] *No, what he means.* . . .

The diphthongization is not equally strong with all speakers, but it seems to be characteristic of an unguarded style of speech. Nor are there invariably perceptibly glided variants in stressed position and before /#/ even with speakers who commonly diphthongize /ij/.

Most glided complex peaks in Cockney are falling diphthongs (3.03). This is hardly the case for /ij/.[1] (1) The end of the glide is at least as prominent as the beginning. (2) There can be no lengthening of the initial element, such as we find in other glided complex peaks: /ih/ may be [ɪ•ə̆], /aj/ may be [ɑ•ɪ̈], etc. (3.052), but /ij/ is never *[ə•ɪ̈], rather [ə̆i•]. (3) Under those conditions where a monophthongal variant occurs this monophthong is identical with the end-point or target position of the glide, not with the beginning: [i•].

/ij/ does not normally occur before pre-consonantal and pre-junctural /l/ in conversational style (3.141). When it does so occur /ijl/ may be a vocoid glide from front close to half-close back, [i•ɤ̆], differing from /il/ [ɪ̈ɤ̆] in that the initial element is closer, fronter, and longer: /fíjl/ [fi•ɤ̆] *feel*, /míjlz/ [mi•ɤ̆z] *meals.*

3.14. Distribution of /i/ Peaks

3.140

When compared with RP the following distributional facts seem noteworthy.

3.141. *Before /l/*

All three /i/ peaks occur before /l/:
/sílij/ *silly*, /ríhlij/ *really*, /síjlin/ *ceiling.*

[1] Nor for /uw/: cf. 3.53.

However, this is the case only when V follows. /ih/ and /ij/ do not occur before /lC/, /l+/, and /l#/ in normal conversational (not necessarily colloquial) style. Words which have /ih ij/ in RP in this position have forms with /i/ in Cockney:

> /fíl/ *feel, fill*; /fíld/ *field, filled*; /ríl/ *real, reel, rill*; /wíl/ *wheel, will*; /stíl+tʃéhz/ *steel chairs.*

Occurrences of /ih/ and /ij/ in such contexts are rare and confined to a somewhat guarded style of speech.

Morphemes which end in /ijl/ in RP, but which have the form /il/ before consonants and junctures in Cockney, may have the latter form even before vowels in Cockney, a position which otherwise permits the occurrence of /ijl/:

> /fílòw+rájt↑/ *Feel all right?* /filíl↓/ *feel ill.*

However, /ijl/ is a fairly common variant in this position:

> /píjləm↓/ *peel them,* /tu+íjlit+sélf↓/ *to heal itself.*

The occurrence of /il/ before V paralleling RP /ijl/ is apparently limited to word boundaries. Thus, before the morpheme /in/ -*ing* there is no variant in /il/: /fíjlin/ *feeling,* in contrast with /fílin/ *filling.*

3.142. /ij/ vs. /i/

The distribution of the complex peak /ij/ vs. the simple peak /i/ is not exactly the same as in RP in unstressed syllables. As in RP there is fluctuation between /ij/ and /i/ in words like *we, me, he, she, be, the* when unstressed. But in two types of context usage seems to be well established. In *he's, she's, he'd, she'd, we'd, we've,* i.e. before a coda consonant, /ij/ is the norm:

> /ijz+nót+túw+bád↑/ *He's not too bad.*

Likewise, before /#/ /ij/ is the usual form:

> /ən+ðáts+wot+térifàjd+mij↓/ *And that is what terrified me.*

In the same way, /ij/ is the norm finally in unstressed syllables generally before /#/, and common also before /+/:

/ləvlij↓/ *Lovely!* /ðij+ég↓/ *the egg.*

However, there is hardly any contrast between /ij/ and /i/ in this position: the occurrence of one or the other cannot be used to distinguish any meanings. On the basis of phonetic similarity the glide [ӡi] and the relatively close monophthong [iˑ] or [i] are considered manifestations of /ij/, whereas any occurrence of the half-close vocoid [ɪ] is interpreted as /i/:

/aj+wə́ndə+wéhrij+íz↓/ ['weӡri'ɪˑz] *I wonder where he is.*

Even before a coda consonant unstressed /ij/ occurs as an alternant to /i/:

/áwzijz/ *houses,* /tʃə́htʃijz/ *churches.*

It is possible that this is the case only before inflectional suffixes.[1]

The pronoun *his* has often the form /(h)ijz/ when stressed:

/it+wózən+íjz↓/ *It was not his,* /it+ízən+íjz+náw↓/ *It is not his now;*

and so has *is* occasionally:

/wot+áj+kənmejk+áwtovit+íjz↑/ *What I can make out of it is* ...

3.143. Intrusive /i/

There is a type of occurrence of /i/ which we might call 'intrusive'[2] when compared with RP. It occurs unstressed as an extra syllable in penultimate position before juncture:

/bjúwriəw/ *bureau,* /idӡípʃiən/ *Egyptian,* /mədӡíʃiən/ *magician,* /mistʃíjviəs/ *mischievous,* /penisíliin/ *penicillin,* /spíniin/ *spinning,* /wést-mínistə/ *Westminster.*

---

[1] Cf. D. Jones, *Pronunciation* § 77.
[2] Cf. 'intrusive r', D. Jones, *Outline* § 759 sq.

These 'slips' seem to be due to a prevailing rhythmical pattern. Important in this connection is the fact that words which have alternants in monosyllabic /jə/ and disyllabic /iə/ after the primary stress in RP generally have the latter form in Cockney:

/əkówdiən/ *accordeon*, /ówdiəns/ *audience*, /owstréiliə/ *Australia*, /kəlámbiə+rə́w/ *Columbia Row*, /əŋgéhriən/ *Hungarian*, /índiənz/ *Indians*, /júwniən/ *union*, /olímpiə/ *Olympia*, /vədʒíniə+rə́wd/ *Virginia Road*.

'Intrusive' when compared with RP is also the /i/ which occurs in certain suffixes: 3rd pers. pres. sing. of verbs and gen. and plur. of nouns after /st/ are commonly /iz/:

/áhstiz/ *asks*, /gə́wstiz/ *ghosts*, /láhstiz/ *lasts*, /pə́wstiz/ *posts*, /joh+bə́stiz+əbrə́wk/ *your busks are broke*;

but not invariably so.

3.144. *Miscellaneous*

According to tradition, Cockney speakers use /i/ in a number of words where RP has /e/.[1] The following forms have been observed:

/əgín/ *again*, /índʒin/ *engine*, /índʒiníh/ *engineer*, /gít/ *get*, /pəzífənz/ *possessions*.[2]

But there are other forms, which are found in a more guarded style: /əgéjn/ (never */əgén/), /éndʒin/, /gét/, /pəzéfənz/. The forms */símətrij/ *cemetery*, */kítʃəp/ *ketchup*, */ívrij/ *every*, */dʒíntəlmən/ *gentleman*, quoted by Matthews and others, have never been found, but the first two are known to some informants.

There are several occurrences of /i/ in unstressed position paralleling other syllable peaks in RP. Thus, /i/ occurs in some words which have /ə/ in RP:

/kánidə/ *Canada*, /fágits/ *faggots*, /gáhdin/ *garden*, /ádik/ *haddock*, /óbstikəl/ *obstacle*, /ówgin/ *organ*.

---

[1] Cf. W. Matthews, *Cockney Past and Present* p. 169 sq.
[2] Cf. occasional spellings in EE's letters: agin, gittin.

Other words have /ej/ in RP:

/bílinzgit/ *Billingsgate*, /krípəlgit/ *Cripplegate*.

Unstressed *by* and *my* regularly have /i/ in Cockney:

/misélf/ *myself*, /miéjprən/ *my apron*, /wij+kéjm+bák+ bibəs/ *we came back by bus*.

Unstressed *you, your* also quite commonly have /i/:

/jinəw/ *you know*, /jirəwn/ *your own*.

On the other hand, *just* (adverb) and *such* may have /i/ not only in unstressed position but also under primary stress:

/dʒíst+íh/ *just here*, /ajwəz+dʒís+gonə+getón/ *I was just going to get on*, /sítʃə+lót/ *such a lot*.

Alternants in accordance with RP forms have been observed for most of the words quoted above.

3.2. /e/ PEAKS

3.21. Simple Peak /e/

3.211. Phonemic Norm and Allophonic Variations

The phonemic norm of the simple syllable peak /e/, as we find it in /més/ [mes] *mess*, does not differ from that of RP. Thus, /e/ is an unrounded, front, between half-close and half-open vocoid.

There are allophonic variants conditioned by the contiguous consonants. It may be tenser and closer before voiced consonants, especially before /d/: /béd/ *bed*.[1] It is somewhat more open and back before /r/: /bérij/ *bury*. It may be slightly labialized after /r w/: /réd/ *red*, /wén/ *when*.

[1] I have not found /e/ to be closer in Cockney than in RP in general, as suggested by D. Jones (*Outline* § 271, *Pronunciation* § 89), I. C. Ward (*The Phonetics of English* §§ 135, 285), and J. D. O'Connor (*New Phonetic Readings* p. 56). The closer variant before /d/ is found in RP too.

Before pre-consonantal and pre-junctural /l/, /e/ is considerably more open and central than the phonemic norm, and often labialized, and the sequence /el/ may be a vocoid glide from a half-open fronted central to a half-close back tongue position, [ɛ̈ɤ̈]: /bél/ [bɛ̈ɤ̈] *bell*, /séldəm/ ['sɛ̈ɤ̈dəm] *seldom*. The centralization and labialization are particularly strong when /el/ is preceded by /tʃ r w/, all of which are themselves labialized: /tʃéltənəm/ ['tʃɛ̈ɤ̈ʔ̩əm] *Cheltenham*, /rélm/ *realm*, /wél/ *well*. The strongly centralized and labialized variant is most likely to be found in rhythmically non-prominent position, i.e. outside the intonation centre and the last syllable of the macrosegment.

3.212. Diphthongization

/e/ is subject to the same variations in length as the other vowels (3.052).

Vocoid glides, [eᵊ] and [eⁱ], are more common in these positions than long monophthongs.[1] The [eᵊ] allophone of /e/ differs from the phonemic norm of /eh/ [eǒ] (3.22) in that the latter is longer and starts with a closer and tenser tongue position. The [eⁱ] allophone of /e/ differs from the phonemic norm of /ej/ [æï] (3.23) in that the latter is longer and starts with a far more open tongue position. The off-glide in /e/ has little perceptual prominence; we indicate this by using a raised symbol.

[eᵊ] is common before voiced consonants:

/néb/ *neb*, /déd/ *dead*, /ég/ *egg*, /séz/ *says*, /ðém/ *them*, /mén/ *men*, /vérij/ *very*;

and it also occurs, less frequently, before voiceless consonants:

/stép/ *step*, /bét/ *bet*, /rétʃ/ *wretch*, /dék/ *deck*, /déf/ *deaf*, /déθ/ *death*, /jés/ *yes*.[2]

[eⁱ] occurs mainly before voiced consonants, especially before /d n/, but also before /g z ʒ m/:

---

[1] Cf. D. Jones, *Pronunciation* § 90.
[2] Also commonly /jéhs/ [je·ǒs], /jɔ́hs/ [jɜ·s].

/béd/ *bed,* /bréd/ *bread,* /déd/ *dead,* /fréd/ *Fred,* /ámsted/ *Hampstead,* /éd/ *head,* /néd/ *Ned,* /réd/ *red,* /ʃéd/ *shed,* /édʒ/ *edge,* /édʒ+rə̀wz/ *hedgerows,* /slédʒ/ *sledge;* /én(d)/ *end,* /éndid/ *ended,* /frén(d)/ *friend,* /én/ *hen,* /mén/ *men,* /spénd/ *spend,* /ðén/ *then;* /bég/ *beg,* /égz/ *eggs,* /lég/ *leg;* /séz/ *says;* /léʒə/ *leisure,* /méʒə/ *measure;* /dʒém/ *gem,* /ðém/ *them.*

There are also occasional occurrences before voiceless consonants: /sìgəréts/ *cigarettes,* /tʃéʃə+strìjt/ *Cheshire Street.*

Although the [e^i] allophone is most likely to be found before a coda consonant, some of the above examples show that it may also occur before an interlude: /éndid/ *ended,* /méʒə/ *measure,* /tʃéʃə/ *Cheshire.*

And though it is most common in rhythmically prominent position it may also occur unstressed non-finally in a macrosegment: /ðen+áhftə+ðát↑/ [ðe^in] *then after that …*

The allophones [e^ə] and [e^i] are apparently in free variation. For factors conditioning the degree of diphthongization in syllable peaks generally, see 3.053.

3.22. Complex Peak /eh/

The phonemic norm of the complex peak /eh/, as we find it in /béh/ [beə̆] *bear,* differs from that of RP by having a closer starting-point. Thus, /eh/ is a vocoid glide where the starting-point is front, between half-close and half-open, with spread lips; the end is central, between half-close and half-open, with neutral lips.[1]

There are allophonic variations in tongue position, less in the starting-point than in the end. The beginning may be somewhat lowered and retracted in unstressed position. The end of the glide varies in the same way as in other Vh syllable peaks

[1] I. C. Ward, *The Phonetics of English* § 219, seems to have observed a disyllabic group, [e·jə]. This is unknown to me.

(3.055): in pre-pausal position the tongue glides to a rather open and back position — half-open or half-open to open, and back central: /béh↓/ *bear.* In non-final position the glide ends with a half-close to half-open, central tongue position: /éhrəplèjn↓/ *aeroplane,* /əféhz↓/ *affairs.*

/eh/ is subject to the same variations in length as the other syllable peaks (3.052). The greater length affects particularly the initial element of the glide, which is sustained. One might transcribe /tʃéh/ [tʃe·ɜ] *chair* vs. /skéhs/ [skeɜs] *scarce.* Monophthongal variants may occasionally occur in unstressed position: /wehrit+íz↓/ *where it is.*

3.23. Complex Peak /ej/

3.231. Phonemic Norm

The phonemic norm of the complex peak /ej/, as we find it in /méjk/ [mæĭk] *make,* differs from that of RP in having a much more open initial element. Thus, /ej/ is an unrounded front[1] vocoid glide, where the starting-point is between half-open and open, and the end is half-close.

There is considerable allophonic variation, both in quantity and in quality, of this syllable peak.

3.232. Allophonic Variations

In tongue position, the starting-point of the glide varies from [ę], i.e. slightly more open than the phonemic norm

---

[1] I. C. Ward (*The Phonetics of English* § 386) and W. Matthews (*Cockney Past and Present* p. 79) are of the opinion that the first element is somewhat retracted and centralized. A similar variant seems to be indicated by the transcription [ʌi] in J. D. O'Connor, *New Phonetic Readings* pp. 56–9. It is possible that this is a variant with some speakers, though it is not common in my experience.

J. Franklyn (*The Cockney* p. 256) has a note on 'breaking up the diphthong into two parts', which I do not quite know how to interpret. The same observation is said to apply to /aw/ and /əw/. If what he has in mind is a *triphthong,* I cannot agree as regards /ej/ and /əw/: no such variant has been observed.

of the simple peak /e/, to [a], i.e. cardinal vocoid No. 4. The variation is conditioned partly (1) by idiolectal differences, the more open variants being considered by the speakers themselves to be more characteristically Cockney and 'rougher' than the closer ones; partly (2) by style, the diphthong being the more open the more conversational the style; and partly (3) by stress and intonation, since the starting-point of the glide may be closer in unstressed position:

/ðejə+nót+bád↑/ [ðẹ̆ĭ] *they are not bad.*

It is also generally closer under primary stress non-finally in the macrosegment than before /#/:

/déj+baj+déj↓/ ['dɛĭ bɑ̆ĭ 'dæ·ĭ] *day by day,*
/méjd+baj+léjdiz↑/ ['mɛĭd bɑ̆ĭ 'læĭdɪz] *made by ladies.*

The end-point of the glide varies in the same way as in other closing diphthongs (3.054). It is particularly open before simple and zero interludes:

/séjlə/ *sailor,* /táks-pèjə/ *tax-payer.*

/ej/ may even have a monophthongal variant. This sound differs from the simple peak /a/ [ɛ] in being less tense, perhaps not quite as front, and usually more open; it may also be longer: [æ·]:

/éjnàj↓/ ['æ·nɑ̱·] *ain't I.*

Monophthongal or near-monophthongal variants of /ej/ are not likely to occur in the last syllable before /#/, i.e. in rhythmically prominent position.

3.233. *Length*

/ej/ is subject to the same variations in length as the other syllable peaks (3.052). The long variants will generally coincide with those that have a very open starting-point (3.232). The greater length affects particularly the initial element of the glide, which is sustained. One might transcribe /méj/ [mæ·ĭ] *May* vs. /méjt/ [mæĭt] *mate.*

3.234. Before /l/

/ej/ does not normally occur before pre-consonantal and pre-junctural /l/ in colloquial style (3.241). When it does so occur /ejl/ may be a monosyllabic two-directional vocoid glide. The starting-point is almost open and not quite front; the change-point is central, or half-close front; the end-point is half-close back: [ǽɜɤ̆] or [ǽĭɤ̆]: /dʒejl/ [dʒǽɜɤ̆] *gaol,* /séjlz/ [sǽɜɤ̆z] *sails.*

3.24. Distribution of /e/ Peaks

3.240

When compared with RP the following distributional facts seem noteworthy.

3.241. Before /l/

All three /e/ peaks occur before /l/:

/sélin/ *selling,* /réhlij/ *rarely,* /séjlin/ *sailing.*

However, this is the case only when V follows. /eh/ and /ej/ do not occur before /lC/, /l+/, and /l#/ in normal colloquial style.[1] Words which have /ej/ in RP in this position are paralleled by forms with /a/ in Cockney:

/pál/ [pǽɤ̆] *pal, pail, pale;* /sál/ [sǽɤ̆] *Sal, sail, sale;* /nálz/ *nails,* /óks+tàlz/ *oxtails,* /rálwèj/ *railway,* /sálz+lèjdij/ *saleslady,* /skál/ *scale,* /wálz/ *Wales.*

Occurrences of /ej/ in such a context are confined to a more guarded style of speech.

Morphemes which end in /ejl/ in RP, but which have the form /al/ before consonants and junctures in Cockney, occasionally have the latter form even before vowels in Cockney, a position which otherwise permits the occurrence of /ejl/:

[1] Nor does /eh/ in RP, as far as my data go.

/álən+θə́ndə↓/ *hail and thunder*, /ˈðərizə+sálon+dáwnˈðə+
stríjt↓/ *there is a sale on down the street*, /wij+àdə+
wáləvə+tájm↓/ *we had a whale of a time*.

The occurrence of /al/ before V paralleling RP /ejl/ is apparently
limited to word boundaries. Thus, before the morpheme /in/
-ing there is no variant in /al/:

/éjlin/ *ailing*, /séjlin/ *sailing*.

3.242. Miscellaneous

According to tradition, Cockney speakers use /e/ in some
words where RP has /i/.[1] This has been observed in /éf/ *if*
(which is more common than /íf/), occasionally also in
/ʃélin/ *shilling*, /sét/ *sit*. /éritəbel/ *irritable* and /mérəkel/
miracle are also forms known to some informants.

Some words which have /a/ in RP are traditionally said to
have /e/ in Cockney. The following forms have been observed:
/élbət/ *Albert*, /bélkənij/ *balcony*, /kétʃ/ *catch*, /démp/ *damp*,
/swéŋk(ij)/ *swank(y)*;

but alternants with /a/ also occur.

The word *yes* has three alternant forms, /jés/, /jéhs/, and /jə́hs/.

3.3. /a/ PEAKS

3.31. Simple Peak /a/

3.311. Phonemic Norm and Allophonic Variations

The phonemic norm of the simple syllable peak /a/, as we
find it in /bád/ [bɛ·d] *bad*, differs from that of RP in being
slightly closer. Thus, it is an unrounded, front, half-open
vocoid.

There are allophonic variants conditioned by the contiguous
consonants. It is somewhat more open before /r/, where it may

---

[1] Cf. W. Matthews, *Cockney Past and Present* p. 170 sq.; H. C. Wyld,
A History of Modern Colloquial English p. 226 sqq.

be almost as open as RP /a/ [æ]: /bárəks/ *barracks*, /márid/ *married*.

Before pre-consonantal and pre-junctural /l/, /a/ is considerably more open and retracted than the phonemic norm, so that the sequence /al/ may be a vocoid glide from a fronted central, between half-open and open, to a half-close back tongue position, with neutral lips, [äɤ̆]: /pál/ [päɤ̆] *pal*, /málkəm/ ['mäɤ̆kəm] *Malcolm*. In unstressed position the beginning of the vocoid glide is still more open and retracted, and Cockney /al/ is similar to RP /aw/, with the exception that the final part of the vocoid glide is rounded and somewhat more fronted in the latter: /kalkə́tə/ [käɤ̆'kʌtˢə] *Calcutta*, /ðəsalvéjʃən+áhmij/ [säɤ̆'væɪ̈ʃən] *the Salvation Army*.

3.312. *Length*

The phonemic norm of /a/ is not perceptibly longer than that of other simple syllable peaks before a simple consonant interlude. The vowels of the stressed syllables in the following pairs of utterances are not noticeably different in length,[1] and the consonant is phonetically ambisyllabic or belongs to the first syllable in both members of the pairs:

/ápij/ *happy*, /kópə/ *copper*; /pátən/ *pattern*, /bə́tən/ *button*; /lákin/ *lacking*, /líkin/ *licking*; /kábin/ *cabin*, /róbin/ *robin*; /ládə/ *ladder*, /stédij/ *steady*; /bágin/ *bagging*, /bégin/ *begging*; /pásidʒ/ *passage*, /mésidʒ/ *message*; /dáʃin/ *dashing*, /kúʃin/ *cushion*; /ávin/ *having*, /évij/ *heavy*; /stámə/ *stammer*, /sə́mə/ *summer*; /fánij/ *Fanny*, /fə́nij/ *funny*; /pális/ *palace*, /póliʃ/ *polish*; /árij/ *Harry*, /ə́rij/ *hurry*.

However, before a complex consonant interlude the length

---

[1] They are not different to our *perception*. Acoustical (physical) measurements may well reveal consistent differences in length between the vowels; cf. a series of studies by R–M. S. Heffner and others on vowel length in American English, *American Speech* vols. 12, 15, 16, 17, and 18.

of /a/ is more comparable to that of the complex peaks, and the (non-phonemic) syllable division after /a/ parallels the one after complex peaks (2.5, 3.04). Thus, the syllable division may be the same in /bándin/ *banding* and /bájndin/ *binding*, viz. in the last part of /n/, whereas it is in the middle of /d/ in /béndin/ *bending*. Likewise, the syllable cut in /fámlij/ *family* parallels the syllabification of /káhmlij/ *calmly* rather than that of /brómlij/ *Bromley*. And the length of the stressed syllable peak in *banding, family* is more comparable to that of *finding, calmly* than to that of *bending, Bromley*.

The greater length of /a/ compared to that of other simple syllable peaks may be still more marked before /C+/ and /C#/, particularly before voiced stops and nasals:

/káb/ *cab* vs. /ríb/ *rib*, /rób/ *rob*, /rə́b/ *rub*;
/bád/ *bad* vs. /bíd/ *bid*, /béd/ *bed*, /gúd/ *good*, /bə́d/ *bud*;
/bág/ *bag* vs. /bíg/ *big*, /bég/ *beg*, /bóg/ *bog*, /bə́g/ *bug*;
/sáŋ/ *sang* vs. /síŋ/ *sing*, /sóŋ/ *song*, /sə́ŋ/ *sung*.

/a/ is subject to the same variations in length as the other vowels (3.052).

The length of /a/ is a purely phonetic feature of the dialect. There is no phonemic contrast between long and short syllable peaks, for example in *can* (noun) and *can* (auxiliary verb).[1] /a/ does not seem to be longer than in many varieties of RP. The conditioning factors for extra length are largely the same as in RP.[2] The length is not morphologically conditioned, however, as suggested by D. Jones for RP: /a/ is not longer before /d/ in adjectives than in nouns. I suggest that any such length differences in RP may be accounted for in terms of

[1] For such a contrast in other English dialects, cf. D. Jones, *Outline* p. 342 n. 22; H. A. Gleason, *An Introduction to Descriptive Linguistics* p. 33 sq.; J. S. Kenyon and T. A. Knott, *A Pronouncing Dictionary of American English*; G. L. Trager and B. Bloch, 'The Syllabic Phonemes of English' p. 230.

[2] Cf. D. Jones, *Outline* § 874 sqq.

stress and intonation: adjectives like *bad, sad* are likely to occur stressed immediately before /#/, a position which is favourable to lengthening.[1]

3.313. *Diphthongization*

Vocoid glides, [εᵉ] or [εⁱ], are more common before /C+/ and /C#/ than the long monophthong [ε·]. They parallel the glided allophones of the simple peak /e/ (3.212), both in their distribution and in the way they differ from the complex peaks /eh/ and /ej/. The phonemic norm of /eh/ [eɜ] is of longer duration, and it starts with a closer tongue position and ends with a more open and retracted one. The phonemic norm of /ej/ [æɪ] differs from the glided allophone of /a/ in that the former is of longer duration and starts with a more open tongue position. The off-glide in /a/ is characteristically front. It has little perceptual prominence; we indicate this by using a raised symbol.

The glided allophone is common before voiced consonants, especially before the alveolar stop and nasal:

/bád/ *bad*, /dád/ *dad*, /glád/ *glad*, /lád/ *lad*, /mád/ *mad*, /sád/ *sad*; /bán(d)/ *band*, /án(d)/ *and*, /lán(d)/ *land*, /mán/ *man*, /sán(d)/ *sand*, /ván/ *van*;

but also before the velar stop and nasal:

/bág/ *bag*, /báŋ/ *bang*, /gáŋ/ *gang*;

and even before other voiced consonants:

/príj+fàb/ *prefab*, /dʒáz/ *jazz*, /prám/ *pram*.

Before voiceless consonants the glide is less noticeable:

/láp/ *Lap*, /fát/ *fat*, /bák/ *back*.

Although glided allophones are most likely to be found before

---

[1] Cf. D. Jones, *Outline* § 878.

coda consonants they also occur before consonant interludes: /rámzgit/ *Ramsgate*, /stándin/ *standing*.

For factors conditioning the degree of diphthongization in syllable peaks generally, see 3.053.

3.32. Complex Peak /ah/

The phonemic norm of the complex syllable peak /ah/, as we find it in /páhs/ [pɑ·s] *pass*, does not differ from that of RP. Thus, it is an unrounded, almost back, open vocoid.[1] The tongue position of the initial part of this complex peak remains essentially the same in all positions, even before preconsonantal and pre-junctural /l/: /kəntráhltə/ *contralto*. Most other syllable peaks have special allophones in this position (3.051). /áhl/ is, in this position, an unrounded back vocoid glide from open to half-close, [ɑɣ̆]: /snáhl/ [snɑɣ̆] *snarl*. The final part, /h/, may be a voiced non-syllabic continuation of the previous segment. More commonly /ah/ ends in a glide towards a central tongue position, [ɑə̆]. The degree of diphthongization is conditioned by the same factors as in other syllable peaks (3.053). There is hardly any perceptual diphthongization in syllables without primary stress non-finally in the macrosegment:

/àhtifíʃəl/ *artificial*, /ahtílərij/ *artillery*.

/ah/ is subject to the same variations in length as the other syllable peaks (3.052). The conditioning factors for length and diphthongization are the same, so that long variants are commonly diphthongized.

[1] The Cockney variant I have come across does not seem to be more truly back than in RP, as suggested by D. Jones (*Pronunciation* §§ 95, 205) and I. C. Ward (*The Phonetics of English* § 145). Nor have I noticed any markedly rounded variants, as suggested by W. Matthews (*Cockney Past and Present* p. 79). J. Franklyn has probably a back, rounded variant in mind when he writes that '*pass* is cockneyized into *parce*, or *pawce*' (*The Cockney* p. 257).

3.33. Complex Peak /aj/

3.331. Phonemic Norm

The phonemic norm of the complex syllable peak /aj/, as we find it in /rájt/ [rɑ̌ɪt] *right*, differs from that of RP in having a more truly back initial element. However, the pronunciation which is suggested in comic literature by the spelling 'oi', e.g. 'foin' instead of 'fine', is not common: the initial element is generally unrounded. Nor can I agree with W. Matthews[1] that the starting-point of the glide is raised as compared with RP, i.e. not quite open. Thus, /aj/ is an unrounded vocoid glide, from back open towards front half-close. The initial element is more back than that of the complex peak /ah/ (3.32). There is considerable allophonic variation, both in quality and in quantity, of this syllable peak.

3.332. Allophonic Variations

The initial element of the complex peak does not vary noticeably, except that it may be somewhat labialized after the onset consonant /w/: /wáj/ *why*, /wájt/ *white*.

The longer variant (3.333) may be a monosyllabic two-directional vocoid glide, with a closer back vocoid glide between the initial and the final element; the labio-velar glide in the middle is shorter and less prominent than the final part: [ɑ̯ᵒɪ̯].[2] This variant occurs only in rhythmically prominent position, especially in the last syllable of the macrosegment when this is also the centre of the intonation: /wénij+dájd↑/ *when he died*.

The end-point of the glide varies in the same way as in other closing diphthongs (3.054). It is particularly open before simple and zero interludes:

/nájlən/ *nylon*, /fájə/ *fire*.

/aj/ may even have a monophthongal variant. This sound differs from the syllable peak /ah/ [ɑ·] in being more truly back,

[1] *Cockney Past and Present* p. 79.
[2] Cf. 3.42 and 3.43 for similar variants of the peaks /oh oj/.

[ɑ·], possibly also slightly closer.[1] A monophthong or near-monophthong is in fact the most common variant before unstressed vowels:

/bájin/ ['bɑ̠·ɪn] *buying*, /lájənziz/ ['lɑ̠·ənzɪz] *Lyons's*,
/tájəd/ ['tˢɑ̠·əd] *tired*, /vájəlin/ ['vɑ̠·əlɪn] *violin*.

The whole sequence /ajə/ may be a long disyllabic monophthong with an intensity dip in the middle, [ɑ̠ɑ̠]:[2]

/wájəlis/ ['wɑ̠ɑ̠lɪs] *wireless*.

When an interlude follows the monophthong is particularly common before /l/:

/nájlən/ ['nɑ̠·lən] *nylon*, /májlən+rə́wd/ *Mile End Road*,
/májlən+bítə/ *mild and bitter*, /ə+pájləvəm/ *a pile of them*;

but it is also common before other consonant interludes:

/dájnin+rùwm/ *dining-room*, /blájmij/ *blimey*,
/ərájvəl/ *arrival*, /its+nájsəvəm/ *it is nice of them*;

and it may even occur before a coda consonant:

/itsə+nájs+sə́nij+rùwm/ ['nɑ̠·s] *it is a nice, sunny room*.

Monophthongal or near-monophthongal variants of /aj/ are less likely to occur in the last syllable before /#/, i.e. in rhythmically prominent position. In unstressed position non-finally in the macrosegment they are fairly common:

/ajwóntə+téljə+sə́mθiŋk↓/ [ɑ̠'wɔntˢə't ˢeljə'sʌmθɪŋk] *I want to tell you something*, /wót+ajwəz+tə́wld↓/ ['wɔʔɑ̠·wəz 'tˢɔ̆d] *what I was told*.

---

[1] The occurrence or non-occurrence of a 'linking' or 'intrusive' /r/ is a clue to the identity of the long back open vocoid: /ah/ is commonly followed by such a segment, whereas /aj/ never, or hardly ever, is (cf. 4.4221): ['trɑ̠·ən 'bi·] *try and be...*, ['bɑ̠·ɪnɪʔ] *buying it* would have had a segment [r] after [ɑ̠·] if the latter had been /ah/; the two utterances have to be analysed as /trájən+bíj/, /bájinit/.

[2] Only occasionally is the monophthong occurring in this context monosyllabic and a manifestation of the /ah/ peak: /dáhrij/ ['dɑ̠·rʒ̆i] *diary*.

3.333. Length

The complex syllable peak /aj/ is commonly longer than in RP. The variations in length are conditioned by the same factors as in other syllable peaks (3.052). The greater length affects particularly the initial element of the glide, which is sustained. One might transcribe /tráj/ [trɑ·ɪ̆] *try* vs. /rájt/ [rɑɪ̆t] *right*.

3.334. Before /l/

Before pre-consonantal and pre-junctural /l/, /aj/ may be monophthongal, so that /ajl/ is a back, open to half-close vocoid glide, [ɑɣ̆]. Alternatively, it is a monosyllabic two-directional vocoid glide from an open back through a half-close central towards a half-close back position; the whole glide is unrounded, [ɑɜ̆ɣ̆] or [ɑɪ̆ɣ̆]: /pájl/ [pɑɜ̆ɣ̆] *pile*, /tʃájld/ [tʃɑɜ̆ɣ̆d] *child*.

3.34. Complex Peak /aw/

3.341. Phonemic Norms

Cockney /aw/ is characteristically different from the RP norm. However, there are also marked differences among Cockney speakers.[1]

One type, occasionally observed,[2] is a long, fully open, front, unrounded monophthong, [a·]: /dáwn+sáwf+íjst↓/ ['dᶻa·n 'sa·f 'ɪ̈ist] *down South-East*.[3]

[1] Cf. D. Jones, *Pronunciation* § 189; W. Matthews, *Cockney Past and Present* p. 78.

[2] In my data, only among men and boys of a less polished type. One woman informant volunteered the description 'rough' for this variant. Cf. Matthews's note on the social conditioning of these variants: 'The monophthong is used only by the coarsest speakers' (*Cockney Past and Present* p. 78).

[3] One of the informants apparently has this pronunciation in mind when she writes (jocularly?) in letters: 'sharting out there' (i.e. shouting), 'darn the lane' (i.e. down), 'there faarsons of em' (i.e. there are thousands of them). Cf. spellings quoted by W. Matthews (*Cockney Past and Present* p. 65) for late 19th century Cockney: abart, art (i.e. about, out), etc.

Another type is a monosyllabic two-directional vocoid glide: the starting-point is almost front, slightly closer than half-open, unrounded; the change-point is almost open; the end-point is half-close, between central and back, possibly rounded, [ɛɑ̆] or [ɛɑ̆ʊ̆], [ɛä̆] or [ɛä̆ʊ̆]: /náw/ [nɛɑ̆] *now*. By far the most common type, in my experience, is an essentially one-directional glide. The phonemic norm, as we find it in /láwd/ [lɛ̆d] or [lɛ̆ʊ̆d] *loud*, differs from RP in having a closer initial element, with lips more spread, and a more fronted, less rounded final element. The starting-point is almost front, slightly closer than half-open, with somewhat spread lips; the end-point is half-close, between central and back, with slightly rounded or neutral lips. Only this type is discussed in some detail in the following paragraphs.[1]

3.342. *Allophonic Variations*

The initial element of this complex peak does not vary noticeably. For an exception, see 3.344.

The end-point of the glide varies in the same way as in other closing diphthongs (3.054). It is particularly open before unstressed vowels, where the most common variant is a long monophthong: /fláwə/ ['flɛ·ə] *flower*.

The monophthongal variant is not limited to this context. It occurs quite frequently before simple interludes, particularly before /t/ and /n/:

/ʃáwtid/ ['ʃɛ·ţɪd] *shouted*, /ðə+ráwtən+áwziz↓/ [ðə 'rɛ·ʔn̩ 'ɛ̞ziz] *the Rowton Houses*, /dáwnin+strìjt↓/ ['dɛ·nɪn ˌstrĭit] *Downing Street*;

but also before other interludes and before coda consonants:

---

[1] W. Matthews (*Cockney Past and Present* p. 79) describes the monophthong (when /aw/ is non-glided) or the beginning of the glide as 'a vowel between the standard *ah* and short *u*', and he transcribes [tʌ:n] or [tʌən] *town*. I have not come across this centralized variant.

/kráwdid+áwt+ìh↓/ ['krɛ̠·dɪd 'ɛ̠·ʔ ˌɪ·ə̌] *crowded out here*,
/ðij+áws+kìjpə↓/ [ði 'ɛ̠·s‚kȋʰpə] *the housekeeper*,
/dríŋkit+dáwn↓/ ['drɪŋkɪt 'dᶻɛ̠·n] *drink it down*.

The monophthongal variant is less likely to occur in the last syllable before /#/ than in other positions. The two occurrences of /aw/ in each of the following utterances should be compared:

/ʃáwtáwt↓/ ['ʃɛ̠·'ṱɛ̠ə̌tˢ] *shout out*, /kəm+dáwn+náw↑/
[kəm 'dᶻɛ̠·n 'nɛ̠ə̌] *come down now*.

The presence or absence of lip-rounding in the final element may be influenced by some of the same factors which determine the tongue position: relatively close tongue position may be accompanied by lip-rounding. Lip-rounding is particularly noticeable before a pause.

3.343. *Length*

The /aw/ peak is always fairly long, commonly longer than in RP. There are variations in length which parallel those of other complex peaks (3.052). The greater length affects particularly the initial element of the glide, which is sustained. One might transcribe /náw/ [nɛ̠·ə̌] *now* vs. /ʃáwt/ [ʃɛ̠ə̌t] *shout*.

3.344. *Before /l/*

Noticeably different variants occur before /l/. Before /lV/ the starting-point of the glide is often more open than the norm, as in /áwlin/ *howling*.

/aw/ does not normally occur before pre-consonantal and pre-junctural /l/ in colloquial style (3.351). When it does so occur, /awl/ may be a vocoid glide from a fully open, between front and back, tongue position to a half-close back one, while the lips are noticeably rounded at the end, [a̠ŏ]: /fáwl/ [fa̠ŏ] *foul*, /táwlz/ [tˢa̠ŏz] *towels*.

3.35. Distribution of /a/ Peaks

3.350

When compared with RP the following distributional facts seem noteworthy.

3.351. Before /l/

All four /a/ peaks occur before /l/:

/pális/ *palace,* /páhlə/ *parlour,* /nájlən/ *nylon,* /áwlin/ *howling.*

However, this is the case only when V follows. /aw/ does not occur before /lC/, /l+/, and /l#/ in normal colloquial style, and the contrast between /ah/ and /aj/ in this position is not too well established either.

Words which have /aw/ in RP in this position are paralleled by forms with /a/ in Cockney:

/ál/ [ä̌ɣ] *owl, howl, ail, hail;* /fál/ [fä̌ɣ] *foul, fail;* /tálz/ [tˢä̌ɣz] *towels, tails, tales.*[1]

Occurrences of /aw/ in such a context are confined to a more guarded style of speech.

The contrast between /ah/ and /aj/ in this position is, possibly, maintained more frequently than the contrast between /a/ and /ej/ and /aw/:

/snáhl/ [snɑ̌ɣ] *snarl* vs. /smájl/ [smɑ̌ɣ] or [smɑǐ̌ɣ] *smile.*

However, instead of the fully back monophthongal variant of /aj/, a slightly more front sound occurs not infrequently, which is identical with /ah/:[2] /smáhl/ [smɑ̌ɣ] *smile.*

Not infrequently words which have /ah/ or /aj/ before preconsonantal and pre-junctural /l/ in RP are paralleled by forms in /a/ in Cockney: *foul, pal, pale, pile, snarl* may all rhyme, all of them ending in /al/ [ä̌ɣ]. In such a style, out of the four

---

[1] Cockney /al/ paralleling RP /ejl/: see 3.241.
[2] Cf. I. C. Ward, *The Phonetics of English* § 205.

/a/ syllable peaks only the simple peak /a/ occurs before /lC/, /l+/, and /l#/.

In words where RP may have /aj/ and /aw/ before unstressed /əl/, Cockney regularly has /ahl/ (or /ajl/ or /al/) and /awl/ (or /al/):[1]

/tráhl/ (or /trájl/ or /trál/) *trial*, /táwlz/ (or /tálz/) *towels*, /váwlz/ (or /válz/) *vowels*, /trálzən+trə́bəlz/ *trials and troubles*.

This is the case even before vowels: /dájlin/ *dialling* rhymes with /smájlin/ *smiling*.

3.352. Miscellaneous

The contrast between /ah/ and /aj/ is not too well established even in other contexts than before /lC/, /l+/, and /l#/. Words which have /aj/ in RP may be paralleled by forms in /ah/ in Cockney: the syllable peak is manifested by a long monophthong, [ɑ·] = /ah/, and the following words may rhyme: *farce* and *nice*, *darning* and *dining*, *Barton* and *biting*, *laugh* and *life*.[2] Likewise: /áhriʃmən/ *Irishman* (cf. /fáhrəwéj/ *far away*), /máhlen+rə́wd/ *Mile End Road* (cf. /máhlin/ *Marlene*). *Mildmay* is regularly /máhmèj/.

In unstressed position RP forms in /aj/ are quite commonly paralleled by Cockney forms in /ah/: /bah+báj+dìh↑/ *bye-bye*, *dear*.

However, in a more guarded style the contrast between /ah/ and /aj/ is observed.

According to tradition, Cockney speakers use /a/ in some words where RP has /e/, for instance in *celery*, *very*, *yellow*.[3] No such forms appear in my data.

---

[1] Cf. D. Jones, *Outline* § 416. Cf. /ojl/ in Cockney in a similar context, 3.452.

[2] Several informants declared that such pairs rhyme sometimes.

[3] Cf. W. Matthews, *Cockney Past and Present* p. 170.

3.4. /o/ PEAKS

3.41. Simple Peak /o/

The phonemic norm of the simple syllable peak /o/, as we find it in /pót/ [pɔt] *pot*, differs from that of RP in being slightly closer. Thus, it is a rounded, back, half-open vocoid. There are allophonic variants conditioned by the contiguous consonants. Both lip-rounding and tongue position are closer after the onset /w/: /wót/ *what*. The vowel is more open before /lV/ and /r/: /fólə/ *follow*, /sórij/ *sorry*. After velar consonants the articulation is more markedly back: /kódlivə/ *codliver*. In unstressed position /o/ is more centralized and slightly closer: /oféndid/ *offended*.

Before pre-consonantal and pre-junctural /l/ the tongue position is almost completely open, and the lips are only slightly rounded or neutral; the sequence /ol/ may be a back vocoid glide from an open towards a half-close tongue position, while the lips are more rounded at the end, [ɒŏ]: /dól/ [dɒŏ] *doll*, /sólv/ [sɒŏv] *solve*.

/o/ is subject to variations in length similar to those of other vowels (3.052), but these variations are less marked. The longer allophone is commonly slightly glided. The glide is towards a central tongue position before apical consonants, [ɔᵊ]: /nód/ [nɔᵊd] *nod*, /kód/ [kɔᵊd] *cod*. Before labials, and particularly before velars, the glide is towards a closer and more rounded vocoid, [ɔº]: /sób/ [sɔºb] *sob*, /bóm/ [bɔºm] *bomb*, /dók/ [dɔºk] *dock*, /dóg/ [dɔºg] *dog*, /sóŋ/ [sɔºŋ] *song*.

3.42. Complex Peak /oh/

The phonemic norm of the complex peak /oh/, as we find it in /dróh/ [drɔ̞ᵊ] *draw*, differs from that of RP in being slightly closer. It is generally a vocoid glide. The starting-point is rounded, back, almost half-open, and the end is unrounded, central, between half-close and half-open. It differs from the complex peaks /ih eh uh/ (3.12, 3.22, 3.52) in that the initial element is relatively longer, the final element less prominent. On the other hand, it is more glided than the phonemic norm of /ah/ and /əh/ (3.32, 3.62).

There are allophonic variants conditioned by the contiguous consonants. Thus, lip-rounding and tongue position are closer after the onset /w/: /wóh/ *war*. In unstressed position /oh/ is more centralized: /nohwíjdʒən/ *Norwegian*.

The longer variant (see below) may be a monosyllabic two-directional vocoid glide, where tongue and lips move briefly through the position of a closer back rounded vocoid before ending in a neutral position; the medial element is shorter and less prominent than the final part: [ɔºɔ̌].[1] This variant occurs only in rhythmically prominent position, especially in the last syllable of the macrosegment: /ðéhfòh↑/ ['ðeɔ̌ˌfɔºɔ̌] *therefore*, /dʒə̀s+bifóh+ðəwóh↑/ [ˌdʒʌs bɪ'fɔ• ðə'wɔºɔ̌] *just before the war*.

The end of the glide varies in the same way as in other Vh syllable peaks (3.055): in pre-pausal position the tongue glides to a rather open and back position — half-open or half-open to open, and back central: /dróh/ *draw*. In non-final position the glide ends with a half-close to half-open, central tongue position: /dróhz/ *draws*. A monophthongal variant, [ɔ•], is common in rhythmically less prominent position: cf. *before* and *war* in the example quoted above.

/oh/ is subject to the same variations in length as the other syllable peaks (3.052). The conditioning factors for length and diphthongization are the same, so that long variants are commonly diphthongized.

3.43. Complex Peak /oj/

The phonemic norm of the complex peak /oj/, as we find it in /dʒójn/ [dʒɔˇɪn] *join*, differs from that of RP in having a

---

[1] Cf. 3.332 and 3.43 for similar variants of the peaks /aj/ and /oj/. I. C. Ward (*The Phonetics of English* § 164) and D. Jones (*Pronunciation* §§ 108, 212) mention this variant, but consider it to be disyllabic.

slightly closer initial element, about the same as the /oh/ peak.
Thus, /oj/ is a vocoid glide where the starting-point is rounded,
back, almost half-open, and the end is unrounded, front,
half-close.

The longer variant (see below) may be a monosyllabic two-
directional vocoid glide, with a closer back vocoid glide between
the initial and the final element; the medial element is shorter
and less prominent than the final part: [ɔºɪ].[1] This variant
occurs only in rhythmically prominent position, especially in the
last syllable of the macrosegment: /inə+kónvòj↓/ [mə 'kɔn‚vɔ°ɪ]
in a convoy, /wə́n+bój↑/ ['wʌn 'bɔ°ɪ] *one boy*.
The end-point of the glide varies in the same way as in other
closing diphthongs (3.054). It is particularly open before simple
and zero interludes: /bójlə/ *boiler*, /indʒójin/ *enjoying*, /implójə/
employer. However, unlike /ej/ and /aj/, /oj/ does not have any
monophthongal variants in this position.

Nor are monophthongal variants common before pre-consonantal and pre-junctural /l/ (cf. 3.051). /ójl/ in this position
may be a monosyllabic two-directional vocoid glide from a
half-open back through a half-close central towards a half-
close back tongue position; only the initial part of the glide is
rounded, [ɔə̆ɣ̆] or [ɔɪ̆ɣ̆]: /bójl/ [bɔə̆ɣ̆] *boil*.

/oj/ is subject to the same variations in length as the other
syllable peaks (3.052). The greater length affects particularly
the initial element of the glide, which is sustained. One might
transcribe /bój/ [bɔ·ɪ̆] *boy* vs. /vójs/ [vɔɪ̆s] *voice*.

3.44. Complex Peak /ow/

The phonemic norm of the complex peak /ow/, as we find it
in /lówd/ [lǫŭd] *lord*, differs from that of RP in being slightly
closer, and glided. It is a back vocoid glide, from between half-
close and half-open to half-close, with progressive rounding
of the lips.

---

[1] Cf. 3.332 and 3.42 for similar variants of the peaks /aj/ and /oh/.

Both lip-rounding and tongue position are closer after the onset /w/ and before labial codas: /wówm/ *warm*, /wówtə/ *water*, /ówf/ *off*, /fówm/ *form*.

The vocoid glide is a narrow one, and a monophthongal variant, [ǫ·], is not uncommon in rhythmically non-prominent position. However, in the last syllable of the macrosegment a glided allophone is the norm: /sə̀w+əv+kóws↓/ *So of course* —. /ow/ does not normally occur before pre-consonantal and pre-junctural /l/ in colloquial style (3.452). When it does so occur the initial element is more open, and /owl/ may be a one-directional back vocoid glide from a half-open to a half-close position; the end of the glide is more truly back than in /ow/, [ɔ̆ŏ]: /ówl/ [ɔ̆ŏ] *all*, /sən+pówlz/ [sŋ̍'pɔŏz] *St. Paul's*.

3.45. Distribution of /o/ Peaks
3.450

When compared with RP the following distributional facts seem noteworthy.

3.451. /oh/ vs. /ow/

The contrast between /oh/ and /ow/ is of a special nature: (1) as a consistent contrast it is limited to certain contexts only; (2) the distribution of /oh/ and /ow/ is partly morphologically conditioned; (3) the speakers are not aware of a difference, or contrast, they consistently make; (4) the distinction is not observed to the same extent by all speakers.

However, we shall still have to postulate a contrast between two syllable peaks, /oh/ and /ow/, with the understanding that in the idiolects of those who do not make such a difference there is only one syllable peak, /oh/, whose phonemic norm is between half-close and half-open, [ǫ·] or [ɔ·], and which may be glided according to 3.42. In the following paragraphs I shall state the distribution of /oh/ and /ow/ in those idiolects where they contrast.

Both /oh/ and /ow/ occur before juncture:

/óh/ *oar, or, ore, awe* vs. /ów/ *all,* /bóh/ *bore* vs. /bów/ *ball,*
/kóh/ *core* vs. /ków/ *call,* /fóh/ *for, four* vs. /fów/ *fall,*
/póh/ *paw, poor, pore, pour* vs. /pów/ *Paul,* /stóh/ *store*
vs. /stów/ *stall,* /tóh/ *tore* vs. /tów/ *tall,* /wóh/ *war, wore*
vs. /wów/ *wall.*

This contrast parallels one between absence and presence of
/l/ in RP: /óh/ *oar, or, ore, awe* vs. /óhl/ *all* (cf. 3.452).

Both /oh/ and /ow/ also occur before /d z/:

/bóhd/ *bored* vs. /bówd/ *board,* /bóhz/ *bores* vs. /bówz/ *balls,*
/fóhz/ *fours* vs. /fówz/ *falls,* /póhz/ *paws, pores, pours* vs.
/pówz/ *Paul's,* /stóhz/ *stores* vs. /stówz/ *stalls,* /wóhz/
wars vs. /wówz/ *walls.*

The occurrence of /oh/ in this context is morphologically conditioned: it occurs only before the verbal and nominal inflectional suffixes /d/ and /z/:

/bóhd/ *bored,* /póhd/ *poured,* /róhd/ *roared;* /bóhz/ *bores,*
/dóhz/ *doors,* /dróhz/ *draws,* /lóhz/ *laws,* /póhz/ *paws,*
pores, pours;

and even in this context it does not occur in morphemes where
RP has /ohl/; instead /ow/ occurs:

/kówd/ *called* (and *cord*), /kówz/ *calls* (and *cause*), /fówz/
falls, /pówz/ *Paul's* (and *pause*), /stówz/ *stalls.*

Elsewhere, only /ow/ occurs before the coda consonants /d z/:

/əbrówd/ *abroad,* /bówd/ *board,* /ków d/ *cord,* /dʒówdʒ/
George, /lówd/ *lord,* /rikówd/ *record,* /sówd/ *sword,* /wówd/
ward; /kówz/ *cause,* /pówz/ *pause;*

and before other coda consonants:

/bówt/ *bought,* /kówt/ *caught, court,* /fówt/ *fort, fault, fought,*
/ʃówt/ *short,* /sówt/ *sort, salt,* /θówt/ *thought;* /pówk/ *pork,*
/tówk/ *talk,* /wówk/ *walk;* /kówf/ *cough,* /ówf/ *off;* /fówθ/

fourth; /kóws/ *course,* /fóws/ *force, false,* /lówst/ *lost,* /sóws/ *sauce;* /fówm/ *form,* /wówm/ *warm;* /bówn/ *born,* /kówn/ *corn,* /drówn/ *drawn,* /lówn/ *lawn,* /wówn/ *warn.*

Likewise, before pre-junctural /l/, in the more guarded style of speech where /l/ is pronounced in this context (3.452), /ow/, and not /oh/, occurs:

/ówl/ *all,* /ʃówlz/ *shawls.*[1]

Before interludes there is less consistency in the distribution of /oh/ and /ow/. Most commonly only /oh/ occurs before /r/:

/kóhrəs/ *chorus,* /dóhrijn/ *Doreen,* /inʃóhrəns/ *insurance,* /dʒóhrin/ *jawing,* /nóhrə/ *Nora,* /póhrin/ *pouring,* /stóhrij/ *story.*

Before other consonants there is a tendency to use /oh/ before a morpheme boundary:[2]

/dóhwèj/ *doorway,* /sóhdəst/ *sawdust,* /ʃóhditʃ/ *Shoreditch,* /ʃóhlij/ *surely,* /johsélf/ *yourself;*

but /ow/ when the morpheme boundary is after the following consonant:

/kówlin/ *calling,* /kówzin/ *causing,* /fówlən/ *fallen,* /fówsiz/ *forces,* /gówdʒəs/ *gorgeous,* /impówtənt/ *important,* /mównin/ *morning,* /nówtij/ *naughty,* /nówməlij/ *normally,* /rikówdə/ *recorder,* /sówsij/ *saucy,* /sówtəv/ *sort of,* /smówlə/ *smaller,* /tówkin/ *talking,* /wówdən/ *warden;*

or where there is no clearly felt morphological boundary after the syllable containing /o/:

[1] Some informants were asked about the sameness or difference of pairs like *bored/board, paws/pause.* They coisndered these forms to be the same. However, when asked to read word lists containing such words they consistently made a difference, [ɔɜ̆] vs. [ǫŭ], whether the /oh/ and /ow/ words were grouped together in separate columns or put in random order.

[2] In such cases there are sometimes alternant forms with /+/ at the morpheme boundary: /dóh+wèj/ *doorway.*

/əkówdiən/ *accordeon*, /ówkwəd/ *awkward*, /bówstəl/ *Borstal*, /kównə/ *corner*, /kówsit/ *corset*, /dówtə/ *daughter*, /lówndrij/ *laundry*, /ówdə/ *order*, /ówdinərij/ *ordinary*, /ówgin/ *organ*, /kwówtə/ *quarter*, /wówtə/ *water*.

However, before an interlude we cannot clearly demonstrate that [ɔɤ̆] and [ǫŭ] are in complementary distribution, nor that they are in contrast: there is too much inconsistency and vacillation in their use.

Since the occurrence of /oh/ is largely morphologically conditioned before the coda consonants /d z/ and before consonant interludes, one might consider /oh/ and /ow/ in complementary distribution in this context, and hence interpret them as variants of the same syllable peak. However, I would like to describe the phonological system independently of the morphological one, and only consider phonological conditioning relevant for complementary distribution (cf. 7.13 (5)).[1] Besides, we still have to account for the contrast between [tɔɤ̆] *tore* and [tǫŭ] *tall*. The latter might have been interpreted as */tóhl/ *tall*, vs. /tóh/ *tore*, had it not been for the fact that *force* and *false*, *sort* and *salt*, *water* and *Walter*, etc., are homonyms (3.452) and can hardly both be considered as containing /l/, */fóhls/ *force*, *false*, */sóhlt/ *sort*, *salt*, */wóhltə/ *water*, *Walter*: they must be interpreted as /fóws/, etc. This is the same peak as that which occurs in *tall*.[2]

[1] For a phonological contrast which seems to be associated with a morphological one, cf. the distribution of [ʌi] and [ae], and of short and long vowels, in Scottish: according to D. Jones (*Pronunciation* §§ 180–1, 431) they are in complementary distribution except before /d z/; in that context [ae] and long vowels occur only before the inflectional suffixes, whereas [ʌi] and short vowels occur before non-inflectional /d z/.

[2] The contrast between /oh/ and /ow/ is not the same as the one found between pairs like *hoarse* and *horse*, *mourning* and *morning* in other dialects of English (cf. D. Jones, *Outline* § 308 and note; I. C. Ward, *The Phonetics of English* §§ 161–3; J. S. Kenyon and T. A. Knott, *A Pronouncing Dictionary of American English* § 98; H. Kurath, 'Mourning and Morning'; G. L. Trager and B. Bloch, 'The Syllabic Phonemes of English' p. 239): these pairs are homonyms in Cockney: /hóws/, /mównin/.

3.452. Before /l/

All four /o/ peaks occur before /l/:

/fólə/ *follow*, /ʃóhlij/ *surely*, /bójlə/ *boiler*, /smówlə/ *smaller*.[1]

However, this is only the case when V follows: /oh/ does not occur before /lC/, /l+/, and /l#/. Nor does /ow/ in normal colloquial style: words which have /owl/ in RP in this position are paralleled by forms with /ow/ in Cockney:

/bówd/ *bald* (and *board*), /kówd/ *called* (and *cord*), /kówz/ *calls* (and *cause*), /fóws/ *false* (and *force*), /pówz/ *Paul's* (and *pause*), /sówt/ *salt* (and *sort*), /wówtə/ *Walter* (and *water*), /wóws/ *waltz*, /ów+rájt/ *all right*, /mjúwzik+òwz/ *music halls*.[2]

Occurrences of /owl/ in such a context are confined to a more guarded style of speech.

In words where RP may have /oj/ before unstressed /əl/, Cockney regularly has /ojl/: /lójl/ *loyal* and /rójl/ *royal* rhyme with /bójl/ *boil*.[3]

3.453. /o/ vs. /ow/

In some contexts RP has alternative forms with /o/ and /ow/.[4] In the older generation /ow/ is the usual variant in Cockney, both before RP /lC/ (there is usually no /l/ in Cockney):

/ówməwst/ *almost*, /owrédij/ *already*, /ówsəw/ *also*, /ówtə/ *alter*, /owðə́w/ *although*, /ówwəz/ *always*, /fóws/ *false*, /fówt/ *fault*, /sówt/ *salt*, /wówltə/ *Walter*;

and before the voiceless fricatives /f θ s/:

---

[1] For the contrast, or lack of contrast, between /ohlV/ and /owlV/, see 3.451.

[2] One informant consistently writes 'walden' for 'warden' in her letters, a spelling which shows that there would be no contrast between two such words.

[3] Cf. /ajl/ in a similar context, 3.351.

[4] Cf. D. Jones, *Outline* §§ 300, 308.

/klówf/ or /klówθ/ *cloth,* /kówfij/ *coffee,* /kówf/ *cough,* /mówf/ or /mówθ/ *moth,* /ówf/ *off,* /ówfən/ *often,* /sówft/ *soft;* /kówst/ *cost,* /kówstə/ *coster,* /króws/ *cross,* /frówst/ *frost,* /ówspitəl/ *hospital,* /lówst/ *lost.*

However, the younger generation more frequently use forms with the simple peak /o/ before the voiceless fricatives, and these are considered by the older generation, too, to be more correct.

In addition, /ow/ regularly occurs in /gówd/ *God,* /gówn/ *gone.*[1]

3.454. /oh/ vs. /uh/

In RP there is, in a number of morphemes, fluctuation between the syllable peaks /oh/ and /uh/, possibly also a third, intermediate peak.[2] In Cockney /oh/ is by far the most common variant: /póh/ *poor,* /ʃóh/ *sure,* /jóh/ *your.*

3.5. /u/ PEAKS

3.51. Simple Peak /u/

The phonemic norm of the simple peak /u/, as we find it in /stúd/ [stʊd] *stood,* differs slightly from that of RP in being a little more fronted. Thus, /u/ is a rounded, between central and back, between close and half-close vocoid.

There are allophonic variants conditioned by the contiguous consonants. /u/ is slightly more back after labials: /púdən/ *pudding,* /pút/ *put,* /búk/ *book,* /búʃ/ *bush;* particularly when /lV/ follows: /púlin/ *pulling,* /búlij/ *bully,* /fúlij/ *fully.* It is also more back after velars: /kúk/ *cook,* /kúʃin/ *cushion,* /gúd/ *good.* After /w/ the lip-rounding is closer: /wúd/ *wood,* /wúmən/ *woman.* After the consonant /j/, and to some extent after the strongly palatalized /ʃ ʒ/, /u/ is centralized, [ü]: /vákjuèjtid/

---

[1] I have not noticed it in *dog,* where J. D. O'Connor seems to have found it: cf. the transcription [do:g] in *New Phonetic Readings* p. 58.
[2] Cf. D. Jones, *Outline* §§ 462–4.

evacuated, /pətíkjuləlij/ *particularly*, /wótʃu+wónt/ *what you
want*. These variations are only slight, and not more marked
than in RP.

Before pre-consonantal and pre-junctural /l/, /u/ is more
truly back and slightly more open, and the phoneme sequence
/ul/ may be a back vocoid glide from just above half-close
towards close, with progressive rounding of the lips, /u̯ŭ/: /búl/
[bu̯ŭ] *bull*, /fúl/ [fu̯ŭ] *full*, /wúlf/ [wu̯ŭf] *wolf*, /wúlwəs/ ['wu̯ŭwəs]
Woolworth's. The glide is narrow, and sometimes hardly perceptible. The presence of /l/ is then manifested by the greater
length and the particularly back quality of the vocoid: /púld/
[pu̯·d] *pulled*, vs. /pút/ [pʊt] *put*.

/u/ is subject to the same variations in length as the other
vowels (3.052), but these are not very marked.

3.52. Complex Peak /uh/

The phonemic norm of the complex peak /uh/, as we find it
in /túh/ [tʊə̆] *tour*, differs from that of RP in having a slightly
fronter starting-point, just as the simple peak /u/ is fronter.
Thus, it is a vocoid glide where the starting-point is rounded,
back central, between close and half-close, and the end is unrounded, central, between half-close and half-open.

There are allophonic variations in the tongue position of the
initial element which parallel those of the simple peak /u/.
After /j ʃ ʒ/ the starting-point is centralized, [ü ə̆]: /fjúhrij/
fury, /dʒúhrij/ *jury*.

The end of the glide varies in the same way as in other Vh
syllable peaks (3.055): in pre-pausal position the tongue glides
to a rather open and back position — half-open or half-open to
open, and back central: /túh/ *tour*. In non-final position the
glide ends with a half-close to half-open, central tongue position:
/túhrist/ *tourist*, /ínfluhns/ *influence*.

Because of the infrequent occurrence of this syllable peak
length variations can hardly be studied systematically. They
are assumed to be the same as in most other syllable peaks
(3.052).

3.53. Complex Peak /uw/

The phonemic norm of the complex syllable peak /uw/, as we find it in /dúw/ [dɜ̌ü] *do*, differs from that of RP in being strongly diphthongized, and considerably more fronted. The tongue glides upwards, but the starting-point may vary: it may be half-close to half-open, or it may be half-close. It is central rather than back, and the lips, which may be neutral at the beginning, are fairly closely rounded at the end: [ɜ̌ü] or [ŭü]. Diphthongization is always accompanied by greater length. The degree of diphthongization is conditioned by the same factors as in other syllable peaks (3.053). In unstressed syllables non-finally in the macrosegment /uw/ is not perceptibly glided, [ü·]. The diphthongization is not equally strong with all speakers, but it seems to be characteristic of an unguarded style of speech. Nor are there invariably perceptibly glided variants in stressed position and before /#/ even with those speakers who commonly diphthongize /uw/.

Most glided complex peaks in Cockney are falling diphthongs (3.03). This is hardly the case for /uw/:[1] (1) the end of the glide is at least as prominent as the beginning; (2) there can be no lengthening of the initial element, such as we find in other complex peaks: /uh/ may be [ʊ·ɜ̌], /aj/ may be [ɑ·ɪ̆], etc. (3.052), but /uw/ is never *[ə·ŭ], rather [ɜ̌ü·]; (3) under those conditions where a monophthongal variant occurs, this monophthong is identical with the end-point or target position of the glide, not with the beginning: [ü·].

/uw/ is more fronted than the norm after the consonant /j/: /júw/ *you*, /kjúw/ *queue*. After /w/ it is more backish and has closer lip-rounding even in the initial part of the glide: /wúwndid/ *wounded*. These variations are not more marked than in RP.

/uw/ does not normally occur before pre-consonantal and pre-junctural /l/ in colloquial style (3.541). When it does so occur, /uwl/ may be a rounded back vocoid glide from half-

---

[1] Nor for /ij/: cf. 3.13.

close towards close, differing from /ul/ [u̯ŭ] in the length of the initial element and in the potential neutral on-glide: /fúwl/ [fu̯·ŭ] or [fə̯u̯ŭ] *fool*.

3.54. Distribution of /u/ Peaks

3.540

When compared with RP the following distributional facts seem noteworthy.

3.541. Before /l/

All three /u/ peaks occur before /l/:

/fúlij/ *fully*, /krúhlij/ *cruelly*,[1] /fúwliʃ/ *foolish*.

However, this is the case only when V follows. /uh/ and /uw/ do not occur before /lC/, /l+/, and /l#/ in normal colloquial style. Words which have /uw/ in RP in this position have forms with /u/ in Cockney:

/fúl/ *fool*, *full*, /púl/ *pool*, *pull*, /skúlz/ *schools*, /lívepul/ *Liverpool*.

Occurrences of /uw/ in such a context are rare, though not quite so rare as /ij/ in a similar context (3.141), and confined to a somewhat guarded style of speech.

/uh/ does not occur in this position either. Words which have /uh/ in RP have either forms with /uwə/, /uw/, or, most commonly, /u/ in Cockney:

/krúl/ [kru̯ŭ] or /krúwl/ [kru̯·ŭ] or /krúwəl/ ['kru̯·u] *cruel*, /fjúl/ or /fjúwl/ or /fjúwəl/ *fuel*, /dʒúlz/ or /dʒúwlz/ or /dʒúwəlz/ *jewels*, /júwʒul/ or /júwʒuwl/ or /júwʒuwəl/ *usual*.

Morphemes which end in /uwl/ in RP, but which have the form /ul/ before consonants and junctures in Cockney, occasion-

[1] A more common variant, instead of /uhl/, is /uwəl/: /krúwəlij/ *cruelly*.

ally have the latter form even before vowels in Cockney, a position which otherwise permits the occurrence of /uwl/:

/in+skúləz+wél/ *in school as well.*

However, /uwl/ is more common in this position:

/fúwlim/ *fool him.*

3.542. /uh/

/uh/ occurs in a few morphemes only, commonly alternating with other syllable peaks. It is a rare variant of the syllable peak in *poor, sure, your,* usually /póh/, /ʃóh/, /jóh/. In less common words, such as *tour, tourist,* /uh/ occurs more freely in alternation with /oh/. It seems to be the only possible syllable peak for the first syllable of *during.*

There is also alternation between monosyllabic /uh/ and disyllabic /uwə/: /áhdjuhs/ or /áhdjuwəs/ *arduous,* /ínfluhns/ or /ínfluwəns/ *influence,* /súhz/ or /súwəz/ *sewers.*

Before /l/ other /u/ peaks are more common (3.541).

3.6. /ə/ PEAKS

3.61. Simple Peak /ə/

3.611. *Stressed /ə/*

The simple syllable peak /ə/ in stressed syllables, i.e. syllables with primary or secondary stress, has considerably varying manifestations in different English dialects. The phonemic norm in Cockney, as we find it in /bə́d/ [bʌd] *bud,* is not the one described for RP,[1] but it does not differ from that of many educated Londoners: it is an unrounded, front, between half-open and open vocoid, not too unlike RP /a/, except that the tongue is not quite so front as in RP /a/, and has no raising at the sides; nor is there any constriction in the pharynx, all

[1] Cf. D. Jones, *Outline* § 334 sqq.

of which is supposed to characterize the RP simple peak /a/.¹
There are few allophonic variations of this syllable peak.
After the consonants /ʃ ʒ r/, and especially after /w/, there may
be some labialization: /ʃə́t/ *shut*, /tʃə́kəl/ *chuckle*, /dʒə́mp/
jump, /rə́f/ *rough*, /wə́ndə/ *wonder*. Before /r/ and /lV/ the tongue
position is slightly more open and retracted: /ə́rij/ *hurry*, /kə́lə/
colour.

A considerably more retracted variant occurs before pre-
consonantal and pre-junctural /l/, and the phoneme sequence
/əl/ may be a vocoid glide from a fronted back, between half-
open and open tongue position towards a back half-close one,
[ʌ̆]: /də́l/ [dʌ̆] *dull*, /bə́lb/ [bʌ̆b] *bulb*, /kə́ltʃə/ ['kʌ̆tʃə] *culture*,
/ə́lsə/ ['ʌ̆sə] *ulcer*, /sə̀ltáhnə/ [ˌsʌ̆'tˢɑ·nə] *sultana*.
The simple peak /ə/ is short. Longer variants occur only in
the last syllable of the macrosegment (cf. 3.052): /its+bréjkin+
ə́p↓/ *it is breaking up*.

3.612. Unstressed /ə/²

The simple peak /ə/ in unstressed position is the central vowel
par excellence. It may vary considerably in tongue position
within the central vocoid area from half-close to half-open;
the setting up of any phonemic norm would be too arbitrary to

¹ Cf. D. Jones, *Outline* § 277 and note. I cannot agree with W. Matthews
(*Cockney Past and Present* p. 80) that this vocoid is 'more central than
the standard sound. It is a vowel between the standard short *u* and
the standard vowel in *bird, worse*, etc.': it is front, not central.

² There is no contrast between the simple syllable peaks [ʌ] and [ə],
as assumed for RP by D. Jones (*The Phoneme* § 148) and M. Swadesh
('On the Analysis of English Syllabics'): [ʌ] never occurs in unstressed
syllables, only under primary or secondary stress, whereas [ə] only occurs
unstressed. *Hiccup* is /íkəp/ ['ıkʌp] (cf. Jones's ['hıkʌp], re-transcribed
in accordance with our system of transcription), and *undone* is either
/ə̀ndə́n/ [ˌʌn'dʌn] or /əndə́n/ [ən'dʌn]; the latter form is homophonous
with *and done*. Jones mentions, but rejects, the possibility of a similar
interpretation for RP when he writes (§ 206) ['hiˌkəp] *hiccup* vs. ['sirəp]
syrup.

be of any use. However, it is always short, and the lip position
is neutral, to the extent that it does not anticipate or continue
the labialization of any following or preceding segment.

Before consonants and internal juncture /ə/ is most truly
central, midway between half-close and half-open: /əbáwt/
about, /tədéj/ *today*, /lə́ndən/ *London*, /féjməs/ *famous*. Before a
terminal contour, particularly when followed by an appreciable
pause, the vocoid is considerably more open and slightly more
back: /dínə↓/ *dinner*, /péjpə↓/ *paper*.[1]

Other special variants, such as the one called 'ə₄' which is
supposed to occur in word-final utterance-medial /rə/,[2] have not
been observed. But there are variants whose nature depends on
the particular segments which precede and follow. Thus, /ə/
is closer and more back when contiguous to velar consonants, particularly between velars: /kəŋgrátjulèjt/ *congratulate*,
/bák əgèjn/ *back again*.

Before /m n ŋ l r/, /ə/ is usually not manifested by any separate
vocoid segment, but by the syllabicity, i. e. the extra length
and the syllable pulse, of the following segment:

/ápəm/ ['ɛpm̩] *happen*, /ə́zbəm/ ['ʌzbm̩] *husband*,[3] /sə́məməm/
['sʌmm̩m̩] *some of them*; /púdən/ ['pʊdn̩] *pudding*, /pə́hsən/
['pɜ·sn̩] *person*, /wútən+síj/ ['wʊʔn̩ 'sə̌i] *would not see*;
/kútəŋ+gét/ ['kuʔŋ 'geʔ] *could not get*; /ʃə́dərin/ ['ʃʌdr̩ɪn]
shuddering, /dərétlij/ [dr̩'eʔlə̌i] *directly*; /bəlíjv/ [bl̩'ɪ̌iv]
believe, /dʒéntəlmən/ ['dʒentl̩mən] *gentleman*, /béθnəl+gríjn/
['beθnɤ 'grə̌in] *Bethnal Green*.

In some cases the distribution of [əC] and [Ç] is conditioned
by the context. Otherwise the two manifestations are in free

---

[1] Cf. similar variations in tongue position, from midway between
half-close and half-open, to half-open, in the /h/ allophones occurring
in the complex peak Vh (3.055).

[2] Cf. D. Jones, *Outline* § 364.

[3] This form, as well as most of the other forms cited in this paragraph, is only one among several possible forms. Thus, *husband* may
also be /ə́zbən/ ['ʌzbən].

variation, though there are certain probabilities of occurrence. Thus, between homorganic stops and nasals /ə/ is almost invariably manifested by the syllabicity of the contoid:

/gáhdən/ ['gɑ·dn̩] *garden*, /kə́mpəmij/ ['kʌmpm̩ɵ̌i] *company*, /béjkəŋ/ ['bæɪ̆kŋ̩] *bacon*.

This is always the case when the /t/ in /tən/ is manifested by [ʔ]:

/gétən/ ['geʔn̩] *getting*, /rótən/ ['rɔʔn̩] *rotten*.

After other consonants, however, /əN/ is more commonly manifested by [əN]: after nasals, nasals plus stops, and /r j w/, [əN] is the rule:

/wúmən/ ['wʊmən] *woman*, /lə́ndən/ ['lʌndən] *London*, /tʃíldrən/ ['tʃɪ̆ðdrən] *children*, /itáljən/ ['ɪ'tˢɛljən] *Italian*, /fríjkwənt/ ['frɪ̆ikwənt] *frequent*;

and after the fricatives /ʃ ʒ/, [əN] is by far the more common variant:

/diskə́ʃən/ *discussion*, /pénʃən/ *pension*, /kəlíʒən/ *collision*, /nohwíjdʒən/ *Norwegian*.

After other fricatives there is more fluctuation, [ən] or [n̩]:

/lísən/ *listen*, /pə́hsən/ *person*, /núwsəns/ *nuisance*; /də́zən/ *dozen*, /fró̄wzən/ *frozen*, /θáwzənz/ *thousands*; /íjvən/ *even*, /sévən/ *seven*.

/ər/ may be variously manifested by [ər] and [ɼ]; the latter is most likely to occur after homorganic consonants:

/dówtərinlòh/ ['dǫ·tɼ̩nˌlɔ̌] *daughter-in-law*, /aj+wə́ndərif/ [ɑ̠· 'wʌndɼɪf] *I wonder if* ..., /áhnsərim+bák/ ['ɑ·nsɼɪm 'bɛk] *answer him back*;

and it also occurs as a variant in other contexts:

/émpərə/ ['empɼə] *emperor*, /néjbərin/ ['næɪ̆bɼɪn] *neighbouring*, /sén+fərəh/ ['sen fɼɜ·] *send for her*.

/əl/, on the other hand, is almost invariably manifested by a

single segment, [ḷ] before vowels, [ɫ̣] or [ɤ] before consonants
and juncture (4.412, 4.413).

Only occasionally is /ə/ manifested by the syllabicity of a
following segment other than nasal or sonorant: /próbəblij/
['prɔbb̥ḷə̌i] *probably*.[1]

3.62. Complex Peak /əh/

The phonemic norm of the complex syllable peak /əh/, as we
find it in /bə́hd/ [bɜ·d] *bird*, differs from that of RP in that the
tongue position is more open and front, the opening between
the jaws is greater, and the lips are slightly rounded, or rather
protruded. Thus, /əh/ is a fronted central, almost half-open,
slightly labialized vocoid. It is long, and may be followed by a
short central off-glide, during which the tongue is slightly
retracted, and, before consonants and internal juncture, also
raised: [ɜ·ə̌] (3.055). However, the off-glide is short and hardly
noticeable, as /əh/ is a central vocoid anyhow. It is audible only
in rhythmically prominent position, viz. in the last syllable of
the macrosegment: /its+méjdəv+fə́h↓/ *it is made of fur*.

There are few allophonic variations of this syllable peak.
The labialization is stronger after /w/, where there may be
actual lip-rounding: /wə́h/ *were*, /wə́hst/ *worst*. Before pre-
consonantal and pre-junctural /l/, /əh/ is more open and central,
and /əhl/ may be a vocoid glide from half-open central towards
half-close back, [ɜɤ̌]: /gə́hl/ [gɜ̱ɤ̌] *girl*, /wə́hld/ [wɜ̱ɤ̌d] *world*.

/əh/ is not necessarily long. It may be short, and in that case
the following (non-phonemic) syllable cut falls as after the simple
syllable peaks /i e a o u ə/, not as after other complex peaks
(2.5, 3.04). This variant occurs especially before /s/: /ðəfə́hs+
tə́hnin/ [ðə'fɜs 'tɜ·nɪn] *the first turning*,[2] but also occasionally

---

[1] On the justification for analysing [Ç] as /əC/, see 7.137.

[2] It is not the same as the stressed simple peak /ə/: it differs from the
latter in being less open and somewhat labialized. However, /ə/ also
occurs in this context, cf. 3.641.

before other consonants: /bə́hn+əlótəv+kə́wl/ ['bɜn ə'lɔʔəv 'kɔ̝ŏ] *burn a lot of coal*. Likewise, the vocoid glide variant of /əhl/ may be short: /gə́hl/ [gɜ̠ɤ̆] *girl*. However, in these contexts the long variant is more common.

3.63. Complex Peak /əw/

The phonemic norm of the complex syllable peak /əw/, as we find it in /ə́wm/ [œʊ̆m] *home*, differs from that of RP in being a considerably more fronted, and also a wider, diphthong. Thus, /əw/ is a vocoid glide where the starting-point is between front and central, half-open, and the end is central, between close and half-close; there is progressive rounding of the lips.[1]

There are small variations in the width of the glide, and in the relative lengths of the two elements, depending on the contiguous segments, and on stress and intonation, but less so than in other complex peaks (3.052, 3.054). Thus, the initial element is relatively longer, and the glide hardly goes beyond a half-close tongue position, before a juncture: /rə́w/ *row*. But before coda consonants the two elements are more equal in length, and the glide reaches its target position: /rə́wd/ *road*, /rə́wst/ *roast*. Even in unstressed syllables the glide is similar to the norm: /ówsəw/ *also*, /télifəwn/ *telephone*.

Monophthongal variants may, however, occur in unstressed

[1] W. Matthews's description (*Cockney Past and Present* p. 79), 'slightly unrounded and centralised, the first element approximating to short *u*, although rather higher and more retracted', does not cover the variants I have come across: the starting-point is front rather than centralized when compared with RP, and it is more front than RP stressed /ə/. Nor do I quite understand J. Franklyn's description (*The Cockney* p. 255 sq.): 'the Cockney takes this short and simple word [i.e. *road*], divides it into two syllables, compounds, and instantly welds them together making a more compact and manageable unit of speech. He does not say *rowd*, he says *roaed*, with a fantastically light glottal stop on the *e*, which, though muted, remains very much in evidence.' If this is meant to suggest a triphthong, or two-directional glide, I cannot agree.

syllables *before* the primary stress. The tongue position is then more retracted: it is a rounded central vocoid, [ö̈]: /əwbéj/ *obey*, /nəwvémbə/ *November*, /grəw+ə́p/ *grow up*. In stressed syllables before the unstressed simple syllable peaks /i ə/ such monophthongal variants also occur, but less commonly: /gə́win/ ['gö̈·ɪn] or /gə́wən/ ['gö̈·ən] *going*, /sə́win+məʃijn/ *sewing-machine*. Markedly different allophonic variants occur before /l/. Before pre-vocalic /l/, /əw/ may be a rounded, fronted back vocoid glide from below half-open towards half-close, [ŏ̈ŏ̆]: /bə́wlə/ ['bŏ̈ŏ̆lə] *bowler*, /rə́wlin/ ['rŏ̈ŏ̆lɪn] *rolling*, /rə́wlit/ ['rŏ̈ŏ̆lɪt] *roll it*. Variants more similar to the phonemic norm also occur in this position, in the same idiolects.

Before pre-consonantal and pre-junctural /l/, /əw/ is still more open and back, and /əwl/ may be a one-directional back vocoid glide from between half-open and open towards half-close. The initial element has little or no lip-rounding, while the final element is well rounded, [ɔ̆ŏ̆]: /rə́wl/ [rɔ̆ŏ̆] *roll*, /sə́wld/ [sɔ̆ŏ̆d] *sold*. This variant occurs only in rhythmically prominent position, viz. in the last syllable of the macrosegment. In less prominent position /əwl/ is not quite so open and back, and is manifested by variants similar to /əw/ before /lV/, so that pre-consonantal and pre-junctural /əwl/ resembles, phonetically speaking, pre-vocalic /əw/. Compare, for example, *whole, roll* in the following utterances:

/ðiə́wláhftə+núwn/ [ðɪ'ŏ̆ŏ̆'lɑ·ftə'nö̈ün] *the whole afternoon*, /ðiə́wl+fámilij/ [ðɪ'ŏ̆ŏ̆ 'fɛ·mɪlə̆i] *the whole family*; /tərə́wlit/ [tə'rŏ̈ŏ̆lɪt] *to roll it*, /ij+rə́wldit/ [i'rŏ̈ŏ̆dɪt] *he rolled it*.

3.64. Distribution of /ə/ Peaks

3.640

When compared with RP the following distributional facts seem noteworthy.

3.641. Stressed /ə/ Peaks

The simple peak /ə/ occurs before /s/ as an alternant to /əh/ in some words where RP has /əh/ only: /bə́st/ or /bə́hst/ *burst*, /kə́s/ or /kə́hs/ *curse*, /fə́st/ or /fə́hst/ *first*, /nə́s/ or /nə́hs/ *nurse*, /pə́s/ or /pə́hs/ *purse*, /wə́s/ or /wə́hs/ *worse*, /wə́st/ or /wə́hst/ *worst*. The informants themselves consider the /ə/ forms 'rougher'.

There is a variant form, /jə́hs/ *yes*, besides /jés/ and /jéhs/. According to tradition, Cockney speakers use /əh/ in some words where RP has /ah/, and vice versa. /əh/, paralleling RP /ah/, occurs, at least as an alternant form, in /bə́hklij/ *Berkeley*, /klə́hk/ *clerk*, /də́hbij/ *Derby*, /fə́h/ *far*, but /ah/ paralleling RP /əh/ has not been observed in words like *dearth, earning, learning, vermin*.[1] The /ah/ alternant in such words seems to be dying out. Thus, one informant could remember her grandfather saying /váhmint/ *vermin*, but she thought the form old-fashioned.

3.642. Unstressed /ə/

In unstressed syllables the simple peak /ə/ has a wider distribution than in RP. It may occur in some words where there is no parallel segment in RP:

/əlóŋəsàjd/ *alongside*, /énərij/ *Henry*, /əmbərélə/ *umbrella*;

but there are variant forms, perhaps more common, without /ə/: /əlóŋsàjd/, /énrij/, /əmbrélə/. On the other hand, words which have an initial /ə/ (or /i/) in RP may occasionally have no such syllable in Cockney:

/ów+kówdən/ *all according*, /ajd+bij+ʃéjmd/ *I'd be ashamed*, /ðətáʃij+kèjs/ *the attaché case*, /lástik/ *elastic*, /ðəléktrik/ *the electric*, /vàkjuéjʃən/ *evacuation*.

A much more widespread phenomenon is the occurrence of

[1] Only one unusual /ah/ occurrence, in /jə́wgàht/ *yogurt*, has been observed.

/ə/ paralleling other syllable peaks in RP.[1] The following list is intended to be illustrative rather than exhaustive. Variant forms in accordance with the RP norm commonly exist.

RP /i/: In initial syllables:

/əléktid/ *elected,* /əlévən/ *eleven,* /əkwípmənt/ *equipment,* /əskéjpt/ *escaped,* /əkspléjn/ *explain.*

/ə/ occurs particularly frequently in medial syllables:

/aktívətij/ *activity,* /áŋgrəlij/ *angrily,* /tʃárətij/ *charity,* /kəmódətij/ *commodity,* /ðəlettrísətij/ [ðəleʔ'trɪsətʃi] *the electricity,* /èksəbíʃən/ *exhibition,* /évəlij/ *heavily,* /ilúwmənéjtid/ *illuminated,* /mílətrij/ *military,* /náhstəlij/ *nastily,* /pəhfəktlij/ *perfectly,* /páwətrij/ *poetry,* /pəblísətij/ *publicity,* /kwóntətij/ *quantity,* /riálətij/ *reality,* /wə́rətin/ *worriting* (i.e. worrying).

In final syllables:

/kávəl/ *cavil,* /fórəd/ *forehead,* /fórən/ *foreign,* /médisən/ *medicine,* /púdən/ *pudding.*

The morpheme *-ing* generally has the form /in/: /kə́min/ *coming,* /kúkin/ *cooking;* likewise: /dáhlin/ *darling,* /íjvnin/ *evening,* /pádintən/ *Paddington,* etc. However, variants in /ən/ also occur: /gə́win/ or /gə́wən/ *going,* /krájin/ or /krájən/ *crying,* /kíjpin/ or /kíjpən/ *keeping,* /lúkin/ or /lúkən/ or /lúkəŋ/ ['lʊkŋ̩] *looking,* /lúwzin/ or /lúwzən/ ['lü•zŋ̩] *losing.* [ən/ is particularly

---

[1] The RP forms given in Jones's *Pronouncing Dictionary* are not, however, in my opinion the only ones. I have not uncommonly heard from presumably RP speakers forms like the ones listed below. As regards /ə/ as a variant for /i/ in 'the penultimate syllables of terminations such as *-ity, -ily'*, D. Jones himself mentions this possibility: *An English Pronouncing Dictionary* p. XXX; cf. also his *Outline* § 262 and *Pronunciation* § 82.

This use of /ə/ is still more widespread in American English; cf. J. S. Kenyon and T. A. Knott, *A Pronouncing Dictionary of American English.*

common where /ə/ is manifested by the syllabicity of the follow-ing segment; after the [ʔ] allophone of /t/ this is the only form:

/kə́tən/ [ˈkʌʔn̩] *cutting,* /gétən/ [ˈgeʔn̩] *getting,* /pútən/ [ˈpʊʔn̩] *putting,* /ʃúwtən/ [ˈʃü·ʔn̩] *shooting,* /və́wtən/ [ˈvœʊ̆ʔn̩] *voting* (or /kə́tin/ [ˈkʌtˢɪn], /gétin/ [ˈgetˢɪn], etc.).[1]

Under similar conditions the preposition *in* has an allomorph /əN/ manifested by a syllabic nasal contoid:

/grəw+ə́pəm+lájf/ [grœ ˈʌpm̩ ˈla̬ĭf] *grow up in life,* /ɹájt+ənðə+kównə/ [ˈɹa̬ĭʔ n̩ðə ˈkɔ̆ŭnə] *right in the corner,* /ðətʃíjf+wə́hdənðij+íŋgliʃ+láŋgwidʒ/ [ðə'tʃĭif ˈwɜ·dn̩ði ˈɪŋgliʃ ˈleŋgwɪdʒ] *the chief word in the English language.*

Compare also /wípəm/ [ˈwɪpm̩] *whip him.*
RP /ih/:

/éspənàhdʒ/ or /éspənèjdʒ/ *espionage,* /àjdəlístik/ *idealistic.*

RP /o/: The preposition *on* has the allomorph /ən/ [n̩] under the same conditions that *in* has such an allomorph. In this context there is thus no contrast between the two prepositions:

/ajl+stáhtən+bə́wθəvjə/ [a̬ў̆ ˈsta·ʔn̩ ˈbœʊ̆θəvjə] *I'll start on both of you.*

RP /oj/: /gáhgəl/ *gargoyle.*
RP /u/:

/aməníʃən/ *ammunition,* /bəkéj/ *bouquet,* /sélələòjd/ *celluloid,* /kómənist/ *communist,* /gədbáj/ *good-bye.*

RP /uh/:

/káʒəltiz/ *casualties,* /véntʃəlij/ *eventually,* /pə́ntʃəlij/ *punctually.*

---

[1] The presence of such allomorphs of the *-ing* morpheme leads to an occasional formal identity between the *-ing* form and the past parti-ciple of the verbs: /íjtən/ [ˈi·ʔn̩] *eating* or *eaten,* /bíjtən/ [ˈbi·ʔn̩] *beating* or *beaten.*

RP /əw/:

/árə/ *arrow*, /bárə/ *barrow*, /félə/ *fellow*, /fólə/ *follow*, /márə/ *marrow*, /piánə/ *piano*, /ʃádə/ *shadow*, /təmáhtə/ *tomato*, /təmórə/ *tomorrow*, /wílbàrə/ *wheel-barrow*, /wídə/ *widow*, /jélə/ *yellow*, /(pə)téjtəz/ *potatoes*.

Forms in /ə/ paralleling RP /əw/ are very common. /əw/ variants occur mainly in less homely words: /fə́wtəw/ *photo*, /réjdiəw/ *radio*, /sə́wəw/ *Soho*.

4. Syllable Margins

4.0. GENERAL SURVEY

4.01. Number and Distribution of Consonants

There are twenty-two consonant phonemes, /p t k b d g f θ s ʃ v ð z ʒ m n ŋ l r h j w/. Three of these, /h j w/, occur in the syllable peak as peak satellites (3.01). All consonants occur as syllable margins, with certain restrictions.

The general restrictions are few in simple margins. In mono-syllables all consonants except /ʒ ŋ/ occur pre-vocalically, as onsets:[1]

/pít/ *pit,* /tít/ *tit,* /kít/ *kit,* /bít/ *bit,* /díd/ *did,* /gít/ *get,* /fít/ *fit,* /θík/ *thick,* /sít/ *sit,* /ʃíp/ *ship,* /vést/ *vest,* /ðís/ *this,* /zíp/ *zip,* /mís/ *miss,* /nít/ *knit,* /lít/ *lit,* /ríd/ *rid,* /hít/ *hit,* /jét/ *yet,* /wít/ *wit;*

and all consonants except /ʒ r h j w/ occur post-vocalically as codas:[2]

/síp/ *sip,* /sít/ *sit,* /sík/ *sick,* /ríb/ *rib,* /híd/ *hid,* /bíg/ *big,* /stíf/ *stiff,* /smíθ/ *smith,* /kís/ *kiss,* /fíʃ/ *fish,* /sív/ *sieve,* /wíð/ *with,* /híz/ *his,* /hím/ *him,* /sín/ *sin,* /síŋ/ *sing,* /síl/ *sill.*

---

[1] /ʒ/ occurs pre-vocalically in the complex margin /dʒ/: /dʒím/ *Jim,* /dʒə́st/ *just.*

[2] /h j w/ occur post-vocalically only as peak satellites, i.e. as part of the syllable peak: /báh/ *bar,* /báj/ *buy,* /báw/ *bow;* cf. 3.01.

There are certain special restrictions. All the potential combinations between syllable peaks and margins, especially between simple peaks and post-peak margins (codas), do not occur. Thus, few consonants (only /t k d ʃ l/?) occur after /u/, and /θ v ð/ combine only with a few vowels as codas. These special restrictions will not be discussed here: they are the same as in RP. Nor shall I deal with the complex margins, where the combinatory possibilities are relatively few, but apparently the same as in RP.[1]

4.02. Preferred and Permitted Consonant Clusters

Only a few notes on preferred and permitted consonant clusters will be added.

In complex onsets and codas there is no combination of phonemically voiced and voiceless consonants.[2] Thus, for example *sḄV-, *sḄrV-, *-VzḄ, *-VsḄ do not occur. But there are frequent combinations of phonemically voiceless consonants with consonants which are phonetically voiced, but which have no voice contrast (4.04), i.e. with nasals and sonorants:

/pléj/ *play*, /smájl/ *smile*, /éls/ *else*, /rént/ *rent*.

In complex interludes combinations of voiced and voiceless consonants are permitted:

/ábsə+lúwtlij/ *absolutely*, /obsíjn/ *obscene*;

---

[1] Statements about the distribution of vowels and consonants in various dialects of English are given, for example, in: L. Bloomfield, *Language* pp. 130–5; B. L. Whorf, 'Linguistics as an Exact Science'; J. D. O'Connor and L. J. M. Trim, 'Vowel, Consonant, and Syllable — a Phonological Definition'; G. L. Trager and H. L. Smith, *An Outline of English Structure* §§ 1.4–1.5; L. G. Jones, 'English Consonantal Distribution'; K. Malone, 'The Phonemic Structure of English Monosyllables'; B. Trnka, *A Phonological Analysis of Present-Day Standard English.*

[2] Possible exceptions are words like /wídθ/ *width*, /brédθ/ *breadth*, /(h)ə́ndrədθ/ *hundredth*. However, these words are commonly /wítθ brétθ (h)ə́ndrətθ/. Cf. C. F. Hockett, *A Manual of Phonology* p. 93.

but they are very rare, and clusters consisting of consonants which are identical as regards the distinctive feature of voicing are preferred: /ápsə+lúwtlij/.

In complex interludes, and even in sequences of consonants interrupted by internal juncture, combinations of homorganic consonants are preferred. This explains the morphophonemic phenomenon known as *assimilation*, which is found in Cockney to the same extent as in RP:[1]

/ébwəd/ *Edward*, /sámwitʃ/ *sandwich*, /əléʃʃuw/ *unless you*...,
/indidʒéʃʃən/ *indigestion*, /ʃúbbij+ðéh/ *should be there*,
/sémp+bák/ *sent back*, /dífrəm+wə́hdz/ *different words*,
/ʃikáhŋ+gə́w/ *she can't go*.

Even distant assimilation, or dilation, may occasionally take place, for instance the occurrence of /ʃ/ for an expected /s/ in the following utterance:

/əgríjŋgrə̀wʃəz+ʃóp/ *a greengrocer's shop*.

The assimilation which occurs in combinations with syllabic contoids may be considered a special kind of dilation. In this case there is assimilation between segments which are not contiguous phonemically, but which are so phonetically. This type of assimilation is very common, in contradistinction to the usual dilation:

/éjpəms/ ['æɪpm̩s] *halfpence*, /dʒə́hməm/ ['dʒɝ·mm̩] *German*,
/rékəŋ/ ['rekŋ̩] *reckon*.

Instead of clusters of several homorganic or near-homorganic consonants there is some preference for simple, or less complex, codas and interludes.[2] It applies particularly to clusters of apical consonants. There is free variation between forms like the following pairs:

---

[1] Cf. D. Jones, *Outline* § 837 sqq.
[2] Cf. the discussion of 'elision', D. Jones, *Outline* § 854 sqq. Cf. also W. Matthews, *Cockney Past and Present* p. 173 sq.

/də́wnt+bəlíjv/ or /də́wn+bəlíjv/ *do not believe,*
/ràwndəbàwt+íh/ or /ràwnəbàwt+íh/ *round about here,*
/ə́wld+strìjt/ or /ə́wl+strìjt/ *Old Street,* /ðij+éldist/ or
/ðij+éldis/ *the eldest,* /pródistən/ or /pródisən/ *Protestant,*
/wiðð́ís/ or /wiðís/ *with this,* /ðəsíksθ+wíjk/ or /ðəsíks+wíjk/
the sixth week.

Such a simplification may be less common in clusters of alveolar apical consonants and dental ones (cf. 4.21).

4.03. Criteria for Classification of Consonants

It is hardly possible to set up a neat and simple classification of the consonants based on distributional data only. Using distribution in different contexts as starting-points we arrive at several sets of classes which are partly similar, partly overlapping, and partly completely different.[1] However, distributional facts are not in conflict with the classification arrived at on the basis of distinctive features (4.04). On the contrary, they support it in many ways. Thus, the voiced/voiceless division is paralleled by the fact that members of the two classes do not combine in complex onsets and codas; /p t k/ form a separate class because of their combinatory possibilities in complex margins in general, and in the onset sCr- in particular; /h j w/ form a separate class because of their occurrence as peak satellites in complex syllable peaks, and /l r j w/[2] show close similarities in their distribution as regards complex onsets. The voiced stops and the fricatives similarly show certain distributional characteristics, though they are not so clear-cut as the groups already mentioned.

4.04. Classification of Consonants

There is a symmetrical system of six stop consonants, three pairs consisting each of a voiceless and a voiced member: /p b/,

---

[1] Cf. e.g. L. Bloomfield, *Language* pp. 130–4; B. Bloch and G. L. Trager, *Outline of Linguistic Analysis* § 3.5.

[2] /h/ does not follow /j w/ or /l r/ in its distribution here.

/t d/, /k g/.[1] There is also a symmetrical system of eight fricatives, paired in the same way: /f v/, /θ ð/, /s z/, /ʃ ʒ/. There are three nasals, whose oral articulations parallel those of the three stop pairs, but which lack the voice contrast: /m n ŋ/.

The remaining consonants, /l r h j w/, are not easily and obviously classifiable. We shall call them oral sonorants, abbreviated to sonorants.[2] Distributionally they fall into two subclasses (4.01, 4.03), and phonetic facts support this sub-classification: /h j w/ are all glides,[3] whereas the phonemic norms of /l r/ are not glides.[4] However, phonologically, when phonemes are considered combinations of a limited set of distinctive features, such a sub-classification is not convenient.

The fricatives have a four-way contrast in point of oral articulation, whereas the stops and the nasals have three only.

---

[1] In view of the fact that the so-called voiced consonants are not always voiced (cf. 4.051), and that at least one 'voiceless' consonant has one voiced allophone (4.13), one might prefer to set up fortis vs. lenis as the distinctive features: English voiceless consonants are generally supposed to be fortes, whereas voiced consonants are lenes. However, such a distinction has little if any basis in instrumental analysis. And even though one has, impressionistically, the feeling that such a distinction accords well with the phonetic facts, I am not prepared to state whether this is a distinction valid for all allophones of the stops and fricatives, any more than the voiceless/voiced distinction is.

[2] The term *sonorant* is here used in a sense which differs slightly from the meaning given to it by Hockett (*A Manual of Phonology* pp. 96, 118): /h/ is included among the sonorants, and the nasals are considered a separate class. Thus, the sonorants may be defined as non-obstruent oral consonants, or as the class of consonants with the widest opening. The term does not necessarily have any acoustical or auditory implication, and for this reason pre-peak /h/, viz. [h], can be called a sonorant.

[3] The onset /h/, when it does occur (4.432), may well be considered a (voiceless) glide: spectrograms of a common variant show a changing spectrum throughout, from a 'neutral' resonance towards the resonance of the following segment.

[4] However, pre-consonantal and pre-junctural /l/ is generally a glide; cf. 4.412, 4.413.

Apart from /j/ and /w/ the sonorants do not easily fit into any overall position system. One may, however, set up a consonant system in terms of distinctive features as suggested in Fig. 7.

		Labial	Apical		Dorsal	
Stop	Voiceless	p	t		k	
	Voiced	b	d		g	
Nasal		m	n		ŋ	
Fricative	Voiceless	f	θ	s	ʃ	
	Voiced	v	ð	z	ʒ	
Sonorant		w	l	r	j	h
			Front	Back	Front	Back

Fig. 7

Classification of Consonants, I

The front/back distinction is obvious in the case of the fricative apicals: dental vs. alveolar. As regards the sonorant apicals, it means that /r/ is more back than /l/ since it is somewhat retroflex.[1] /h/ is back in relation to /j/ not because it is considered a glottal sonorant:[2] its resonance depends on the following or the preceding vowel (3.03, 4.431). But it is never as front as the palatal /j/: not even in /hi-/, where it glides towards front close, or in /-ih/, where it glides away from front close.

The description 'dorsal' applies to /h/ as well as to /k g ŋ ʃ ʒ j/ because it is a (non-syllabic) vocoid (3.03, 4.431) in whose articulation neither the lips nor the tip of the tongue are involved: as in any other vocoid, the main body of the tongue is slightly humped up.

[1] For the complicating fact that /l/ is not always an apical contoid at all, but a velar vocoid, see 4.412, 4.413.

[2] Or fricative: cf. H. Kurath, 'The Binary Interpretation of English Vowels. A Critique', especially p. 116 sq.

Such a classification has the advantage of keeping the number of distinctive features at a minimum and giving a near-symmetrical system. However, I do not insist on such a classification. A possible alternative is given in Fig. 8.

		Labial	Apical		Dorsal		
Stop	Voiceless	p	t		k		
	Voiced	b	d		g		
Nasal		m	n		ŋ		
Fricative	Voiceless	f	θ	s	ʃ		
	Voiced	v	ð	z	ʒ		
Sonorant			l	r	j	h	w
			Front	Back	Front	Central	Back

Fig. 8
Classification of Consonants, II

The double articulation of /w/ — it is labio-velar — enables us to put it in the labial category in one type of classification, and in the dorsal category in another. The latter classification may have certain advantages. Thus, the articulation of the tongue only, not of the lips, is picked out as the relevant feature for a sub-division of the sonorants. (This is not possible in the case of the stops, nasals, and fricatives.) And it may seem to give more adequate expression to the phonetic facts about /h j w/ both as peak satellites and as onset consonants.

A third possibility, avoiding the awkwardness of considering /r/ more back than /l/ — awkward because their points of articulation do not differ very much — is to set up a classification of the apical fricatives and sonorants more in accordance with the traditional consonant chart: see Fig. 9.

Little seems to be gained by this relabelling, and four new distinctive features have to be accommodated in the system.

3⁷9 2̄5̄

Table I gives a list of all consonant phonemes,their phonemic labels, in terms of distinctive features, and a short phonetic description of their phonemic norms, in terms of the traditional IPA consonant chart.

		Labial	Apical		Dorsal		
Stop	Voiceless	p	t		k		
	Voiced	b	d		g		
Nasal		m	n		ŋ		
Fricative	Voiceless	f	Dental	Alveolar	ʃ		
			θ	s			
	Voiced	v	ð	z	ʒ		
Sonorant			Lateral	Retro-flex	Front	Central	Back
			l	r	j	h	w

Fig. 9

Classification of Consonants, III

4.05. Allophonic Variations

4.050

There are certain allophonic variations which apply to a number of consonants.

4.051. Voicing

Among the stops and fricatives one member of each pair is labelled voiceless, the other voiced: /p t k f θ s ʃ/ are voiceless, whereas /b d g v ð z ʒ/ are voiced. However, there are allophonic variations which make the distinction less absolute. There is no difference from RP in this respect. The 'voiceless' consonants have no allophones with any perceptible voicing,[1] but the so-called voiced consonants are not always

---

[1] There is one exception: one allophone of /t/ is a voiced flap (4.13).

Lincoln Christian College

Symbol	Distinctive Features	Phonetic Description
p	voiceless labial stop	voiceless bilabial stop
t	voiceless apical stop	voiceless alveolar stop
k	voiceless dorsal stop	voiceless velar stop
b	voiced labial stop	voiced bilabial stop
d	voiced apical stop	voiced alveolar stop
g	voiced dorsal stop	voiced velar stop
f	voiceless labial fricative	voiceless labio-dental fricative
θ	voiceless front apical fricative	voiceless dental fricative
s	voiceless back apical fricative	voiceless alveolar fricative
ʃ	voiceless dorsal fricative	voiceless palato-alveolar fricative
v	voiced labial fricative	voiced labio-dental fricative
ð	voiced front apical fricative	voiced dental fricative
z	voiced back apical fricative	voiced alveolar fricative
ʒ	voiced dorsal fricative	voiced palato-alveolar fricative
m	labial nasal	voiced bilabial nasal
n	apical nasal	voiced alveolar nasal
ŋ	dorsal nasal	voiced velar nasal
w	labial sonorant[1]	voiced labio-velar vocoid glide
l	front apical sonorant	voiced alveolar lateral
r	back apical sonorant	voiced post-alveolar (retroflex) frictionless continuant
j	front dorsal sonorant	voiced palatal vocoid glide
h	back dorsal sonorant[1]	vocoid or vocoid glide[2]

Table I

The consonant phonemes: distinctive features, and
phonetic description of phonemic norms

[1] If my second, alternative, consonant classification is adopted, /h/ is a central dorsal sonorant, and /w/ is a back dorsal sonorant.

[2] As to the particular quality of the vocoid (glide), cf. 3.03, 4.431.

fully voiced. Between other voiced segments they are fully voiced:

/rə́bə/ *rubber*, /ʃádə/ *shadow*, /bégə/ *beggar*, /ʃívə/ *shiver*, /mə́ðə/ *mother*, /bízij/ *busy*, /méʒə/ *measure*; /lə́mbə/ *lumber*, /lówndrij/ *laundry*, /áŋgrij/ *angry*, /évrij/ *every*, /ənðén/ *and then*, /bénzin/ *benzine*, /índʒin/ *engine*.

After a terminal contour, particularly where there is an appreciable pause, and at the beginning of an utterance the consonants may be partly voiceless, in their initial stage:

/báj/ *buy*, /déj/ *day*, /gə́w/ *go*, /və́wt/ *vote*, /ðéh/ *there*, /zúw/ *zoo*.

In the first element of a complex syllable onset the voicelessness may extend through the greater part of the consonant:

/bríŋ/ *bring*, /dʒúwn/ *June*, /glúw/ *glue*, /vjúw/ *view*.

Before a terminal contour the voicelessness is more marked. However, only in the fricatives may it extend not only all through the final consonant but also through part of the preceding consonants:

/klə́bz/ *clubs*, /dʒówdʒ/ *George*, /tʃéjndʒd/ *changed*, /nájvz/ *knives*, /səprájzd/ *surprised*.

The nasals and the sonorants have no contrast of voicing. The phonemic norm of the nasals is voiced, and there are no noticeably (fully or partly) voiceless allophones. /h/ is voiceless as an onset consonant and voiced as a peak satellite. The remaining sonorants, /l r j w/, have voiced phonemic norms, but there are noticeably voiceless allophones: these consonants are partly voiceless after voiceless consonants, especially after voiceless stops; /r j/ may be fully voiceless in this position:

/plíjz/ *please*, /klə́mzij/ *clumsy*, /flóh/ *floor*, /slə́w/ *slow*; /prés/ *press*, /tráj/ *try*, /kráj/ *cry*, /fráj/ *fry*, /θríj/ *three*, /ʃríjk/ *shriek*; /pjúw/ *pew*, /kjúw/ *queue*; /twélv/ *twelve*, /kwówtə/ *quarter* .

There are no voiceless allophones when a juncture occurs between the voiceless consonant and the sonorant:

/stópt+réjnin/ ['stɔpt 'ræĭnɪn] *stopped raining* vs. /stóp+ tréjnin/ ['stɔp 'tr̥æĭnɪn] *stop training*; /bák+jáhd/ ['bɛk 'jɑ·d] *back yard* vs. /lóŋ+kjúw/ ['lɔŋ 'kçü·] *long queue*;

and this is also generally so in an interlude when there is a nonphonemic syllable cut between them:

/séprit/ ['sep-rɪʔ] *separate* vs. /séjkrid/ ['sæĭ-kr̥ɪd/ *sacred*.

4.052. Miscellaneous

Other allophonic variations concerning classes of consonants are the aspiration and affrication of stops (4.122), the glottalization of stops (4.123), and the nasal and lateral release or the lack of release of stops (4.124).

4.1.   STOPS

4.11. Phonemic Norms and Allophonic Variations

The phonemic norms of the six stop consonants are bilabial (/p b/), alveolar (/t d/), and velar (/k g/). The first member of each pair is voiceless, the second is voiced:

/páh/ *par*, /báh/ *bar*, /táh/ *tar*, /dáhn/ *darn*, /káh/ *car*, /gáhd/ *guard*.

There are allophonic variations, most of which parallel those of RP. Thus, the labial stops may be labio-dental before the labiodental fricatives /f v/:

/ajl+rápit+ə́pfohjə/ *I'll wrap it up for you*.

The apical stops are dental before the dental fricatives /θ ð/:

/éjtθ/ *eighth*, /àtðə+fíniʃ/ *at the finish*, /líjdðə+wéj/ *lead the way*.

The sequence apical stop plus front apical fricative may even be manifested by a single phonetic segment, a dental stop: [t̪] = /tð/, [d̪] = /dð/ (cf. 4.21):

/gótðə+péjpəz+ɪn↑/ ['gɔt̪ə 'pæɪpəz ˌɪn] *Got the papers in?*

Before the fricatives /ʃ ʒ/, which are palatalized and labialized (4.21), the apical stops are also somewhat palatalized and labialized:

/tʃék/ *check*, /kwéstʃən/ *question*, /dʒíjn/ *Jean*, /pídʒin/ *pigeon*.

In the clusters /tr dr/, /t d/ are post-alveolar or slightly retroflex:

/tráj/ *try*, /dráj/ *dry*.

The velar stops show considerable allophonic variation in point of articulation, depending on the contiguous vowels. They are front velar near front vowels:

/kíjp/ *keep*, /síjk/ *seek*, /gíjs/ *geese*, /bíg/ *big*;

and back velar near back vowels:

/kówt/ *caught*, /tówk/ *talk*, /gówd/ *God*, /bóg/ *bog*.

These variations are not greater than in RP. The same is true of the amount of lip-rounding occurring in the clusters /kw gw kr gr/:

/kwíjn/ *queen*, /əkwájə/ *acquire*, /láŋgwidʒ/ *language*, /kráj/ *cry*, /gríjn/ *green*;

and before rounded vowels:

/kúwl/ (or /kúl/) *cool*, /gúws/ *goose*.

4.12. Allophonic Variations

4.120

Certain allophonic variations apply to several or all of the stops.

4.121. *Voicing*

The phonemic norm of /p t k/ is voiceless. /p k/ have no allophones with any perceptible voicing. /t/ has as one of its allophones a voiced flap (4.13).

The phonemic norm of /b d g/ is voiced. They are, however, subject to variations in the degree of voicing: at least partly voiceless allophones occur (4.051).

4.122. *Aspiration and Affrication*

The phonemic norm of the voiceless stops is aspirated. There are allophonic variations in the degree of aspiration, just as in RP. The aspiration is particularly strong after juncture before a stressed vowel:

/páhs/ *pass*, /tájm/ *time*, /kə́m/ *come*;

but it is also fairly strong before an unstressed vowel:

/pətéjtə/ *potato*, /təbákə/ *tobacco*, /kəmín/ *come in*;

and as a simple interlude before a stressed vowel:

/səpə́wz/ *suppose*, /əták/ *attack*, /bikə́m/ *become*.

The stops are much less aspirated as or in an interlude before unstressed vowels:

/hápij/ *happy*, /prítij/ *pretty*, /lə́kij/ *lucky*; /áhftə/ *after*, /máhstə/ *master*, /báhṣkit/ *basket*;

and in a complex syllable onset:

/spówt/ *sport*, /stáht/ *start*, /skáj/ *sky*.

Before other consonants the stops are not aspirated:[1]

/sprín̠/ *spring*, /skríjm/ *scream*, /dʒípsij/ *gipsy*, /ámpʃə/ *Hampshire*, /kóknij/ *Cockney*, /síklij/ *sickly*, /fákt/ *fact*.[2]

---

[1] Unless one considers the (full or partial) voicelessness of the sonor-ants after voiceless stops a manifestation of the aspiration of the stops: cf. 4.051.

[2] Cf. the nasal and lateral release of stops, and the lack of any special release, 4.124.

Before internal juncture there is generally no aspiration either, and we find the same allophones as before consonants, including nasally and laterally released stops:

/bént+ə́wvə/ *bent over,* /bák+dóh/ *back door,* /nót+ʃóh/ *not sure,* /brík+léjn/ *Brick Lane.*

Before a terminal contour there is free variation between an aspirated stop and a non-released stop:

/stóp↓/ *Stop!* /bə́t‖/ *But* — /kəm+bák↑/ *come back.*

The conditioning factors for aspiration are the same as in RP. However, Cockney differs from RP in the *degree* of aspiration, especially of /t/, to a certain extent also of /k/. There is actually more than mere aspiration: there is real *affrication* in positions favourable to strong aspiration: [tˢ] and [kˣ].[1] /k/ is audibly affricated only before a terminal contour, /bák↓/ [bɛkˣ] *back,* whereas /t/ may be affricated even as an interlude before unstressed vowels, i.e. in a position where RP is supposed to have little aspiration:[2]

/tíj/ [tˢə́i] *tea,* /ətów/ [ə'tˢo̜ʊ] *at all,* /sít↓/ [sɪtˢ] sit, /bétij/ ['betˢə̜i] *Betty.*

/bétij/ ['betˢə̜i] *Betty* differs from /bétsij/ ['betsə̜i] *Betsy* in the length of the fricative [s], possibly also in the resonance of the latter.

Though voiced stops are not commonly aspirated or affricated in any dialect of English, /d/ is frequently affricated in Cockney

----

[1] Cf. D. Jones, *Pronunciation* § 230, and W. Matthews, *Cockney Past and Present* p. 80. Matthews finds this affricated variant of 'initial t' 'particularly among women'. I do not believe that the alveolar stop is more affricated among women than among men. However, men tend to use a higher percentage of [ʔ] allophones (cf. 4.15), and this fact may give the impression that there is stronger affrication among women.

[2] I am not too sure that this is actually so. Strongly aspirated allophones of /t/ are frequently found among supposedly RP speakers in this position: /bétə/ ['betʰə] *better.*

in the same positions as /t/ is, but not to the same extent: /bád↓/ [bɛdᶻ] *bad*, /dík↓/ [dᶻɪkˣ] *Dick*.

When /d/ is thus affricated before a terminal contour the fricative off-glide is generally voiceless, though lenis, and also the stop part is partly voiceless (cf. 4.051). In pre-peak position the fricative off-glide is voiced.

4.123. Glottalization

Voiceless stops occurring as coda or as the first part of a complex interlude frequently have a secondary glottal articulation: there is a closure at the glottis slightly before, or simultaneously with, the oral closure. The glottal closure is released before the oral one:

/ə́p/ [ʌpˀ] *up*, /fílip/ ['fɪlɪpˀ] *Philip*, /púts/ [pʊt' s] *puts*, /káptin/ ['kɛpˀtˢɪn] *captain*, /ətráktiv/ [ə'trɛkˀtˢɪv] *attractive*, /igzáklij/ [ɪg'zɛkˀlə̆i] *exactly*, /séprit/ ['sepˀrɪʔ] *separate*.

This pre-glottalization may be slightly more common among men than women (cf. the wider use of the [ʔ] allophone of /t/ among men, 4.15), but it is not restricted to Cockney: it is common also among RP speakers in the South.[1]

4.124. Miscellaneous

The stops are nasally released before nasals:

/áknij/ *Hackney*, /kídnij/ *kidney*, /ə́wpəm/ ['œŭpm̩] *open*;

and /t d/ are laterally released before lateral allophones of /l/:

/dʒéntlij/ *gently*, /médlin/ *meddling*, /dʒéntəlmən/ ['dʒent̞l̩mən] *gentleman*.

As the examples show, the nasal and the lateral release take

---

[1] Cf. P. Christophersen, 'The Glottal Stop in English'; J. D. O'Connor, 'RP and the Reinforcing Glottal Stop'; B. S. Andrésen, 'The Glottal Stop in the Received Pronunciation of English.'

place even before unstressed /ə/, viz. when this vowel is manifested by the syllabicity of the following nasal or lateral. All stops are unreleased before other stops, i.e. the articulators are brought into position for the second stop before the release of the first one; a juncture may intervene: /rápt/ *wrapped*, /sit+dáwn/ *sit down*, /ákt/ *act*, /bɔ́hd+kèjdʒ/ *bird cage*, /ég+kɔ̀p/ *egg-cup*.

These variations are the same as those found in RP.[1]

4.13. The Voiced Flap

/t/ has a voiced allophone, [t̬], which differs from /d/ in being shorter, more flap-like, and without the affrication which may be part of /d/. It occurs mainly as a simple interlude, between syllable peaks:

/bétə/ ['bet̬ə] *better*, /ʃáwtid/ ['ʃe̬t̬ɪd] *shouted*, /gitáwt/ [gɪ't̬e̬t̬ˢ] *get out*, /ówspitəl/ ['o̬·spɪt̬ɫ] *hospital*, /pútən/ ['put̬n̩] *putting*.

The last two examples show the occurrence of [t̬] before a syllabic contoid = /əC/. It also occurs, though less frequently, in a complex interlude after /n l/ before a vowel:

/wóntə+méjk/ ['wɔnt̬ə 'mæǐk] *want to make*, /dʒibrówltə+ wówk/ [dʒɪ'brɔ̬·ɫt̬ə 'wǒŭk] *Gibralta Walk*.

It never occurs otherwise than in or as an interlude, never as an onset or a coda.

Stress is not a conditioning factor for the occurrence of [t̬]: both the preceding and the following syllable may be stressed, or one of them only, or none:

/ʃɔ́tɔ́p/ ['ʃʌ't̬ʌp] *shut up*, /juwv+gótit/ [jü·v 'gɔt̬ɪʔ] *you have got it*, /gitɔ́p/ [gɪ't̬ʌp] *get up*, /ðáts+notim/ ['ðɛts nɔt̬ɪm] *that is not him*.[2]

[1] D. Jones, *Outline* §§ 578, 590, 600 sqq.

[2] The stress mark is put *before* [t̬], because it could not very well be put in the middle of it; [t̬] is, however, ambisyllabic.

Nor do morphological considerations seem to play any important rôle for the use of the [ṭ] allophone. It may be most frequent in the middle of a word or at the end of a word (before a vowel in the following word), but it also occurs word-initially, provided there is no juncture before the word:

/wij+ád+təgə́wtə+wə́hk/ [wi ˈɛd tˢəˈgœŭ̈ṭə ˈwɜ·k] *we had to go to work,*

/aj+də́nə+áwtə+kə́tit/ [ɑ̱ɪ ˈdᶻʌnə ˈɛ̰̍ṭə ˈkʌṭɪʔ] *I do not know how to cut it.*

Rate of delivery is a conditioning factor, however: [ṭ] never occurs in slow style, when the speaker is reducing his tempo in hesitation or before a pause, etc.

To the extent that the use of [ṭ] is not stylistically conditioned (cf. 4.15) it must be considered an allophone in free variation with [tˢ] and [t] and partly with [ʔ] in certain contexts: as a simple interlude or as part of a complex interlude after /n l/, at a normal rate of speech.

There is no doubt about the contrast between [ṭ] and [d]: /rájtin/ [ˈrɑ̱ĭṭ̍m][1] *writing* vs. /rájdin/ [ˈrɑ̱ĭdɪn] *riding,* /ʃətə́p/ [ˌʃʌˈṭʌp] *shut up* vs. /fèdə́p/ [ˌfeˈdʌp] *fed up.* Only occasionally does /d/ [d] actually occur in a morpheme where comparison with RP would lead us to expect /t/: /sádis+fàjd/ [ˈsɛdɪsˌfɑ̱ĭd] *satisfied.*

Nor can [ṭ] be considered an allophone of the /r/ phoneme. There is a rare flap allophone of /r/ (4.421), but it is not quite identical with the flap occurring in [ˈbeṭə] *better*: the flap allophone of /r/, [ɾ], is probably post-alveolar, and the contact is made with the very tip of the tongue, while [ṭ] is alveolar and part of the blade of the tongue is involved in the contact. The two flaps occasionally occur in the same context, and are thus in contrast: /bétə/ [ˈbeṭə] *better* vs. /vérij/ [ˈveɾə̆i] *very.*

Sometimes the usual allophone of /r/, a post-alveolar frictionless (or slightly fricative) continuant, occurs in words where

[1] One out of several possible forms.

one would expect /t/:[1] ['sta·rɪd] *started*, ['gɔrɛ̰ŋ'rœʊ̆n] *got our own*. These must be considered instances of an unusual distribution of /r/: /stáhrid/, /górawrɔ́wn/. The two forms ['sta·ṭɪd] and ['sta·rɪd] *started* do not exemplify a variation between two allophones of the same phoneme, but an alternation between two allomorphs of the same morpheme: /stáhtid/ and /stáhrid/. For [ṭ] and [r] (or [ɾ]) are not interchangeable in VCV: in a great number of words, such as *around, sorry, very*, only [r] (or [ɾ]) occurs. On the other hand, [ṭ] is very frequently in variation with [t] and [tˢ], with which it never contrasts but with which it is always interchangeable in this context. Thus, [ṭ] can only be considered an allophone of the /t/ phoneme.

4.14. The Glottal Stop[2]

4.140

The glottal stop, [ʔ], is a frequent allophone of /t/ in interludes and codas. It never occurs as an onset consonant.

4.141. In Codas

The glottal stop occurs most freely as a simple coda, where the following internal juncture is followed by a consonant, any consonant, not only the few consonants before which [ʔ] is common in RP according to some writers:[3]

/páht+tájm/ ['pa·ʔ 'tˢa̰ɪm] *part time*, /gót+kówt/ ['gɔʔ 'kǫ̆tˢ] *got caught*, /gét+dáwn/ ['geʔ 'dḛn] *get down*,

---

[1] One informant writes in a letter (jocularly?) 'your gorem' for 'you('ve) got them'.

[2] For the use of [ʔ] in English in general, see D. Jones, *Outline* p. 151 n. 15; D. Jones, *Pronunciation* § 233 sq.; W. Matthews, *Cockney Past and Present* pp. 80, 167 sq.; E. Dieth, *Vademekum der Phonetik* p. 99 sq.; P. Christophersen, 'The Glottal Stop in English'; J. D. O'Connor, 'RP and the Reinforcing Glottal Stop'; B. S. Andrésen, 'The Glottal Stop in the Received Pronunciation of English'.

[3] Cf. D. Jones, *Pronunciation* § 233.

/wót+fóh/ ['wɔʔ 'fɔ̌] *what for*, /ðát+stə́f/ ['ðɛʔ 'stʌf]
that stuff, /nót+ðát/ ['nɔʔ 'ðɛʔ] *not that*, /jəgót+mij/
[jə'gɔʔ mǐi] *you got me*, /bət+ríhlij/ [bəʔ 'rɪ̌lə̌i] *but really*,
/íjt+wèjv/ ['ĩiʔ 'wæ̌ĭv] *heat wave*.

The juncture may also be followed by a vowel:

/stáht+əbíznis/ ['stɑ·ʔ ə'bɪznɪs] *start a business*,
/nót+onðə+kétʃ/ ['nɔʔ ɔnðə 'ketʃ] *not on the catch*,
/aj+mét+əh/ [ɑ̌ǐ 'meʔ ɜ·] *I met her*, /spít+at+im/ ['spɪʔ
ɛʔ ɪm] *spit at him*, /wájt+éh/ ['wɑ̌ǐʔ 'e·ə̌] *white hair*,
/wot+évərit+íz/ [wɔʔ 'evərɪʔ 'ɪz] *whatever it is*, /bət+aj+
míjn/ [bəʔ ɑ̌ǐ 'mǐin] *but I mean*.

Much less frequently does the glottal stop occur in a complex
coda, and then apparently only as the second and last part of
a coda whose first element is /n/ or /l/, or occasionally other
consonants:

/ʃiwózənt+ðéh/ [ʃɪ'wɔzn̩ʔ 'ðe·ə̌] *she was not there*,
/gə́vmənt+wə́hk/ ['gʌvmənʔ 'wɜ·k] *government work*,
/wént+ə́p+lə́vlij/ ['wenʔ 'ʌp 'lʌvlə̌i] *went up lovely*,
/juw+spójlt+it/ [jü 'spɔ̌ǐ̃ʔ ɪʔ] *you spoiled it*,
/tʃést+nə́t+tríj/ ['tʃesʔ 'nʌʔ 'trə̌i] *chestnut tree*;

or as the first element of a coda whose second and last member
is /s/:

/kárəts/ ['kɛrəʔs] *carrots*, /fágits+ən+píjz+púdən/ ['fɛgɪʔs n̩
'pi·z 'pudn̩] *faggots and peas pudding*,
/wóts+ðəmátə/ ['wɔʔs ðə'mɛʔə] *what is the matter*,
/séprit+bíts/ ['seprɪʔ 'bɪʔs] *separate bits*.

The glottal stop is also common as a simple coda before a
terminal contour:

/itsə+sə́ht↓/ [ɪtsə 'sɜ·ʔ] *it is a cert*, /kwájt+əlót↓/ ['kwɑ̌ǐʔ
ə'lɔʔ] *quite a lot*, /ʃijz+ʃówt↓/ [ʃiz 'ʃɒ·ʔ] *she is short*,
/péj+pàkit↓/ ['pæ̌ǐ ˌpɛkɪʔ] *pay packet*, /aj+fəgót+it↓/ [ɑ̌ǐ
fə'gɔʔ ɪʔ] *I forgot it*.

Before a terminal contour, [ʔ] is most likely to occur when no appreciable pause follows; when the speaker slows down in hesitation [tˢ] may be more common.

4.142. In Interludes

The glottal stop also occurs frequently as a simple interlude, particularly before syllabic nasals and sonorants, i.e. before unstressed /əm ən əŋ əl/, where it is by far the most common allophone of /t/:[1]

/bótəm̩/ [ˈbɔʔm̩] bottom, /pútəm/ [ˈpʊʔm̩] put them, /brítən/ [ˈbrɪʔn̩] Britain, /tótənəm/ [ˈtˢɔʔn̩əm] Tottenham, /pátən+brájən/ [ˈpɛʔn̩ ˈbrɑ·ən] Pat and Bryan, /bótəl/ [ˈbɔɫ] or [ˈbɔʔɤ] bottle, /lítəlítəlij/ [ˈlɪʔl̩ˈɪʔl̩ǒi] Little Italy.

A common variant of /t/+ the morpheme -ing is [ʔn̩]:

/sítən/ [ˈsɪʔn̩] sitting, /kʌ́tən/ [ˈkʌʔn̩] cutting, /wéjtən/ [ˈwæɪ̆ʔn̩] waiting.

The glottal stop does not occur quite so frequently as a simple interlude before vocoids, at least not among women speakers (cf. 4.15). However, among men and children, and among women in colloquial style, [ʔ] is common:[2]

/bétə/ [ˈbeʔə] better, /páhtij/ [ˈpɑ·ʔi·] party, /pətéjtə/ [pəˈtˢæɪ̆ʔə] potato, /sátədij/ [ˈsɛʔədǒi] Saturday, /stáhtid/ [ˈstɑ·ʔɪd] started, /wówtə/ [ˈwǫ·ʔə] water.

As a simple interlude [ʔ] has only been found after a stressed before an unstressed syllable peak; when [ʔ] occurs between vocoids under other stress conditions it is always followed by a juncture:

[ɪʔˈɪz] /it+íz/ it is, [bəʔ ɪʔ ˈwɔz] /bət+it+wóz/ but it was, [ˈpʊʔ ˈʌp] /pút+ʌ́p/ put up.

[1] In this position it is also of frequent occurrence in RP.

[2] In one family I found the children saying /sítin/ [ˈsɪʔɪn] sitting, /rájtin/ [ˈrɑɪ̆ʔɪn] writing, etc., whereas the mother said /sítən/ [ˈsɪʔn̩], /rájtən/ [ˈrɑɪ̆ʔn̩]. The latter forms were supposed to be 'better'.

[ʔ] is far less common in a complex interlude. When it does so occur, it seems to be used most often before /n/ or /l/:

/páhtnə/ ['pɑ·ʔnə] *partner*, /ítlə/ ['ɪʔlə] *Hitler*, /imíjdjətlij/ [ɪ'mi·djəʔlə̆i] *immediately*, /əpéhrəntlij/ [ə'peə̆rə̆ʔlə̆i] *apparently*;

and only occasionally before other consonants:

/átkinz/ ['ɛʔkɪnz] *Atkins*, /pótmən/ ['pɔʔmən] *potman*.

4.143. Survey of the Distribution of the Glottal Stop

Paragraphs 4.141—4.142 show that the glottal stop does not occur with equal frequency in all positions. It is particularly frequent as a simple interlude before syllabic contoids and as a simple coda before /+C/, positions where it is also quite common in RP. It is not quite so common as a coda before /#/, and still less so before /+V/. It is least frequent as an interlude before vocoids.

That [ʔ] is more common as a coda than as an interlude (except before a syllabic contoid) may be seen from utterances like the following (cf. particularly the use of [ʔ] as a coda and of [t̡] as an interlude):

/ðáts+wotit+íz↑/ ['ðɛts wɔt̡ɪʔ 'ɪz] *that is what it is* (recorded in this way on several occasions),

/ʃijz+gótit↓/ [ʃiz 'gɔt̡ɪʔ] *she has got it*, /tə́hndit+əbít+ bétə+náw↑/ ['t̩ˢɜ·ndɪʔ ə'bɪʔ 'bet̡ə 'nɛ·ə̆] *turned it a bit better now*, /jùwkəd+gétit+ðén↑/ [ˌjə̆ükəd 'get̡ɪʔ 'ðen] *you could get it then*, /pétikəwt+léjn↓/ ['pet̡ɪkœŭʔ 'læ̆ɪn] *Pettycoat Lane*, /getáwtəvit↓/ [ge't̪ɛ̆ə̆t̪əvɪʔ] *get out of it*, /aj+fəgét+woti+kówd+isèlf↓/ [ɑ̆ɪ fə'geʔ wɔt̡ɪ 'kọ̆ŭd ɪˌsë̆ɣf] *I forget what he called himself.*

The relative lack of frequency of [ʔ] in a complex coda is seen from utterances like the following:

/wóts+ðəmátə↓/ ['wɔts ðə'mɛʔə] *what is the matter*, /ef+wíj+gèt+eni+bénəfits↑/ [ef 'wi· ˌgeʔ enɪ 'benəfɪts] *if we get any benefits.*

However, not infrequently will *all* occurrences of /t/ as interludes and codas in an utterance be manifested by the glottal stop. The following examples are taken from women speakers:[1]

/ðəlítəl+béjbi+ʃáwtid+áwt↓/ [ðə'lɪʔl̩ 'bæɪ̆bɪ 'ʃe̯ə̯ʔɪd 'e̯ə̯ʔ] *the little baby shouted out,* /ijz+nót+gótit+jét↑/ [i•z 'nɔʔ 'gɔʔɪʔ 'jeʔ] *he has not got it yet,* /pútit+on+əbítə+péjpə↓/ ['puʔɪʔ ɔn ə'bɪʔə 'pæɪ̆pə] *put it on a bit of paper,* /sówtit+áwt↓/ ['sɔ•ʔɪʔ 'e̯ə̯ʔ] *sort it out.*

A young boy is the source of the following utterance, containing almost exclusively [ʔ] allophones of /t/:

/kəz+áj+dúw+kwájt+əlót+əmúwvin+əbáwt↓   wèl+àj+get+
[kəz'ɑ̆ɪ'dü• 'kwɑ̆ɪʔ ə'lɔʔ ə'mü•vɪn ə'be̯ə̯ʔ   ˌwel̩ ˌɑ̆ɪ geʔ
'Cause I do quite a lot of moving about.   *Well, I get*

áp↑   sít+áp+ən+sìt+áp| ən+gèt+dáwn+əgèjn↑ pút+mij+
'ʌp   'sɪʔ 'ʌp ən ˌsɪʔ 'ʌp ən ˌget 'de̯ə̯n ə̩geɪ̆n 'puʔ mi
up, *sit up and — sit up and get down again,*   *put my*

fíjt+áp+on+ðə+síjt| ənów+ðərést+əvit↑/
'fi•ʔ 'ʌp ɔn ðə 'si•ʔ n̩'ɔ• ðə'rest əvɪʔ]
feet up on the seat,   *and all the rest of it.*

4.144. Paralleling Consonants Other than /t/ in RP

Sometimes morphemes which contain consonants other than /t/ in RP, and whose main allomorphs in Cockney likewise contain these other consonants, have a variant form with the [ʔ] allophone of /t/. The glottal stop occurs only in those phonological contexts which otherwise permit the occurrence of [ʔ], viz. as interludes and codas.

Most frequently [ʔ] parallels /k/ in RP, in simple or complex interludes:

/rétən/ ['reʔn̩] *reckon,* /rétənàjz/ ['reʔəˌnɑ̆ɪz] *recognize,* /sótə/ ['sɔʔə] *soccer,* /téjtən+áp/ ['tˢæɪ̆ʔn̩ 'ʌp] *taken up,* /ðej+pítəm+áp/ [ðæɪ̆ 'pɪʔəm 'ʌp] *they pick them up,*

[1] Women vs. men: cf. 4.15.

/əfétʃən/ [ə'feʔʃən] *affection*, /bátwədz/ ['bɛʔwədz] *back-wards*, /kótnij/ ['kɔʔnə̆i] *Cockney*, /ðəléttrit↓/ [ðə'leʔtrɪʔ] *the electric*, /lájtlij/ ['lɑɪ̆ʔlə̆i] *likely* (homophonous with *lightly*), /práttikəl/ ['prɛʔtɪkl̩] *practical*, /tetníjk/ [tˢeʔ'niˑk] *technique;*

and in codas:

/əbát+rúm/ [ə'bɛʔ 'rʊm] *a back room*, /lájt+ðát↓/ ['lɑɪ̆ʔ 'ðɛʔ] *like that*, /rábitən+pówt+fədínə/ ['rɛbɪʔn̩ 'pɒ̆ʊ̆ʔ fə'dᶻɪnə] *rabbit and pork for dinner*, /ðəwíjt+bifóh↓/ [ðə'wiˑʔ bɪ'fɔ̆ə̆] *the week before*, /brówtəm+bát↓/ ['brɒˑʈəm 'bɛʔ] *brought them back*, /ənúw+bút↓/ [ə'nüˑ 'bʊʔ] *a new book*, /lút↓/ ['lʊʔ] *look*, /əbáwtə+wíjt↑/ [ə'bɛ̆ˑʈə 'wiˑʔ] *about a week*, /gávmənt+wə́ht↓/ ['gʌvmənʔ 'wɜˑʔ] *government work.*

[ʔ] may also parallel /kt/ in RP:

/drétlij/ ['dreʔlə̆i] *directly*, /kəlét+ðəpléjt/ [kl̩'eʔ ðə'plæɪ̆tˢ] *collect the plate.*

Nor is [ʔ] unusual where RP has /p/, in interludes:

/ə+kə́tələ+wíjks/ [ə 'kʌʔlə 'wiˑks] *a couple of weeks*, /əkwítmənt/ [ə'kwɪʔməntˢ] *equipment*, /éjtəmij/ ['æɪ̆ʔm̩iˑ] *halfpenny*, /píjtəl+júwstuw/ ['piˑʔl̩ 'jüˑstüˑ] *people used to...* /pétəməns/ ['peʔm̩əns] *peppermints*, /θrútəms/ ['θrʊʔm̩s] *threepence;*

or in codas:

/tʃáts/ [tʃɛʔs] *chaps*, /əkə́t+əv+tíj/ [ə'kʌʔ əv 'tˢə̆i] *a cup of tea*, /əgrúwt+ðat+méjk+ə̀p/ [ə'grüˑʔ dɛʔ 'mæɪ̆k ˌʌp] *a group that make up...*, /práts/ [prɛʔs] *perhaps*, /ət+ðətót+əviz+vójs/ [əʔ ðə'tˢɔʔ əvɪs'vɔ̆ɪ̆s] *at the top of his voice*, /ə́t+ðərúwm/ ['ʌʔ ðə'rə̆üm] *up the room*, /ðəkówlət+pèjpəz/ [ðə'kɒˑləʔ ˌpæɪ̆pəz] *the call-up papers;*

or it may parallel RP /pt/:

/két+maj/ ['keʔ mɑɪ̆] *kept my...*

Much less frequently does the glottal stop parallel a voiced stop in RP. Very occasionally it may be found where RP has /g/:

/əbít+bútkəjs/ [ə'bɪʔ 'buʔ₁kæɪ̆s] *a big book-case;*

but less rarely where RP has /d/. [ʔ] is quite frequent in the negative form of the auxiliaries *could, did, had, need, should, would* before a syllabic nasal:

/kútəm+fájnd/ ['kʊʔm̩ 'fa̰ĭnd] *could not find,* /wi+dítənt/ [wɪ 'dᶻɪʔn̩tˢ] *we did not,* /ij+átəŋ+gót/ [i 'ɛʔŋ 'gɔʔ] *he had not got...,* /ʃútəŋ+gét+ðèh/ ['ʃʊʔŋ 'gɛʔ ₁ðeɔ̆] *should not get there,* /wij+wútən+ávit/ [wi 'wʊʔn̩ 'ɛvɪʔ] *we would not have it;*

and occasionally it occurs before syllabic nasals in other morphemes:

/gáhtən/ ['gɑ•ʔn̩] *garden,* /ðij+ə́wltənz/ [ði 'ɔ̆ŏʔn̩z] *the old ones.*

Nor is [ʔ] uncommon where RP has /d/ in simple, or occasionally complex, codas:

/brét+ən+bə́tə/ ['breʔ n̩ 'bʌʔə] *bread and butter,* /kút+gét/ ['kʊʔ 'geʔ] *could get,* /étwət+kə́mz+ín/ ['eʔwəʔ 'kʌmz 'ɪn] *Edward comes in,* /gówt+nə́wz+wén/ ['gʊ̆ʔ 'nœŭz 'wen] *God knows when,* /gút+gówd/ ['gʊʔ 'gɔ̆ŭd] *good God,* /ʃij+át+təsít+làjk+ðát/ [ʃi 'ɛʔ tə'sɪʔ ₁la̰ĭk 'ðɛʔ] *she had to sit like that,* /ðə+wíndərət+gówn/ [ðə 'wɪndərəʔ 'gʊ̆n] *the window had gone,* /gòt+kílt+ðat+nájt/ ['gɔʔ 'kĭ̆ʔ ðɛʔ 'na̰ĭʔ] *got killed that night,* /ðij+ə́wlt+fówt+bə̀s/ [ði 'ɔ̆ʔ 'fʊ̆ʔ ₁bʌs] *the Old Ford bus,* /rét+kə́htənz/ ['reʔ 'kɛ•ʔn̩z] *red curtains,* /təgèt+rít+əv+ðát/ [tˢə₁geʔ 'rɪʔ əv 'ðɛtˢ] *to get rid of that,* /sáks+əv+wút+fɪəm+íz+fə́hm/ ['sɛks əv 'wʊʔ frəm 'ɪz 'fə•m] *sacks of wood from his firm.*

There are some rare occurrences of [ʔ] where RP has other consonants than stops, e.g. paralleling RP /v/:

/gítəm/ ['gɪʔəm] *give them,* /ət+kóws/ [əʔ 'ko̯ŭs] *of course,*
/ðəbátələt+brítən/ [ðə'bɛʔ|əʔ 'brɪʔŋ] *the Battle of Britain,*
/əbótələt+wískij/ [ə'bɔʔ|əʔ 'wɪskə̆i] *a bottle of whiskey.*

4.15. /t/ Allophones: A Survey

Paragraphs 4.11–4.13 indicate several rather strikingly
different allophones of the /t/ phoneme. Their occurrence is
partly phonologically conditioned, but to a large extent they
are in free variation or stylistically, i.e. extra-linguistically,
conditioned.

In onsets, i.e. as a simple onset or as part of a complex onset,
only voiceless alveolar stop allophones occur, with aspiration
or affrication according to 4.122.

/t/ as a coda consonant has one additional allophone, viz.
[ʔ]. In a complex coda the alveolar stop is by far the most
common allophone. Only after /n l/ or before /s/ do we find [ʔ],
and even there [t] (or [tˢ], [tʰ]) is much more common. However,
as a simple coda [ʔ] occurs freely and with a high frequency,
in variation with the alveolar stop.

In interludes there is a third allophone, [t̬]. In complex interludes the voiceless alveolar stop is by far the most common
allophone; for certain exceptions, mainly before or after /n l/,
see 4.13 and 4.142. In a simple interlude the glottal stop allophone occurs only after a stressed syllable peak before an
unstressed one, V́tV.[1] This is the only context where all three
allophones, [t] (or [tˢ], [tʰ]), [t̬], and [ʔ], occur. In V́tV́ only [t̬]
occurs, whereas in VtV́ and VtV the voiceless alveolar stop and
the voiced alveolar flap are in free variation.

Only the voiceless alveolar stop occurs as a variant in all
positions (with one exception: V́tV́). The greatest amount of
fluctuation is found in simple interludes and simple codas.

In those contexts where different allophones may occur,

[1] V is here any unstressed syllable peak; V́ is any syllable peak with
primary or secondary stress.

the use of one or the other is apparently not correlated with stress conditions[1] or with the particular type of syllable peak preceding and following: [ʔ] and [ṭ] occur just as freely contiguously to complex peaks as to simple ones. However, the rate of delivery, speed and pauses, may be of importance for the choice of allophones: [ṭ] occurs less freely in slow style (4.13), and [ʔ] is not so likely to occur as a coda in hesitating speech, before a long pause (4.141).

Stylistic and social factors are of greater importance, however, and social sub-types of the dialect may be distinguished by means of the /t/ allophones. Generally speaking, a wide use of [ʔ], in those contexts where, according to 4.143, it is less frequent, is considered by the speakers themselves to be an indication of 'rough' speech, and it is found most frequently among men and boys, and among children who have not yet been subjected to the corrective influence of the schools. Women are more likely to 'mind their P's and Q's', which in this particular case means using an alveolar stop or flap as allophone of /t/. The alveolar flap is considered the normal, 'correct' variant, whereas the alveolar stop, at least when it is strongly affricated in V́tV, is looked upon as being too 'posh' for a Cockney to use: ['betˢə] (/bétə/ *better*) is 'posh', ['beṭə] is normal, and ['beʔə] is 'rough'. Thus, whereas a man may use the [ʔ] allophone of /t/ almost in all positions where it may occur, irrespective of whom he is talking to, a woman may show considerably more fluctuation, and the relative frequency of the various allophones will to some extent depend on the character of the interlocutor (whether the informant's own family or the analyst), the general setting of the utterance (whether at the club or in the informant's home), and the extent to which the informant is absorbed by *what* she is saying, forgetting *how* she says it.

---

[1] Certain stress patterns *prevent* the occurrence of [ʔ] in a simple interlude altogether: see the fourth paragraph of 4.15.

4.16. Distribution of Stops

4.160

When compared with RP the following distributional facts seem noteworthy:

4.161. The [ʔ] *Allophone*

/t/ occurs, manifested by its [ʔ] allophone, in an allomorph of a number of morphemes where RP has only allomorphs with some other stop consonant or /v/ (4.144).[1]

4.162. /t/ instead of /k/

/t/ occurs, manifested by a voiceless alveolar stop allophone, in a variant form of a few morphemes where RP has /k/ only:

/áhst/ *ask*, /bə́st/ *busk*: /aj+wúdən+áhstim+sìj↑/ *I would not ask him, see*, /if+ajm+áhstin+juw↓/ *if I am asking you*, /joh+bə́stiz+əbrə́wk↓/ *your busks are broke.*

The infinitive/present and the preterite are homonyms: no alveolar suffix is added to the infinitive form /áhst/:[2]

/ajl+áhst+ə+pəlíjsmən/ *I'll ask a policeman*,
/aj+áhst+ə+pəlíjsmən/ *I asked a policeman*.

4.163. Voiced instead of Voiceless

The voiced stops are supposed to be used in certain words in Cockney where RP has voiceless stops.[3] In my data this occurs only in common variant forms of *beetle* (/bíjdəl/)

---

[1] On the phonemic interpretation of [ʔ], see D. Jones, *The Phoneme* § 620, which favours the same solution as the one adopted here. For some theoretical problems, see 7.32 of the present study.

[2] One informant writes in a letter: 'We were ask if there were any question.' This suggests at least that there is no phonemic difference between the present and the preterite forms.

[3] Cf. H. C. Wyld, *A History of Modern Colloquial English* p. 312 sq.; W. Matthews, *Cockney Past and Present* p. 174.

and *Protestant* (/pródistənt/), and at least one informant has heard forms with /b/ for /p/ in *Baptist, capable, cripple, deputy*.[1]

On the other hand, the voiceless stop /k/ is common in a variant form of *God*, /kówd/, used as an interjection.

4.164. Labial Stop instead of Labial Fricative

Labial stops occur instead of the voiced labial fricative in a variant form of a few words:

/sébəm/ ['sebm̩] *seven*, /sépən+tíjn/ ['sepm̩ 'tˢ ɪ̈in] *seventeen*, /gə́bənə/ ['gʌbn̩ə] *governor*.

4.165. Excrescent Stops

/t k d/ occur in certain morphemes where there is no parallel segment in RP. This is in accordance with Cockney tradition,[2] but in the present data this 'excrescent' consonant is restricted to a very few words:

/əkrówst/ *across*, /nə́θiŋk/ *nothing*,[3] /róŋk/ *wrong*, /gáwnd/ *gown*, /ə́wndə/ *owner*, /spójldz/ *spoils*;

and at least one informant has heard /váhmint/ *vermin*. Only in *-thing* constructions does the excrescent consonant occur with any regularity or consistency. Very occasionally *-ing* forms, which regularly end in /in/ or /ən/, have forms in /iŋk/: /gríjtiŋk/ *greeting*. On the other hand, *-thing* words may, very rarely, have forms in /in/, on the analogy of the *-ing* forms.

---

[1] On the occasional occurrence of /d/ instead of the voiced flap allophone of /t/, for instance in *satisfied*, see 4.13.

[2] Cf. W. Matthews, *Cockney Past and Present* pp. 80, 163; H. C. Wyld *A History of Modern Colloquial English* pp. 290 sq., 309.

[3] Cf. occasional spellings in letters from an informant: 'somethink' 'anythink'.

4.2 FRICATIVES

4.21. Phonemic Norms and Allophonic Variations

The phonemic norms of the eight fricative consonants are labio-dental (/f v/), dental (/θ ð/), alveolar (/s z/), and palato-alveolar (/ʃ ʒ/). The labio-dental and dental fricatives are flat, whereas the alveolar and palato-alveolar ones are grooved, the groove being wider in the palato-alveolar fricatives than in the alveolar ones:[1]

/fél/ *fell*, /vést/ *vest*, /θéft/ *theft*, /ðén/ *then*, /sét/ *set*, /zíp/ *zip*, /ʃél/ *shell*, /méʒə/ *measure*.

The phonemic norm of /f θ s ʃ/ is voiceless, and they have no voiced allophones. The phonemic norm of /v ð z ʒ/ is voiced, but they are subject to allophonic variations in the degree of voicing, to a greater extent than the voiced stops: partly or fully voiceless allophones occur (4.051).

There are also other minor allophonic variations, which parallel those of RP. Thus, the labial fricatives /f v/ may be bilabial before other bilabial consonants; a juncture may intervene: /əpéhrəv+búwts/ *a pair of boots*. /s z/ may be dental before the dental fricatives /θ ð/: /wótsðə+tájm/ *what is the time*. In a complex interlude /ð/ may be manifested, not as a separate segment, but in the dental quality of a preceding apical segment whose phonemic norm is otherwise alveolar: [t̪] = /tð/, [d̪] = /dð/, [s̪] = /sð/, [z̪] /zð], [n̪] = /nð/:[2]

/gótðə+péjpəz+ìn/ ['gɔt̪ə 'pæɪpəz ˌɪn] *got the papers in?*
/əkrówsðə+rə́wd/ [ə́krɒ̆s̪ə 'rœŭd] *across the road,*
/inðə+frə́nt/ [ɪn̪ə 'frʌnt] *in the front.*

---

[1] On flat vs. grooved articulation, see K. L. Pike, *Phonetics* p. 121.

[2] [t̪], [d̪], [s̪], [z̪], [n̪] seem to alternate with [t̪ð], [d̪ð], [s̪ð], [z̪ð], [n̪ð] only, never with [t̪θ], [d̪θ], [s̪θ], [z̪θ], [n̪θ]. It is therefore convenient to interpret these dental segments as /tð dð sð zð nð/, never as /tθ dθ sθ zθ nθ/.

The contrast between the following utterances rests on the dental vs. the alveolar quality of the voiceless apical stop; it is admittedly rather tenuous:

/pə́wstðə+létə/ ['pœŭst̪ə 'letˢə] *post the letter* vs.

/pə́wstə+létə/ ['pœŭstə 'letˢə] *post a letter*.

With many speakers /ʃ ʒ/ differ somewhat from those of RP. The teeth are kept close together, as in RP. The lips are protruded, but they are kept fairly parallel, so that there is less lip-rounding than is shown in D. Jones, *Outline* Fig. 101.[1] However, the main difference is that /ʃ ʒ/ are more palatalized than in RP. This applies to /ʃ ʒ/ in all contexts, but the palatalization is of course particularly strong near close front vowels: /ʃíjp/ *sheep*, /fíʃ/ *fish*, /dʒíjn/ *Jean*, /tʃéjndʒ/ *change*.

4.22. Distribution

4.220

The distribution of the fricatives in Cockney differs only in a few respects from RP.

4.221. *Interchange of /v/ and /w/*

There is no example in the present data of the interchange between /v/ and /w/, which has been thought characteristic of the London dialect.[2]

4.222. *|t d| or |f v| instead of |θ ð|*

Traditionally, morphemes containing /θ ð/ in RP commonly show forms with /t d/ or /f v/ in Cockney.[3] There are only a couple of examples in my data of the former variants:

[1] Cf. the acoustically 'clearer' [ʃ] of D. Jones, *Outline* § 729.

[2] See e.g. W. Matthews, *Cockney Past and Present* p. 177 sq; H. C. Wyld, *A History of Modern Colloquial English* p. 292. Both consider this an obsolete feature of Cockney.

[3] See e.g. W. Matthews, *Cockney Past and Present* pp. 80, 177 sq., 162 sq.; H. C. Wyld, *A History of Modern Colloquial English* p. 291; J. Franklyn, *The Cockney* p. 251.

/táwzən/ *thousand*, /bétnəl+gríjn/ *Bethnal Green,*
/ðəbéjd/ *the bathe;*

but /f v/ paralleling RP /θ ð/ are quite common:[1]

/áhfə/ *Arthur*, /béfnəl+gríjn/ *Bethnal Green*, /klówfs/ *cloths,*
/éjpəf/ *halfpenny worth*, /fáwzən/ *thousand*, /frəw/ *throw;*
/bóvəd/ *bothered*, /məvərən+fáhvə/ *mother and father,*
/smúwv/ *smooth*, /wévə/ *whether.*

4.223. /ʒ/

/ʒ/ has a more limited distribution than in RP: it never
occurs as a simple coda. Words which have or may have
/ʒ/ as a simple coda in RP[2] are paralleled by forms with /dʒ/
in Cockney:

/báridʒ/ *barrage*, /béjdʒ/ *beige*, /kámǝflàhdʒ/ *camouflage,*
/éspǝnèjdʒ/ or /éspǝnàhdʒ/ *espionage*, /gáridʒ/ *garage,*
/rúwdʒ/ *rouge.*

Thus, /ʒ/ occurs only in a complex onset, coda or interlude preceded by /d/, and as a simple interlude:

/dʒə́dʒ/ *judge*, /dídʒə/ *did you*, /májndʒə/ *mind you,*
/méʒə/ *measure*, /káʒəltiz/ *casualties.*

A certain number of morphemes are supposed to contain
/dʒ/ in Cockney, paralleling RP /z/. Such forms are very rare
in my data, and occur as an occasional variant only:[3]

/mjudʒíʃən/ *musician*, /skwíjdʒ/ *squeeze.*

---

[1] One informant writes (jocularly?) in a letter: 'farsons of People'
(i.e. thousands of people), 'git on wiv em' (i.e. get on with them).

[2] Cf. D. Jones, *Outline* § 739 n. 34.

[3] Cf. W. Matthews (*Cockney Past and Present* p. 178), who says of
final /dʒ/ for /z/ that it 'is not generally used by Cockneys'. J. Franklyn
(*The Cockney* p. 232 sq.) does not recognize it as a regular Cockney feature either. However, he considers /s/ to be the regular Cockney form.
spelling 'They are suppoced to suppoce'. I have never heard such a form.

4.224. Missing Fricatives

Some morphemes may have allomorphs without fricatives somewhat more frequently than in RP. Thus, unstressed *of*:

/əlót+ənúw+fláts/ *a lot of new flats;*

and unstressed *they, them, their*:[1]

/fóhrej+gét+bád/ *(be)fore they get bad,* /nə́wbədij+séj+nə́θiŋk+túwəm/ *nobody say nothing to them,* /aj+sóhrəm/ *I saw them,* /tuw+eh+bódij/ *to their body;*

and even stressed or unstressed *that*:

/atiz+ríhlij+trúw/ *that is really true,*
/áts+wot+ðej+də́n+tùwəs/ *that is what they done to us.*

In addition, there may be, more sporadically, absence of an expected fricative:

/joh+sélz/ *yourselves,* /gísit/ *give us it,* /sə́miŋk/ ['sʌmĩk] or /sə́nin/ ['sʌnɪn] *something.*

4.3. NASALS

4.31. Phonemic Norms and Allophonic Variations

The phonemic norms of the three nasal consonants are bilabial (/m/), alveolar (/n/), and velar (/ŋ/). They are always voiced: /sám/ *Sam,* /sán(d)/ *sand,* /sáŋ/ *sang.*

There are allophonic variations, most of which parallel those of RP. Thus, the labial nasal may be labio-dental before the labio-dental fricatives /f v/: /kə́mfət/ *comfort,* /ìmfəméjʃən/ (also /ìnfəméjʃən/) *information.* The apical nasal is dental before the dental fricatives /θ ð/: /inðéh/ *in there.* The phoneme sequence apical nasal plus front apical fricative may even be manifested by a single phonetic segment, a dental nasal, [n̪] =

---

[1] One informant's letters contain frequent spellings like 'I was gittin em', 'you sling em'.

/nŏ/ (4.21): /ə́p+ənŏij+éh/ ['ʌp n̩i 'eŏ]¹ *up in the air.* Before the phonemes and phoneme sequences /ʃ tʃ dʒ/, which are palatalized (4.11, 4.21), the apical nasal is itself somewhat palatalized: /éjnʃənt/ *ancient,* /lə́ntʃ/ *lunch,* /tʃéjndʒ/ *change,* /índʒəd/ *injured.* The velar nasal shows considerable allophonic variations in point of articulation, depending on the preceding syllable peak. It is front velar after front vowels, /bríŋ/ *bring,* and back velar after back vowels, /róŋ/ *wrong,* but these variations are hardly greater than in RP.

4.32. Nasalization of Vocoids

The nasal consonants may be manifested, not as a separate segment, but in the nasality of a preceding syllable peak whose phonemic norm is otherwise not nasal or nasalized:

/əpéhrəntlij/ [ə'peŏrə́ʔlŏi] *apparently,* /əpójntmənts/ [ə'pɔ̃ĩʔmənts] *appointments,*² /aj+wént+wiŏ+dʒúwn/ [ɑ· 'wẽʔ wɪŏ 'dʒŏün] *I went with June,* /əpájnt+ənə+áhf/ [ə'pɑ̃·ʔ n̩ə 'ɑ·f] *a pint and a half,* /májnjə+píjzən+kjúwz/ ['mɑ̃·jə 'pĩizən 'kjŏüz] *mind your P's and Q's,* /ŏəstéjt+jurín/ [ŏə'stæĩt juˈrĩ] *the state you are in,* /nə́θiŋk/ ['nʌθĩk] *nothing,* /sə́mθiŋk/ ['sʌmθĩk] *something.*³

¹ [n̩] is syllabic in this utterance.
² The nasality extends all through /oj/, as well as through other complex peaks.
³ The word *something* occurs in a number of variant forms. The following have been recorded, and there are doubtless more: /sə́mθiŋ/ ['sʌmθɪŋ], /sə́mθiŋk/ ['sʌmθɪŋk], or ['sʌmθĩk], /sə́miŋk/ ['sʌmĩk], /sə́miŋ/ ['sʌmĩŋ], /sə́mik/ ['sʌmɪk], /sə́min/ ['sʌmĩ], /sə́mŏiŋ/ ['sʌmŏɪŋ], /sə́nθin/ ['sʌnθɪn], /sə́nŏiŋk/ ['sʌ̃ŏĩk], /sə́nŏik/ ['sʌ̃ŏɪk], /sə́nin/ ['sʌnin]. Cf. the transcription ['sʌ̃ʔĩ] in D. Jones, *Pronunciation* § 258, the spellings quoted by W. Matthews (*Cockney Past and Present* pp. 71, 75), 'somethin', 'suthin', and by J. Franklyn (*The Cockney* p. 252), 'sumink', and G. B. Shaw's spelling in *Captain Brassbound's Conversion,* 'sathink'.

In the present data, only /n/ and /ŋ/ are ever manifested in this way. It is likely, however, that a larger corpus of text would show /m/ manifested in the same way.[1]

This type of nasalization, which is phonologically relevant, should be distinguished from a weaker form of nasality, which is considered a characteristic of Cockney,[2] and which is widespread among my informants. This latter type of nasalization is non-contrastive on the phonemic level, but it is a factor in the complex of features generally called voice quality. It is especially strong in a nasal context:

/its+nájs↓/ [ɪts 'nã̇·s] *it is nice,* /fə́nij↓ ínit↓/ ['fʌ̃nɪ̃ 'ɪ̃nɪ̃ʔ] *funny, is it not,* /wen+ə́p/ [wẽn 'ʌ̃p] *went up;*

but it is not limited to this context:

----

[1] The phonetic manifestations of /n/ and /ŋ/ are identical in this context, and there is no contrast between them. One might therefore prefer to consider all nasalized vocoids as /Vn/ (or, alternatively, as /Vŋ/). The data show a tendency to neutralization of the contrast between the nasals before certain consonants, with a decided preference for [m] before labial consonants and [ŋ] before velar consonants (4.331), but pre-consonantal [m n ŋ] must still be considered occurrences of three different nasal phonemes. It is therefore convenient to make the same analysis of the nasalized vocoid, and I interpret it as /Vŋ/ before velar consonants, as /Vm/ if it is ever found before labial consonants, and as /Vn/ in other contexts.

[2] A number of writers have made a point of nasalization in Cockney, but they do not always distinguish between the two types of nasalization indicated above. D. Jones (*Pronunciation* § 392) gives examples only of our weaker type of nasalization ([ãɪnt ʃə 'kãmɪ̃n]), but in the transcribed passage (pp. 207–9) he has indicated nasalization only in cases where it is, in my opinion, phonologically relevant ([θɛ̃ʔ] *thank,* [dʒɛ̃ʔomən] *gentleman,* etc.). I. C. Ward (*The Phonetics of English* § 232 and the transcribed passage pp. 235–7) does not distinguish between sub-phonemic and phonemic nasalization (e.g. [ãɪ dʌʊ θɪ̃ʔ soʊ] *I do not think so.* J. D. O'Connor (*New Phonetic Readings* pp. 56–9), when he gives an attempted transcription in Cockney, uses the nasalization symbol only 'when the nasalisation is significant, i.e. when the nasal consonant has disappeared.' See also W. Matthews, *Cockney Past and Present* p. 77 and E. Dieth, *Vademekum der Phonetik* p. 99.

/pə́tnij/ ['pʌ̃ʔnə̆ĭ] *Putney*, /ðij+ə́wld+áws/ [ði 'ɔ̆ŏd 'ḛ̃ə̃s]
the old house, /əzðej+lájt/ [əzðɛĭ 'lɑ̃ĭʔ] *as they like.*

This weaker, phonemically non-relevant form of nasalization
is not marked in the transcriptions.

4.33. Distribution

4.330

The distribution of the nasals in Cockney differs only in a
few respects from RP.

4.331. Assimilation

As in RP, morphemes whose main allopmorphs end in /n/
have allomorphs in /m/ before labial consonants and in /ŋ/
before velar consonants. This is extremely common in rapid
colloquial style. An internal juncture may intervene:

/wútən/ ['wʊʔn̩] *would not*, but /wútəm+péj/ ['wʊʔm̩ 'pæĭ]
would not pay; /áwzin/ *housing*, but /áwzim+bíznis/
housing business; /kútən/ ['kʊʔn̩] *could not*, but /kútəm+
fájnd/ ['kʊʔm̩ 'fɑ̃ĭnd] *could not find*; /dúwin/ *doing*, but
/dúwim+mij+ə́wn+dʒób/ *doing my own job*; /(ð)ən/ *than*,
but /móhəm+wot+juθíŋk/ *more than what you think*;
/átən/ ['ɛʔn̩] *had not*, but /ij+átəŋ+gót/ [i• 'ɛʔŋ 'gɔʔ]
he had not got.

This kind of 'assimilation' is especially frequent in unstressed
syllables, but it is also quite common in stressed syllables:

/lén(d)/ *lend*, but /lémmi+səm+mə́nij/ *lend me some money*;
/káhn/ *can't*, but /káhŋ+gét/ *can't get.*

Before other than labial and velar consonants the contrast
between the three nasals is well established:

/émtij/ *empty* vs. /séntim/ *sent him*, /dʒámd/ *jammed* vs.
/bán(d)/ *band* vs. /báŋd/ *banged*, /fámlij/ *family* vs. /mánlij/
manly vs. /dáŋlin/ *dangling.*

4.332. Unstressed /in/ instead of /iŋ/

There is no contrast between the apical and the dorsal nasal in post-peak margins in unstressed syllables. Only /n/ normally occurs, thus regularly in the verbal *-ing* forms:[1]

/drípin/ *dripping*, /fə́sin/ *fussing*, /gítin/ og /gítən/ ['gɪʔn̩] *getting*;

and also in other morphemes containing unstressed /iŋ/ in RP:

/bíldin/ *building*, /mównin/ *morning*, /ʃílin/ *shilling*.

The same applies to words containing unstressed /-iŋ-/ in RP in simple interludes, and in complex interludes or codas before consonants other than velars:

/bə́kinəm+pális/ *Buckingham Palace*, /bílinzgit/ *Billingsgate*, /ízlintən/ *Islington*, /túw+ʃílinz/ *two shillings*.

Only extremely rarely does /iŋ/ occur as a variant form, except before velar consonants, where it is the norm (cf. 4.331):

/séjiŋ+kwík/ *saying quick*, /lúkiŋ+glàhs/ *looking-glass*.

Only one morpheme has unstressed /iŋ/ in its main allomorph, viz. *-thing*: /nə́θiŋk/ *nothing*, /sə́mθiŋk/ *something*.[2] In stressed syllables, i.e. syllables with primary or secondary stress, /iŋ/ frequently occurs: /dájmən+ríŋ/ or /dájmən+rìŋ/ *diamond ring*.

Morphemes which are supposed to contain /iŋ/ paralleling RP /in/ or /ən/ as a Cockney characteristic[3] regularly have forms with /in/ or /ən/ in the present data:

/káptin/ *captain*, /tʃíkin/ *chicken*, /kúʃin/ *cushion*, /gáhdin/ or /gáhdən/ *garden*, /kítʃin/ *kitchen*, /línin/ *linen*, /páhdən/ *pardon*.

---

[1] Occasional spellings in letters from an informant bear out this pronunciation: 'comin', 'gittin', 'shartin' (i.e. shouting), 'Xmas pudens'.

[2] For other variants, see p. 126 n. 3.

[3] See W. Matthews, *Cockney Past and Present* p. 176; H. C. Wyld, *A History of Modern Colloquial English* p. 290; D. Jones, *Pronunciation* § 287.

A few words are supposed to contain a medial nasal segment in Cockney not paralleled by any segment in RP.[1] Out of these, only /skélintən/ *skeleton* occurs in my data, never, for example, */mílintrij/ *military*, only /mílətrij/.

4.4. SONORANTS

4.40. The remaining five consonants, /l r h j w/, are better treated individually than as a group. Although they share certain characteristics (4.03—4.05), each of them presents its own problems, phonetically as well as phonemically.

4.41. /l/

4.411. Phonemic Norm and Allophonic Variations

The allophone of /l/ which occurs as a simple onset is considered to be its phonemic norm. It is a voiced alveolar lateral contoid: /lə́k/ *luck*, /láhdʒ/ *large*. After voiceless consonants in the same phonetic syllable /l/ is partly voiceless, with some friction: /plíjz/ *please*, /flóh/ *floor* (4.051).

4.412. Vocoid Resonance

4.4121. Anticipating and Continuing Vocoid Position. There are variations in tongue position conditioned by the contiguous syllable peaks. The tongue position of the vocoid will, to some extent, be anticipated by, or continued in, /l/, so that the front part of the tongue is slightly raised near front vocoids, and the back part of the tongue is humped up near back vocoids: /l/ has various 'vowel resonances',[2] i.e., in our terms, vocoid resonances.

The resonance is most palatal or front before the high front vowel: /líjv/ *leave*; gradually less so before mid front, low, central, and back vowels: /léd/ *led*, /lák/ *lack*, /lə́k/ *luck*, /lúk/ *look*,

[1] Cf. W. Matthews, *Cockney Past and Present* p. 176.
[2] Cf. D. Jones, *Outline* § 665 sqq.

/lók/ *lock*; more and more velar in post-peak position, least so after the high front vowel: /fíl/ *fill*; gradually more so after the mid front, low, central, and back vowels: /fél/ *fell*, /pál/ *pal*, /páhl/ *pearl*, /fúl/ *full*, /fówl/ *fall*.

4.4122. 'Clear' vs. 'Dark' l. It is usual to set up two main allophones of /l/ in most British dialects: 'clear l' and 'dark l', i.e. a lateral with palatal resonance and a lateral with velar resonance.[1] The former occurs only in onsets and interludes before vowels and /j/,[2] the latter in interludes and codas before other consonants and juncture. There may be a better physiological and acoustical justification for making a division between these two types in Cockney than in RP. In Cockney postpeak /l/ has a marked velar quality, and the velarization may be said to be phonologically relevant, which the laterality is not in this position: the most common allophone in pre-consonantal and pre-junctural position is a non-syllabic velar vocoid, [ɣ̆], where there is no contact between the tip of the tongue and the teeth ridge. We have not postulated 'lateral' as a distinctive feature for /l/ (4.04), so that this need not worry us. However, we do label /l/, phonologically, as a 'front apical sonorant', and this description obviously does not fit the [ɣ̆] allophone. This is a case where the distinctive features postulated for a phoneme do not apply to all its allophones.[3]

4.413. Allophonic Variations of 'Dark l'

4.4131. Lateral or Vocoid. The back vocoid and the strongly velarized lateral are largely in free variation before consonants and juncture. The syllabic lateral, i.e. /əl/, may possibly be more

[1] See e.g. D. Jones, *Outline* §§ 659, 668 sq.

[2] Clear l may also occur before the central vocoid [ə˙] used as a hesitation signal: /it+wəz+ówl?/ [ɪʔ wəz 'ɒ˙lə˙] *it was all* —.

[3] For other cases, see 7.13, 7.23. B. Bloch and G. L. Trager (*Outline of Linguistic Analysis* § 3.4) are of the opinion that the velar allophone is lateral too, and consider lateral opening as the 'characterizing phonetic feature' of /l/.

frequent after another alveolar contoid than in other positions:

/lítəl/ ['lɪtɫ̩] *little*, /médəl/ ['medɫ̩] *medal*, /tə́nəl/ ['tʌnɫ̩] *tunnel*;

and /l/ before another, pre-vocalic, and hence 'clear' /l/ is usually lateral, even if internal juncture intervenes:

/əfúl+ĺəwd/ [ə'fuɫ 'lœʊ̆d] *a full load*, /əlítəl+ĺəŋgə/ [ə'lɪtɫ̩ 'lɔŋgə] *a little longer*.

But such phonological conditioning is of minor importance. There are conditioning factors of a stylistic nature, however: there are more lateral allophones in slow, careful enunciation than in colloquial style. Likewise, words and phrases with a formal connotation will commonly have the lateral allophone. Thus, in the recorded data of one informant who generally uses the vocoid allophone, all occurrences of *gentleman* have the lateral allophone, /dʒéntəlmən/ ['dʒentɫ̩mən]. However, the vocoid allophone occurs quite as frequently in the speech of women as of men and children, in the speech of those who pay more attention to how they speak as of the 'rougher' type.

On the whole, a back vocoid is the most common allophone before consonants and juncture.

4.4132. Allophonic Variation of the Vocoid. There is considerable allophonic variation of the vocoid, both in tongue and lip position. It is a non-syllabic vocoid *glide*, except when it is a manifestation of the unstressed phoneme sequence /əl/; in the latter case it is a syllabic monophthong, [ɤ]. The following remarks apply to the end-point of the glide, and to the monophthong.

Unrounded cardinal vocoid No. 7, slightly fronted, may be considered as the norm, and [ɤ] has been chosen as a convenient symbol for this general allophonic type of /l/.

The tongue position is closer after close vocoids than after open ones:

/fíl/ [fĭɤ̆] *fill*, /fúl/ [fu̠ɤ̆] *full*; /bə́lb/ [bʌɤ̆b] *bulb*, /sólv/ [sɒɤ̆v] *solve*;

and it is not quite so back after front or central vocoids (/fíl/, /bɔ́lb/) as after back ones (/fúl/, /sólv/).

The lip position of the vocoid is indifferent. It is commonly unrounded, but some labialization may be present. It is generally rounded after rounded vocoids:

/kówld/ [kɔŏd] *called*, /fúl/ [fʊ̆] *full*, /ɔ́wld/ [ɔ̆d] *old*;

and the lip-rounding may be more marked in emphatic, careful enunciation. Thus, in the last syllable of a macrosegment, particularly when it is also stressed, there is commonly lip-rounding:

/ijz+əgúd+tʃájld/ [i·z ə'gʊd 'tʃɑ·ŏd] *he is a good child.*[1]

4.4133. Allophonic Variation of the Preceding Syllable Peak. The allophonic variants of the syllable peaks differ strongly from the phonemic norms before pre-consonantal and pre-junctural /l/ (3.051).

4.414. Distribution

When compared with RP the following distributional facts seem noteworthy.

There is an unusual limitation on the syllable peaks which may occur before pre-consonantal and pre-junctural /l/ in normal colloquial style. Any stressed simple syllable peak may occur under these conditions:

/fíl/ *fill*, /fél/ *fell*, /pál/ *pal*, /dól/ *doll*, /fúl/ *full*, /gɔ́l/ *gull*;

but out of the complex peaks only /oj əh əw/ are well established; morphemes containing /ojl əhl əwl/ in RP are always paralleled by similar forms in Cockney:

/bójl/ *boil*, /gɔ́hl/ *girl*, /rɔ́wl/ *roll*.

[1] In the phonetic transcription [ŏ] is used as the phonetic symbol for most variants of the vocoid allophone of /l/. [ŭ] and [ŏ] are used after rounded vocoids.

Other complex peaks before /1C 1+ 1#/ in RP are either paralleled by simple peaks in Cockney, or there are several variant forms. /ih/ and /ij/ hardly ever occur in this position; instead there are forms with /i/:

/ríl/ *real*, /fíl/ *feel*.

/uh/ and /uw/ are also rare; instead there are forms with /u/:

/fjúl/ *fuel*, /fúl/ *fool*.

Instead of /ej/ and /aw/ Cockney commonly has forms with /a/:

/pál/ *pale*, /fál/ *foul*;

and RP /ah/ and /aj/ are either commonly both paralleled by /ah/ in Cockney:

/snáhl/ *snarl*, /páhl/ *pile*;

or, in a more colloquial style, by /a/:

/snál/ *snarl*, /pál/ *pile*.

Unstressed /ə/ following a complex peak is rare before /l/. RP disyllabic sequences are paralleled by single syllables in Cockney:

/trájl/ (or /trál/) *trial*, rhyming with /májl/ (or /mál/) *mile*; /rójl/ *royal*, rhyming with /bójl/ *boil*; /táwl/ (or /tál/) *towel*, rhyming with /fáwl/ (or /fál/) *foul*.

On the other hand, RP forms with /l/ before a consonant or a juncture may be paralleled by forms without any /l/ in Cockney.[1] Thus, RP /owl/ is often paralleled by Cockney /ow/: /ów/ *all*.[2] In unstressed position /l/ may also frequently be missing in rapid style: /kéhfənəs/ *carefulness*, /sivéstə/ *Silvester*,

---

[1] For a similar phenomenon in 'careless speech' in RP, cf. D. Jones, *Pronunciation* § 305.

[2] For the sake of easier comparison, in the present study the RP sound system is analysed in a way which closely parallels the analysis of Cockney. It is for this reason that RP [ɔ·l] *all* is interpreted as /owl/. It is possible that a better analysis would be /ohl/.

/aj+dúwit/ *I'll do it*. In /máhmèj/ *Mildmay* (the name of a well-known hospital of the district) /l/ is regularly missing; the syllable peak is regularly /ah/, not /aj/.

However, potentially, in slow, formal style of speech more similar to RP, particularly when it is necessary to bring out differences in meaning more clearly, all syllable peaks with the exception of /eh/ and /oh/ may occur before pre-consonantal and pre-junctural /l/. Even then /ij/ is extremely rare.[1]

In a few words pre-vocalic ('clear') /l/ has another distribution than in RP. A common variant form of *only* is /ə́wnij/, without any /l/ phoneme. On the other hand, Cockney /l/ is paralleled by RP /n/ in /tʃímlij/ *chimney*.

4.42. /r/

4.421. *Phonemic Norm and Allophonic Variations*

The phonemic norm of /r/ is a voiced oral post-alveolar frictionless continuant. The lips are well protruded, so that even the following vowel may be somewhat labialized: /réd/ *red*, /grə́w/ *grow*, /vérij/ *very*.

Fricative allophones occur after voiceless consonants and /d/ in the same phonetic syllable, the friction being particularly strong after /t/ and /d/: /prés/ *press*, /kráj/ *cry*, /fráj/ *fry*, /θríj/ *three*, /ʃríjk/ *shriek*, /tráj/ *try*, /dráj/ *dry*.

After voiceless consonants /r/ is also voiceless, or partly devoiced. It is completely voiceless after /t/, but it may be voiced in its final part after other voiceless consonants: /tráj/ *try*, /práwd/ *proud* (4.051).

The voiced post-alveolar flap allophone, [ɾ],[2] is extremely rare. It has been observed occasionally with a few speakers only, and then more frequently in the cluster Cr, /príj+fàb/

---

[1] For a more detailed discussion of the distribution of the syllable peaks before pre-consonantal and pre-junctural /l/, cf. 3.141, 3.241, 3.351, 3.452, 3.541.

[2] Cf. D. Jones, *Outline* §§ 750, 753.

preƒab, /bríŋ/ *bring,* /fríj/ *free,* /θrúw/ *through,* /évrij/ *every,*
than as a simple interlude, /sèpəréjʃən/ *separation,* /vérij/ *very.*
In any case it occurs only in words which are emphasized.

4.422. *Distribution*

4.4220. The distribution of /r/ in Cockney differs only in a
few respects from RP.

4.4221. *Linking and Intrusive* /r/. In many idiolects /r/ is
the usual means of bridging a hiatus between two syllable
peaks when the first peak is Vh or unstressed /ə/. This occurs
not only where the spelling has 'r', in which case RP may have
the same form, the so-called linking r:[1]

/íhrəm+séj/ *hear them say,* /ðehráwziz/ *their houses,*
/fáhrəwéj/ *far away,* /ohrénibodij/ *or anybody,* /juhróptiks/
your optics, /əjəhrən/ *a year and*..., /áhftərəm/ *after them;*

but also where no 'r' occurs in the spelling, and this /r/, the so-
called intrusive r, is less generally used and accepted in RP:[2]

/ðəsínəmahrəz/ *the cinema as*..., /dróhrit/ *draw it,*
/róhrənjən/ *raw onion,* /dʒóhrin/ *jawing,* /gív+jərədʒób/
give you a job, /káhbinèjtid+səwdəríz+fərìndidʒéʃʃən/
carbonated soda is for indigestion, /nót+ərəwp/ *not a hope.*[3]

---

[1] Cf. D. Jones, *Outline* § 756.

[2] Cf. D. Jones, *Outline* § 759, and *Pronunciation* § 361 sq. One of the
informants writes 'I wonder our Eva's getting on' (i.e. how), but this
need not necessarily mean that there is an intrusive /r/, only that *our*
is monosyllabic and homophonous with *how*, i.e. /aw/.

[3] This is not the usual way of bridging the hiatus after the unstressed
indefinite article: it is more common to use the form /ən/: /fájn+ənəwm+
fòh+ðəm/ *find a home for them.* Curiously enough, in the few cases
where /ər/ has been recorded for the indefinite article it has only been
where the next word starts with /h/ in RP. In such cases the indefinite
article may also be left out altogether: /aj+ad+áws+ðèn/ *I had (a)
house then* (in contradistinction to a flat), /ðej+wútən+əht+éhrən+
joréd/ *they would not hurt (a) hair on your head.*

The use of linking and intrusive /r/ is not limited to this context. Linking /r/ may also occur when a potential preceding /ə/ is missing, so that there is no hiatus to bridge:

/áhftrəm/ *after them,* /ówltrit/ *alter it,* /rimémbrit/ *remember it,* /áwvrit/ *over it,* /gúd+frisélf/ *good for himself.*

Both linking and intrusive /r/ may occur after other syllable peaks than Vh and unstressed /ə/. Thus, linking /r/ occurs after unstressed /i o u/:

/báj+jiráwn/ *buy your own,* /wirájðə/ *we are either...,* /jorájz/ *your eyes,* /péj+forit/ *pay for it,* /jurélθ/ *your health,* /jurənájs+gáhl/ *you are a nice girl;*[1]

and after /ij ej aw uw/, both stressed and unstressed:[2]

/wìjrán+lákij/ *we are unlucky,* /ðejráp+ðéh/ *they are up there,* /awráwn/ *our own,* /wén+juwrin+béd/ *when you are in bed,* /júwrow+rájt/ *you are all right.*[3]

Intrusive /r/ has been observed only after /aj aw/ and unstressed /u/, but it is possible that its limited occurrence is due to the limitation of our texts. It is found only once after /aj/,[4] but repeatedly after /u aw/:

[1] It is probably possible to interpret these as /ih oh uh/, since there is hardly any actual *contrast* between /ih/ and /i/, /oh/ and /o/, /uh/ and /u/ in such a context: the occurrence of one for the other could hardly serve to distinguish meanings.

[2] It may be a mere coincidence that linking /r/ occurs only after these complex peaks in my data. It may possibly occur after any complex peak.

[3] It is possible to interpret unstressed /ij uw/ as /ih uh/, for the reasons given in n. 1. The occurrence of linking /r/ after /ej aw/ and stressed /ij uw/ may be considered parallel to its occurrence after a consonant, where a potential preceding unstressed /ə/ is missing: *we are, they are, our, you are* have two alternant forms before a vowel: /wijr/ and /wijər/, /ðejr/ and /ðejər/, /awr/ and /awər/, /juwr/ and /juwər/.

[4] On the occurrence and non-occurrence of intrusive /r/ as a clue to the distinction between monophthongal /aj/ and /ah/, see p. 65 n. 1.

/ðej+dɔ́wnt+téjk+jurəbawt+tén+mínits/ *they do not take you about ten minutes,* /əfóh+stóhri+ájráws/ *a four-storey high house,* /ij+tɔ́wld+mij+áwrij+méjdit/ *he told me how he made it,* /djuw+nɔ́w+awrɔ́wld+ʃij+íz/ *do you know how old she is.*

Intrusive /r/ is common before or in the middle of the central vocoid used as a hesitation signal, [rə·] (after a syllable peak) or [ərə·] (after a consonant):

/fər? gɔ́hlz/ [fərə· 'gɜ̌z] *for girls,* /bjúwtifəl+fúwd ? tʃíkin/ ['bjü·ʈɪfɤ 'fü·d ərə· 'tʃɪkɪn] *beautiful food, chicken* —[1]

/r/ never occurs finally in a microsegment. In the following utterances linking or intrusive /r/ occurs *after* the terminal contour, as an onset consonant:[2]

/ij+éjntə+sɔ́h| rijz+bín+in+prízən/ *he ain't a sir, he has been in prison,* /ðej+ɔ́wvəròwlju| rən+fájnd+áwt/ *they overall you and find out.*

Such utterances are rather rare: usually there are morphemic variants without /r/ at a terminal contour.

It is possible that the use of linking (and intrusive) /r/ is on the decrease: it is observed slightly less frequently among young people. But it is probably more a characteristic of the individual idiolect than of certain age or class groups. In some idiolects the hiatus may be bridged by the glottal stop;[3] in other idiolects there may be an open hiatus.

In the present data there is no correlation between the absence of a potential linking /r/ and the occurrence of /r/ in the pre-

---

[1] The phonological interpretation of this hesitation signal is not too clear. It can hardly be considered a phoneme on the same level of analysis as the other phonemes. Its quality is that of a long unstressed /ə/.

[2] This statement is intended to simplify the phonological description. Phonetically, /r/ is ambisyllabic here. Cf. p. 231.

[3] There is then a juncture before [ʔ]. The glottal stop as an allophone of /t/ never occurs in this position (4.14). [ʔ] after a juncture is not considered a separate phoneme: it is a manifestation of the juncture.

ceding syllable, as suggested for RP:[1] /ij+méjksju+róhron+télij/ *he makes you roar on telly* (i.e. television).

But there does seem to be some correlation between the occurrence of /r/ and stress: linking /r/ is less common before a stressed syllable. And even though it does occur at a terminal contour it is more rare in such cases. It is most common within a close-knit grammatical construction or meaning group. Thus, when it does occur before a stressed syllable it is almost exclusively in such set phrases and compounds as

/awrə́wn/ *our own,* /ðəríz/ *there is,* /fərínstəns/ *for instance,* /fáhðərin+lóh/ *father-in-law,* /píktʃəráwziz/ *picture houses.*

Cf. also the absence of one of the two potential linking /r/'s in each of the following utterances, viz. in *brother* and *never*:

/wij+ád+əbrə́ðə+ə́wvərin/ *we had a brother over in* ...,
/wij+névə+íhrəm+séj/ *we never hear them say* ...

4.4222. Miscellaneous.

W. Matthews[2] mentions metathesis of /r/ in a number of words as an old and traditional characteristic of Cockney: 'perdooce', 'childern', 'hunderd', etc. From a synchronic point of view this means, not that /r/ has changed places with the contiguous unstressed /ə/, when compared with RP forms, but that there is no /r/ at all. Such forms do occur occasionally:

/tʃíldən/ *children,* /ə́ndəd/ *hundred,* /íntədúws/ *introduce,* /sékətərij/ *secretary;*

but they are not a prominent feature of present-day Cockney.

/r/ may also be missing where RP has CrV-. This has been observed only after phonologically labial or phonetically labialized consonants, thus repeatedly after /b/ and /f/ in

[1] Cf. D. Jones, *Outline* § 757.
[2] *Cockney Past and Present* p. 175 sq.

/béd/ *bred,* /bíŋ/ *bring,* /bówt/ *brought,* /bɔ́wtən/ [ˈbœŭʔn̩]
broken, /fíj/ *three,*

and occasionally also in other words after /b f ʃ/:

/fàbikéjʃən/ *fabrication,* /sáfən+íl/ *Saffron Hill,* /fénz/
friends, /ʃúwd/ *shrewd,* /ʃə́gd/ *shrugged.*

However, the present data are too limited to allow us to decide
whether the limitation of the phenomenon to this context is a
mere coincidence or not.

On the occasional occurrence of /r/ in morphemes whose main
allomorphs have /t/, see 4.13.

4.43. /h/

4.431. *Phonemic Norm and Allophonic Variations*

/h/ is a non-syllabic vocoid whose nature depends on the peak
nucleus of the same syllable (3.03, 4.04). As an onset consonant
it is a voiceless anticipation of the following peak nucleus. As
a peak satellite it is a voiced continuation of the preceding peak
nucleus, or, alternatively, especially after /i e u/, a voiced
vocoid glide towards a central, half-close to half-open, unrounded vocoid position.

The allophonic variations of /h/ as part of the syllable peak
are discussed in 3.055, 3.12, 3.22, 3.32, 3.42, 3.52, and 3.62.

The phonemic norm of the onset consonant /h/ is a voiceless,
oral, non-plosive sound (a continuant, or a glide) of a slightly
fricative nature. Since there is no friction-causing obstruction
in the cavities above the larynx one might call it a glottal fricative. Whether the weak frictional noise characterizing /h/ is
mainly due to friction at the glottis or simple cavity friction
is not too clear.[1] The articulating organs above the glottis are
in the position for the following vocoid, or glide towards such
a position.

---

[1] On the distinction between local friction and cavity friction, see
K. L. Pike, *Phonetics* pp. 71, 138 sq.

4.432. Distribution

/h/ occurs only immediately preceded or followed by a vowel. It does not occur in post-peak margins. The following discussion is limited to pre-peak /h/. The distribution of /h/ as a peak satellite is discussed in 3.01, 3.141, 3.241, 3.35, 3.45, 3.54, 3.641.

[h] before the syllable peak as a contrasting segment with a distribution paralleling that of RP belongs to a somewhat formal style of speech, and occurs particularly when the informants make an effort to speak 'correctly'. Most adult informants know where there 'should' be [h],[1] but even when they are on their guard there are apt to be 'slips' and erratic pronunciations, the same words being sometimes pronounced with and sometimes without [h]. In conversation with people from a higher social stratum they may frequently be observed to correct themselves, after having 'dropped an h'. In such a style [h] may often be missing in well-known names or in other household words, even if it is generally retained otherwise.

However, most commonly there is great inconsistency in the use of pre-peak [h], and in really colloquial style its presence or absence cannot be considered contrastive; it may be missing in words where RP has it, and on the other hand it may occur where it is paralleled by no segment in RP, but never consistently one way or the other. Its status may be compared to that of pre-peak [ʔ], which has no phonemic, though possibly a stylistic, value in English (*fester Einsatz*). Like [ʔ] it is most likely to occur in heavily stressed syllables, under emphasis, and it is always preceded by a juncture:

/háw+didju+gét+ih↓/ *How did you get here?* /əzə+hə́wl↓/ *as a whole* ..., /in+hə́hràws↑/ *in her house,* /nə̀w+aj+héjnt↓/ *no, I ain't,* /aj+àd+hə́h↓/ *I had her,* /émfəsajz+háw+jusìŋ↓/ *emphasize how you sing,* /tájm+tuget+hə́p↓/

---

[1] Children are much more uncertain. Thus, a group of girls rehearsing a play had great difficulty in putting their h's in the proper places.

time to get up, /tíj+héjtʃ/ *t, h* (spelling), /əh+hérənz/ *her errands,* /foh+hə́h↑ héniwèj↓/ *for her, anyway,* /ajl+hén+ ðat+stóhrij↑/ *I'll end that story;*

though it is not limited to that position:

/aj+lájt+hìlz↓/ [ɑ̌ɪ 'lɑ̌ɪʔ 'hɪ̆ɣz] *I like eels,* /ʃijz+lówst+həh+pléjt↓/ *she has lost her plate.*

Like [ʔ] its use varies from one speaker to the next: some informants (mostly women?) only rarely have pre-peak [h], whereas others (e.g. frequently children) use it almost regularly under primary stress at the beginning of a microsegment which would otherwise begin with a vowel.[1, 2]

/h/ does not form part of any complex syllable margin, in any style of speech. Where RP may have the onset /hj/ Cockney has /j/ only: /júw/ *hue,* /júwdʒ/ *huge,* /júwmən/ *human,* /júwmə/ *humour.*

4.44. /j/

4.441. Phonemic Norm and Allophonic Variations

The phonemic norm of /j/ is a voiced palatal vocoid glide.

As a peak satellite it is a voiced unrounded non-syllabic vocoid glide towards a high front tongue position or, in /ij/, alternatively a non-syllabic continuation of the preceding seg-

[1] I cannot agree with W. Matthews (*Cockney Past and Present* p. 80 sq.), who states that 'The aspiration of normally initial vowels ... is not a rule of Cockney and is, indeed, rather rare. I have heard the aspiration from some older Cockneys, particularly when they were trying to be dignified and correct, but I have not heard it from younger Cockneys, except accidentally.'

[2] Letters from a woman informant have frequent mis-spellings which indicate both the absence of an expected [h]: 'freds bike as ad its chips', 'thats me usband', 'thats ow it tis I was gitten em', 'so you ad a nice oliday with yer dad', 'I wonder our Eva's getting on' (i.e. how), 'What a terrible thing as appened in the Swiss Alps'; and the inconsistency of its use: 'they came ome and Mrs B... had the doctor home to him'.

ment (cf. 3.03). The allophonic variations of /j/ as part of the syllable peak are discussed in 3.054, 3.13, 3.232, 3.332, 3.43. Pre-peak /j/ is the same as in RP. Thus, it is closer before close vowels, as in /jídiʃ/ *Yiddish*, than before open ones, as in /jáhd/ *yard*. After voiceless consonants, especially after voiceless stops, in the same phonetic syllable /j/ is voiceless or partly devoiced, with some friction, [ç]: /θáŋkju/ [ˈθɛŋkçʊ] *thank you* (cf. 4.051). After /d/ there may be some friction in /j/, which is, however, fully voiced: /djúhrin/ *during.*[1]

4.442. Distribution

/j/ occurs only immediately preceded or followed by a vowel. It does not occur in post-peak margins.

The following discussion is limited to pre-peak /j/. The distribution of /j/ as a peak satellite is discussed in 3.01, 3.14, 3.241, 3.35, 3.452.

/j/ occurs as a simple pre-peak margin:

/jídiʃ/ *Yiddish,* /jét/ *yet,* /jáhd/ *yard,* /júws/ *use,* /jə́ŋ/ *young.*

According to tradition, pre-peak /j/ occurs in Cockney in a number of words where it is not paralleled by any segment in the most common forms of RP, such as in *ear.*[2] This does not occur in the present data.

In pre-peak complex margins /j/ occurs almost exclusively before /u/ peaks. Only rarely does it occur before other vowels: /mjáw/ *miaw,* /pjánə/ *piano.*

Even before /u/ the occurrence of /j/ is subject to greater limitations than in RP.[3] As in RP it never occurs after /ð ʃ ʒ ŋ r w/. Nor does it normally occur after /t d θ s z n l h/. RP forms with Cju- are paralleled by Cockney forms with Cu-:

---

[1] /j/ is not common in this context: cf. 4.442.
[2] Cf. H. C. Wyld, *A History of Modern Colloquial English* p. 308.
[3] Cf. D. Jones, *Outline* § 817.

/túwzdij/ *Tuesday*, /stúwdənt/ *student*, /kóstùwm/ *costume*, /sìtuw+éiʃən/ *situation*; /dúwk/ *duke*, /prədúws/ *produce*, /rézidùw/ *residue*; /enθúwziàzəm/ *enthusiasm*; /súwt/ *suit*; /rizúwm/ *resume;* /núw/ *new*, /nuwmə́wniə/ *pneumonia*, /dʒénuin/ *genuine*; /lúw/ *Lew*, /ilúwminèjt/ *illuminate*, /ápsəlùwt/ *absolute*; /húwdʒ/ *huge*.[1]

Only formal style has variants with Cju-: /tjúwn/ *tune*, /édjukèjt/ *educate*. Even after other consonants there are variant forms without /j/, though they are comparatively rare:

/kúw+gáhdənz/ *Kew Gardens*, /rikúwpərèjt/ *recuperate*, /fúw/ *few*, /múwzik/ *music*.

/j/ regularly occurs after /p b g v/ in pre-peak margins:

/dispjúwt/ *dispute*, /bjúwtifəl/ *beautiful*, /áhgjumənt/ *argument*, /vjúw/ *view*.

4.45. /w/

4.451. Phonemic Norm and Allophonic Variations

The phonemic norm of /w/ is a voiced labio-velar vocoid glide.

As a peak satellite it is a voiced non-syllabic vocoid glide towards a high back tongue position, with progressive rounding of the lips, or, in /uw/, alternatively a non-syllabic continuation of the preceding segment (cf. 3.03). The allophonic variations of /w/ as part of the syllable peak are discussed in 3.054, 3.342, 3.44, 3.53, 3.63.

Pre-peak /w/ is the same as in RP. Thus, it has closer lip-rounding before rounded vowels, as in /wúwnd/ *wound*, than before unrounded ones, as in /wéj/ *way*. After voiceless stops /w/ is partly devoiced: /twélv/ *twelve*, /kwówtə/ *quarter* (cf. 4.051).

---

[1] This is a rather formal form. In more colloquial style the usual form is /júwdʒ/; cf. 4.432.

4.452. Distribution

/w/ occurs only immediately preceded or followed by a vowel. It does not occur in post-peak margins. The following notes refer to pre-peak /w/. The distribution of /w/ as a peak satellite is discussed in 3.01, 3.352, 3.45, 3.541.

/w/ occurs as a simple pre-peak margin:

/wínd/ *wind*, /wést/ *west*, /wájf/ *wife*, /wónt/ *want*, /wúd/ *wood*, /wə́n/ *one*;

and as the last element of pre-peak complex margins:

/twínz/ *twins*, /kwíjn/ *queen*, /swíŋ/ *swing*, /skwót/ *squat*.

There are the same pre-peak clusters as in RP, with the exception that /hw-/ never occurs: in morphemes where RP speakers might have forms with /hw-/ Cockney shows forms with /w-/:

/wítʃ/ *which*, /wéðə/ *whether*, /wéh/ *where*.

Some morphemes have alternative forms without /w/ in unstressed syllables, where RP has /w/ only: /ínədz/ *inwards*, /sə́mən/ *someone*, /əgúdən/ *a good one*.

On the earlier Cockney interchange between /v/ and /w/, see 4.221.

5. Spectrographic Analysis

5.1. INTRODUCTION

This is an impressionistic-auditory study of Cockney. For our purposes such an analysis has more point than an instrumental investigation. It has been my effort to catch the dialect as it is actually spoken, in everyday life, in the street, in the home. A laboratory setting is not conducive to bringing out such a speech form. The speakers of the dialect are aware that their speech differs from what they can hear on the wireless, from what is taught in school, from what is considered 'correct' English. Many of them are ashamed of their own dialect in front of strangers. At least, they often try to adopt another speech form in such a situation, a speech form which is different in all respects: in vocabulary, grammar, phonology. I have frequently had occasion to notice this even in the homes of my informants: the style used when they talk among themselves may change when they address the analyst. The type of speech elicited in a laboratory would therefore probably be rather formal.

I have, of course, made tape recordings, in order to have a permanent record. However, these were all made in the homes of the informants, where they would feel most at ease, over a cup of tea. The quality of the recordings is therefore not good enough to give valuable data for instrumental acoustical analysis.

In spite of this I have subjected some of my recordings to spectrographic analysis,[1] without, however, attaching too much importance to my findings. I have made spectrograms of one part of the data which is better suited than the rest for such instrumental analysis, viz. some recorded word lists, read by EE and MM. A basic difficulty is, of course, that in reading such a list the informants are apt to use a rather formal style. It is all the more interesting to note that even some of the more elusive features of Cockney are retained in these recorded word lists.

There are two types of problem one might appropriately study by means of such spectrograms. (1) Is it possible to find acoustical correlates to the articulatory facts we have observed concerning the particularly Cockney variants of the various phonemes? This would be a purely *phonetic* study. (2) Do the acoustical facts bear out our phonemic conclusions? In particular, can we find confirmation, in the acoustical data, of certain unexpected phonemic groupings we have had to make — unexpected when compared with RP — such as the lack of contrast between, or coalescence of, several syllable peaks before pre-consonantal and pre-junctural /l/ (4.414), and the contrast between word pairs like *board* and *bored* (3.451)? This would be a *phonemic* study, or a phonetic study highly relevant for our phonemic analysis.

5.2. PHONETIC PROBLEMS

The word lists were drawn up for the purpose of studying the syllable peaks. Each syllable peak was put systematically in different contexts, and I have attempted to give similar contexts, including contiguous consonants, the position relative to the terminal contour, and stress, to each peak. A partly

[1] By means of the Kay Electric Company's Sonagraph, of the University of Oslo.

conflicting principle was the attempt to use only familiar words. Three typical series are the following ones:

/i/: *pit, bid, pin, pretty, mirror, silly, fill, milk, children, council, houses*;

/ih/: *beer, beard, fierce, theatre, clearing, nearly, really, real*;

/ij/: *bee, bead, beat, meaning, feeling, feel, field, lovely*.

The data are limited: only two informants were used, each of them reading the list only once. The data are not of a type suitable for spectrographic analysis: female voices are generally too high-pitched for an accurate reading of the formant frequencies even in the broad-band spectrograms of the Sonagraph: besides, we have already noted that the recordings were made under poor conditions. For these reasons many spectrograms are difficult to read. Therefore I attach no importance to the absolute figures I have obtained for the formant frequencies of the several syllable peaks, and they are not published here.

However, the syllable peaks can be compared with each other for easily recognizable acoustical features, and these can be seen against the background of what is known about the acoustical structure of other English dialects.[1] The spectrograms, poor as they are, at least bring out the following points, noted in the course of this study.

Syllable Peaks. The first element of a complex syllable peak is often sustained, and particularly before a terminal contour. Thus, the [ɪ] part of /ih/ is more sustained in *beer* than in *beard* and *fierce*, the [æ] part of /ej/ is more sustained in *pay* than in *paid*, and the [ɔ] part of /oj/ is more sustained in *boy* and *convoy* than in *noise* (3.052).

---

[1] A number of studies have appeared since Martin Joos published his *Acoustic Phonetics* in 1948, in various periodicals, especially in the *Journal of the Acoustical Society of America*. The best collection of spectrograms, showing the characteristic formant patterns of the various sounds, published to date is still *Visible Speech* by R. K. Potter, G. A. Kopp, and H. C. Green.

/i/ *Peaks.* The formant values of the first part of /ih/ are between those of the simple peak /i/ and the sustained part of /ij/. Thus, the spectrograms support our impression that /ih/ is rather close and front (3.12). /ij/ in monosyllabic utterances is glided. The initial part, [ɜ̆], is a brief on-glide only. It is the last part which is sustained (3.13), and this has the formant structure of a relatively close vocoid.

/e/ *Peaks.* /e/ is [i]-glided before voiced coda consonants in monosyllables, viz. in *bed, dead, egg* (3.212). The first part of /ej/ has an [æ]-like formant pattern (3.231).

/a/ *Peaks.* The simple peak /a/ is [e]-glided at least once, in *pan* (3.313). /aj/ has a brief [u]- or [o]-like glide in the middle in several utterances, e.g. *pie, wide* (3.332). The first part of /aw/ has an [æ] or [ɛ]-like formant pattern, clearly a fronter and closer vocoid than /ah/. No triphthongal variants occur, but there is at least one near-monophthongal [ɛ·], in *thousand* (3.341, 3.342).

/o/ *Peaks.* There is one instance of /oj/ with a short medial [u]- or [o]-like glide (3.43).

/u/ *Peaks.* /uw/ in monosyllabic utterances is glided. The initial part, [ɜ̆], is a brief on-glide only. It is the last part which is sustained (4.53).

/ə/ *Peaks.* The stressed simple peak /ə/ has an [æ]-like formant pattern (4.611). The formant patterns of the initial part of /əh/ and /əw/ are rather similar. There are not sufficient data on the characteristic formant structure of front, half-open, rounded vocoids to determine whether /ə/ in these contexts is [œ]-like in structure (3.62, 3.63).

/l/. Almost all occurrences of pre-junctural and pre-consonantal /l/ are manifested by vocoids, as far as it is possible to read this out of the spectrograms (4.4131).

5.3. PHONEMIC PROBLEMS

The difference between /oh/ [ɔə] and /ow/ [ɒʊ] clearly appears in the spectrograms in the different nature of the off-glide: /póh/ *pour*, /bóhd/ *bored* vs. /bówd/ *board*, /bówt/ *bought* (3.451). As might be expected, the recorded word lists show certain inconsistencies in the syllable peaks used before pre-junctural and pre-consonantal /l/ (4.414). A comparison between a phonemic, auditory, analysis of these recorded word lists and the spectrographic analysis gives the following results.

In almost all recordings of words with /ih/ or /ij/ in RP in such a context, the simple peak /i/ occurs. There are two exceptions: once *feel* is recorded as /fíjl/, and once *real* is analysed as /ríəl/. The spectrograms bear out this analysis: all recordings of words like *feel* and *real* show the same formant pattern as *fill*, with the two exceptions mentioned. The spectrogram of /fíjl/ [fiˑɤ̌] shows a long, sustained [i] part, whereas /fíl/ [fɨ̌ɤ̌] shows the formants smoothly changing all through; in /ríəl/ ['rɪɤ̌] the last part, [ɤ̌], is sustained.

In the same way, the formant patterns of *full* and *fool*, both /fúl/, appear the same, and *boil* and *royal*, analysed as /bójl/ and /rójl/, show the same pattern. All recordings of words containing /owl/ in RP have formant patterns similar to /ow/.

When reading words containing RP /ejl al ahl ajl awl/ the informants show considerable vacillation. Two patterns emerge from the phonemic analysis of the recordings: RP /ejl al awl/ are all rendered as /al/, and RP /ahl ajl/ are given as /ahl/. The spectrograms show corresponding similarities: /al/ shows the formant pattern of a smooth glide from a fairly front open vocoid towards a back, closer one, and /ahl/ has a long sustained [ɑ]-like pattern. In those cases where the informants make a distinction between /ejl/ and, for example, /al/, a short medial [ɪ]-like glide appears on the spectrogram: [æˡɤ̌]. In the same way, when /ajl/ is distinguished from /ahl/, there is a similar glide in the middle of /ajl/, [ɑˡɤ̌].

6. Earlier Notes on Cockney

6.0. A number of writers have, between them, covered most of the material presented in this study, though they may have done so in other terms, and only briefly or in scattered notes. We shall examine some of the more systematic and comprehensive studies in the field.

6.1. PHONETIC STUDIES

6.10. There are brief references to Cockney variants, for example in the following handbooks on phonetics:

D. Jones, *An Outline of English Phonetics*;
D. Jones, *The Pronunciation of English*;
I. C. Ward, *The Phonetics of English*.

J. D. O'Connor, in *New Phonetic Readings* p. 56 sq., gives a brief survey of the phonetics of Cockney. H. C. Wyld, in *A History of Modern Colloquial English*, has notes on the Cockney sound system from a historical point of view. W. Matthews gives, in *Cockney Past and Present*, a survey of many aspects of the London dialect, but is primarily concerned with tracing Cockney characteristics back in the history of the dialect. The dialect he is concerned with is Cockney 'as it is spoken in the North of London' (p. 81). J. Franklyn's *The Cockney* has numerous, though somewhat unsystematic, notes on features of the Cockney dialect, particularly in the section 'Language'.

In these publications the following points are dealt with. All comparisons are with RP.

6.11. Syllable Peaks

/ih/ — closer starting-point (3.12): Jones, *Outline* § 441, *Pronunciation* § 199; Ward § 216.

/ij/ — diphthongized (3.13): Jones, *Outline* § 251, *Pronunciation* §§ 72 and 207; Ward § 120; O'Connor p. 56; Matthews p. 78.

RP /ijl/ = Cockney /il/ (3.141): Jones, *Pronunciation* § 72; Ward § 123. But we find no reference to the parallel relationship between RP /ihl/ and Cockney /il/ (3.141) and between RP /uh/l or /uwl/ and Cockney /ul/ (3.541), or to the lack of contrast between /ejl/, /al/, and /awl/ and between /ahl/ and /ajl/ in Cockney (3.241, 3.351).

Final RP /i/ = Cockney /ij/ (3.142): Jones, *Pronunciation* § 77; Ward § 131.

RP /ə/ = Cockney /i/ in *just, such* (3.144): Matthews p. 171. 'Intrusive' /i/ (3.143): Cf. the spelling 'parient', Matthews p. 71.

RP /e/ = Cockney /i/ in certain words (3.144): Matthews p. 169 sq.

/e/ — lengthened or diphthongized (3.212): Jones, *Outline* § 876, *Pronunciation* § 90 (diphthongized in 'the South').

RP /i/ = Cockney /e/ in certain words (3.242): Matthews p. 170 sq.; Wyld p. 226 sqq.

/eh/ — closer starting-point (3.22): Jones, *Pronunciation* § 205; Ward § 219; O'Connor p. 57; monophthongal variant (3.22): Jones, *Pronunciation* § 205.

/ej/ — more open starting-point (3.231): Jones, *Outline* §§ 58 and 388, *Pronunciation* § 164; Ward § 386; Matthews p. 79.

/a/ — closer (3.311): Ward §§ 141 and 285; O'Connor p. 56; Matthews p. 79; cf. Franklyn's spellings with 'e', 'thet' p. 254 and 'thenk' p. 241.

/a/ — diphthongized (3.313): Jones, *Pronunciation* § 93 (in 'the South'); cf. Franklyn's spellings 'ea' ('Leanberf', i.e. Lambeth, p. 254) and 'ae' ('faenks', i.e. thanks, p. 241), which may be intended to suggest glided allophones.

/ah/ — diphthongized (3.32): Jones, *Pronunciation* § 98 (with 'some Southern people').

/aj/ — more back, and sometimes rounded, starting-point (3.331): Jones, *Pronunciation* § 177 and p. 207; Ward § 204; O'Connor p. 57; Matthews p. 79; cf. Franklyn's spellings with 'oi', 'soize', 'foive', etc., p. 254.

/aj/ — monophthongal variants (3.332): Jones, *Pronunciation* § 189; Matthews p. 79.

/aw/ — front, sometimes closer starting-point (3.341): Jones, *Outline* §§ 58 and 420, *Pronunciation* § 189; Ward § 285; O'Connor p. 57.

/aw/ — monophthongal or with an unrounded off-glide only (3.341, 3.342): Jones, *Outline* § 58, *Pronunciation* § 189; Ward § 210; Matthews p. 78. Franklyn's story about the RP speaker's *pear switch* being understood by the Cockney as *power switch*, i. e. a confusion between RP /eh/ and Cockney /awə/ (/aw/?), indicates a diphthong with a front, close starting-point and an unrounded off-glide.

/aw/ — a two-directional glide (3.341): Franklyn *may* be having such a triphthongal variant in mind when he describes /aw/ (as well as /ej/ and /əw/, which, however, in my data have no such triphthongal variants) in the following way: 'The Cockney takes this short and simple word, divides it into two syllables, compounds, and instantly welds them together making a more compact and manageable unit of speech.' There is even supposed to be 'a fantastically light glottal stop' in the middle. He suggests the spellings 'deahn' or 'deoun' (p. 255 sq.).

/oj/ — closer starting-point (3.43): Jones, *Pronunciation* § 197; Ward § 213; O'Connor p. 57.

/oh ow/ — closer and more rounded, often with a central off-glide, sometimes a two-directional glide with greater lip-rounding in the middle (3.42, 3.44): Jones, *Pronunciation* §§ 108 and 212; Ward §§ 159, 164, and 285; O'Connor p. 56 sq.

The contrast between /oh/ and /ow/ (3.451): D. Jones *may* be having such a contrast in mind when he states that some people (not specified as to dialect) distinguish for instance between [so:d] *sword* and [sɔ:d] *sawed* (*Pronunciation* § 114). The same contrast may be implied in O'Connor's transcriptions pp. 57–9, [o:] vs. [oə]: [o:] *all*, [o:f] *off*, [o:rɑiʔ] *all right*, [o:ʔ] *ought*, [do:g] *dog*, [ko:ʔ] *caught*, [ko:d] *called*, [ko:s] *course*, but [doə] *door*, [doəz] *doors*, [floə] *floor*, [noə] *nor*.

RP /owl/ = Cockney /ow/ (3.452): Franklyn has spellings like 'warnuts' (i.e. walnuts, p. 66), 'War-r-zies' (i.e. Walls's, p. 89), and Matthews quotes the spelling 'ou right' (i.e. all right, p. 68) from the late nineteenth century. Cf. also O'Connor's transcriptions pp. 57–9: [o:] *all*, [ko:d] *called*, cf. [ko:s] *course*.

RP /uh/ = Cockney /oh/ (3.454): Jones, *Pronunciation* § 216; Ward § 224.

/uw/ — centralized and diphthongized (3.53): Jones, *Pronunciation* § 123 and p. 207; Ward §§ 171 and 285; O'Connor p. 57; Matthews p. 78; cf. Franklyn's spellings 'yeou' (i.e. you, p. 254) and 'deuin' (i.e. doing, p. 256.)

RP /uhl/ = Cockney /ul/ (3.541): Franklyn may have had this in mind when he wrote 'croolty' (i.e. cruelty, p. 83), though the spelling suggests rather /uwl/.

/ə/ — front, open (3.611): Jones, *Pronunciation* § 132; Ward § 175 (a); O'Connor p. 56.

/əh/ — more open (3.62): Jones, *Pronunciation* § 140.

/əw/ — more open starting-point (3.63): Jones, *Outline* § 401, *Pronunciation* § 170; Ward § 285; more front: Ward § 200; Matthews p. 79; more open and front: O'Connor p. 57.

RP /əhs/ = Cockney /əs/ (3.641): Matthews p. 171.

RP /ah/ = Cockney /əh/ in certain words, and vice versa (3.641): Matthews pp. 171 sq. and 181 sq.; Wyld p. 212 sqq.

Initial unstressed /ə/ missing (3.642): Matthews p. 172.

Unstressed /ə/ paralleling other syllable peaks in RP (3.642): Matthews p. 172.

A tendency to lengthen the 'short' vowels (3.04): Jones, *Outline* § 879.

'Drawling', lengthening of all syllable peaks (2.9, 3.052):
Ward §§ 226, 285, 294; Matthews p. 77.

Nasalization (2.9, 4.32): Jones, *Pronunciation* § 392; Ward
§§ 204, 232, and 285; O'Connor p. 56; Matthews p. 77.

6.12. Syllable Margins

Aspiration and affrication of stops (4.122): Jones, *Pronunciation* § 230; Ward §§ 242, 285, and 386; O'Connor p. 57;
Matthews p. 80; Franklyn p. 243.

/t/ voiced allophone (4.13): Jones, *Pronunciation* § 232; Ward
§ 250 (b); Matthews p. 174; Franklyn p. 243, cf. his spellings
'Gorra loit' (i.e. Got a light?) p. 82 and 'S' marra' (i.e. What
is the matter?) p. 258. O'Connor transcribes with [d], e.g.
['pud iʔ] *put it*. The phonemic interpretation made by these
authors is not quite clear, however, since it does not appear
unambiguously whether they consider the sound described as
a member of the /t/ phoneme, or as a /d/ or /r/. In *The Phoneme*
(§ 311) D. Jones favours the inclusion of the flap among the
allophones of the /t/ phoneme.

[ʔ] as an allophone of /t/ and paralleling other consonants
in RP (4.14): Jones, *Pronunciation* §§ 234, 250, 258; Ward
§ 250 (e); O'Connor p. 57; Matthews pp. 80, 167 sq.; Franklyn
p. 242.

RP /k/ = Cockney /t/ in *ask* (4.162): Jones, *Pronunciation*
§ 247; Franklyn p. 289.

RP voiceless stop = Cockney voiced stop in certain words
(4.163): Matthews p. 174; Wyld p. 312 sq.

RP unstressed /vən/ = Cockney /pən/ or /bən/ (4.164):
Jones, *Pronunciation* §§ 273 and 328; Franklyn p. 259.

'Excrescent' /t k d/ (4.165): Jones, *Outline* § 657, *Pronunciation*
§ 288; Ward § 260; Matthews pp. 80, 163; Wyld pp. 290 sq.
and 309.

RP /θ ð/ = Cockney /f v/ (4.222): Jones, *Pronunciation*
§§ 331 and 335; Ward § 278 (iv); Matthews pp. 80 and 162;
Wyld p. 291.

Post-peak /l/ — a strongly velarized lateral or a back vocoid (4.412, 4.4131): Jones, *Pronunciation* § 298 and p. 207; Ward §§ 267 and 285; O'Connor p. 56; Matthews p. 80.

Allophonic variations of the syllable peaks before post-peak /l/ (3.051, 4.4133): Jones, *Outline* § 847 (V), *Pronunciation* § 299 sq.; Ward §§ 167, 175 (a), 198, 205, 268, and 285; Franklyn p. 253 sq. O'Connor (pp. 57–9) indicates it systematically in his transcription: [æŏ] for /el/, [ɑŏ] for /ajl/, [ɔu] for /əwl/.

'Intrusive' /r/ (4.4221): Ward § 274; Matthews p. 177.

Missing and 'intrusive' /h/ (4.432): Jones, *Outline* § 58, *Pronunciation* § 372; O'Connor p. 57; Matthews pp. 80 sq. and 163 sq.; Wyld pp. 294 sqq. and 310 sq.; Franklyn p. 262.

/j/ — missing in pre-peak complex margins (4.442): Matthews p. 172.

Pre-peak /w/ — missing in unstressed syllables (4.452): Matthews p. 175; Wyld p. 296 sq.

6.2. WRITTEN COCKNEY

6.20. In addition, there are various attempts to suggest characteristics of the Cockney sound system in *writing*.

6.21. Phonetic Transcription

Jones (*Pronunciation* pp. 207–9), Ward (pp. 235–7) and O'Connor (pp. 56–9) have made regular phonetic transcriptions, and other attempts have appeared from time to time, for example in *Le Maître Phonétique*. Such transcriptions may be quite accurate and consistent, but they often leave unsolved certain phonemic problems, such as the phonemic status of the glottal stop (4.14, 7.32), the voiced contoid, often a flap, which occurs in words like *letter* (to which phoneme does it belong? /t/, /d/ or /r/? cf. 4.13), nasalization (is there only one type? cf. 4.32), the phonemic interpretation of the syllable peaks before 'dark l' (4.414; the transcriptions sometimes seem to suggest a neutralization of certain contrasts, but this is not clearly stated).

6.22. Cockney in Literature

Normal orthography has been used extensively to indicate Cockney variants, but this method is bound to be less systematic and consistent, and it is often rather ambiguous. Matthews uses inadvertent spellings to trace present-day characteristics of Cockney back to earlier centuries. This is a safer method, though less easy to use, than to rely on normal literature, in which the author deliberately mimics his Cockney characters. The latter type of indication of Cockney is frequently used, particularly in comic literature. Sometimes the author limits himself to a few items of vocabulary and certain characteristics of grammar; at other times he also tries to suggest the pronunciation.

Charles Dickens was among the first writers to make extensive use of this method, for example for the speech of Sam Weller. But the Dickensian type of Cockney has come under heavy fire, for instance from G. B. Shaw,[1] who considers this conventionalized stage Cockney most misleading, representing a form of speech which either never existed or which has disappeared. Shaw's attempts at rendering Cockney have, in their turn, been severely criticized by J. Franklyn (p. 226 sqq.), who, among other things, accuses Shaw of inconsistency, of mixing up several types of Cockney, and of neglecting grammar and idiom. However, Franklyn is himself, on occasion, inconsistent and ambiguous in his Cockney orthography, and he actually favours only a light sprinkling of phonetically spelled words: the spelling should be 'phonetic only in easily recognizable words' (p. 237). Cf. p. 271: 'Correct idiom, syntax, and (of course incorrect) general grammar, conveying the words a Cockney would speak to express the thoughts and emotions a Cockney would have, with here and there a light phonetic spelling to indicate dialect.'

---

[1] The note on 'English and American Dialects', appended to *Captain Brassbound's Conversion*.

6.23. Shaw's Cockney

We shall look a little closer at Shaw's Cockney. I have chosen him rather than any other author because he is well known, because he has indicated Cockney pronunciation more consistently and more extensively than any other serious writer I know of, and because he supposedly knew something about phonetics.

Shaw's Cockney has been the subject of much controversy. We shall limit ourselves to a look at the Cockney spellings in his dramatic works. The pronunciation of Drinkwater in *Captain Brassbound's Conversion* is indicated throughout, whereas the only consistent attempts in *Pygmalion* are found in the opening pages. For several characters in *Major Barbara*, but particularly for Bill Walker, there are Cockney spellings throughout. In addition, sprinklings of Cockney orthography are found for Burgess in *Candida*, Lickcheese in *Widowers' Houses*, several characters in *Man and Superman*, and Hodson in *John Bull's Other Island* (fairly consistently in a dialogue with Matthew Haffigan in Act III).[1]

Quite frequently the supposedly Cockney spellings indicate pronunciations which might occur in RP. For example, an unusual orthography may simply suggest the occurrence of /ə/ in unstressed syllables, assimilations, simplification of complex consonant clusters, etc.:

> *C*: 'dunno' (i.e. /dənə́w/ *don't know*), 'grajally' (/grádʒəli/ *gradually*), 'moddle' (/módəl/ ['mɔdɫ̩] *model*), 'spose' (/spə́wz/ *suppose*), 'praps' (/práps/ *perhaps*), 'Nortn Folgit' (/nówtən+fólgit/ ['nɒ̆ŭtn̩] *Norton Folgate*), 'frenliness' (/frénlinis/ *friendliness*), 'the lars word' (/ðəláhs+wə́hd/ *the last word*);
>
> *P*: 'tuppence' (/tə́pəns/ *twopence*), 'f'them' (/fəðəm/ *for them*), 'deah' (/díh/ *dear*);
>
> *CBC*: 'knollidge' (/nólidʒ/ *knowledge*).

---

[1] In the rest of this chapter the following abbreviations are used: *C* = *Candida*, *CBC* = *Captain Brassbound's Conversion*, *JB* = *John Bull's Other Island*, *MB* = *Major Barbara*, *P* = *Pygmalion*.

When real Cockney variants seem to be involved, Shaw's spellings can be used to support many of our findings. But there is some inconsistency.

/i/ *Peaks.* The diphthongal nature of /ij/ (3.13) is clearly suggested in the spellings 'bəyee, cəyee, dəyee' (i.e. the letters b, c, d, *P*), where the actual phonetic symbol ə is used. In the article 'The Simplified Spelling Reform' Shaw uses the spelling 'Ber-ee, Ser-ee, Der-ee'.

The spellings 'reely' (really, *P*) and 'reel' (real, *JB*) *may* be indicative of the close variant found in Cockney (3.12).

Spellings like 'git' (get) and 'sence' (since), 'sperrit' (spirit) (all from *MB*) suggest the interchange between /i/ and /e/ which is found in Cockney (3.144, 3.242). But we also find the spelling 'gat' (get, *MB*).

/e/ *Peaks.* The open starting-point of /ej/ (3.231) is clearly indicated in the spellings 'i' and 'y', used fairly consistently in all of Shaw's dramatic works, e.g. 'Lidy' (Lady), 'Dily Mile' (Daily Mail), 'brines' (brains), 'sy' (say), 'fythful' (faithful) (all from *CBC*). Only occasionally are there other spellings, e.g. 'caibles' (cables, *JB*).

Shaw generally keeps /ej/ distinct from /aj/, for which he chooses other spellings, cf. 'civlawzytion' (presumably /sìvlaj+zéjʃən/ civilization, *CBC*).

/a/ *Peaks.* The close variant of /a/ (3.311) is consistently indicated by the spelling 'e', e.g. 'cherrity' (charity), 'thenk' (thank), 'vennity' (vanity) (all from *CBC*). However, no attempt is made to show that there is any contrast between /e/ and /a/: 'ends' in Shaw's orthography might mean both 'hands' and 'ends'. And it must be a slip on Shaw's part when he writes 'selvytion' (salvation, *MB*): /a/ before 'dark l' has rather *open* variants.

There is much less consistency in the orthography for /ah/. *C* shows a variety of forms: 'ar' ('harsk', i.e. ask), 'awr' ('Pawrk', i.e. park), 'or' ('gordon', i.e. garden), but in the other publications 'aw' is the usual form, e.g. 'awsk' (ask, *MB*). However, this spelling is also used for other syllable peaks, and it is not quite clear what variant Shaw has in mind. 'ar' is, of course, a common spelling for /ah/, but Shaw uses it in words which are spelled otherwise in normal orthography. The spellings 'ar', 'aw', and 'or' might perhaps all of them indicate back, rounded variants, which other phoneticians have found to be a characteristic of Cockney.[1]

/aj/ is generally indicated by 'aw', e.g. 'wawf' (wife), 'pawrit' (pirate), 'secrifawce' (sacrifice) (all from *CBC*), a spelling which is also used for other purposes. Other spellings are 'oy' ('voylence', i.e. violence, *CBC*), 'oi' ('Oi', i.e. I, *JB*), 'y' ('Kyzer', i.e. Kaiser, *JB*). These spellings are probably meant to indicate back rounded variants (3.331). The spelling 'Ahyee' (i.e. I, *P*) suggests the extreme lengthening of this diphthong (3.333), and 'ah' ('trah it', i.e. try it, and 'frahtnd', i.e. frightened, both *CBC*) indicates a monophthongal variant (3.332). The spelling 'awy' ('Awy', 'Wawy', i.e. the letters i and y, a rendering of children reading the alphabet in 'The Simplified Spelling Reform'), on the other hand, may suggest a triphthongal pronunciation (3.332), or, possibly, simply lip-rounding of the initial element, [ɔ̈ɪ].[2]

/aw/ is consistently written 'ah', e.g. 'Brarsbahnd' (Brass-bound), 'ahses' (houses) (both from *CBC*), and this may suggest a monophthongal variant, or at least a variant which has an *unrounded* off-glide (3.341).

/o/ *Peaks.* /o/ may be written 'o' (in 'wot', i.e. what, only in *JB*, *MB*, *CBC*), but in *CBC* it is much more frequently 'or' e.g. 'cornduck' (conduct), 'Jornson' (Johnson), 'storp' (stop). I assume that both these spellings are meant to suggest a close variant (3.41). But sometimes 'or' *may* indicate /ow/ rather than /o/ (3.453), e.g. 'orspittle' (hospital, *MB*), 'orf' (off, *MB*),

---

[1] Cf. p. 63 n. 1.

[2] The latter interpretation has been suggested to me by Professor Paul Christophersen.

'gorspellin' (gospelling, *MB*), 'lorst' (lost, *CBC*), 'corfee' (coffee, *CBC*), 'corster' (coster, *CBC*).

There is no indication of any contrast between /oh/ and /ow/ (3.451). Where we might expect to find either of these there is a variety of spellings: often 'or' (e.g. 'lor' law, 'thort' thought, 'Drinkworter' Drinkwater, all from *CBC*) or 'aw' ('lawd' lord, 'bawn' born, both from *CBC*), but also 'our' ('thourt' thought, *C*), 'awr' ('cawrse' course, *C*), 'ore' ('pore' poor, *CBC*), and 'oah' ('afoah' before, *CBC*). It is difficult to interpret this material, where much of the 'Cockney' effect is produced by simply interchanging orthographies all equally common for /oh/ or /ow/; this applies particularly to 'or' and 'aw'.

The peak /oj/ occurs only on a few occasions in Cockney spellings, and it is then either 'aw' ('spawl' spoil, *P*, and 'chawce' choice, *CBC*) or 'woy' ('bwoy' boy, *CBC*). The former spelling is ambiguous, since it is also used for other syllable peaks. The latter *may* perhaps suggest a triphthongal variant (3.43).

/u/ *Peaks*. The diphthongal nature of /uw/ (3.53) is clearly indicated in the spellings 'tə-oo' (two, *P*), 'yə-oo' (you, *P*), 'bə-oots' (boots, *P*), where the actual phonetic symbol ə is used. 'Worterleoo' (Waterloo, *CBC*) and 'Kioo' (the letter q, 'The Simplified Spelling Reform') also suggest the same pronunciation; but such spellings are rare.

'crool' (cruel, *CBC*) may suggest the occurrence of /u/ or /uw/, instead of /uh/, before 'dark l' (3.541).

/ə/ *Peaks*. Stressed /ə/ is rather consistently spelled 'a', e.g. 'cappətə-ee' (cup of tea, *P*), 'blad' (blood, *JB*), 'nathink' (nothing, *CBC*). This suggests a front, open variant (3.611).

It is difficult to interpret the few unusual spellings for /əh/: 'clorgyman' (clergyman, *C*), 'detormined (determined, *C*), 'yorr' (year, *C*) *may* suggest /ah/ rather than /əh/ (3.641), and 'ur' ('gurl' girl, *C*) is only another way of spelling /əh/. But we are informed in *CBC* that *turn* is pronounced 'as teun with the eu sounded as in French', and this may indicate the rather open, front, slightly rounded variant which has been observed (3.62). On the other hand, the following spellings from *CBC* all clearly suggest the peak /ə/ rather than /əh/ (3.641): 'pusson' person, 'wuss' worse, 'nass' nurse, 'fust' first, 'suvvice' service; only the last word is rather unexpected in this connection.

In *P* Eliza's interjection *oh*, presumably /əw/, is spelled in a number of ways of the type 'ah-ah-ah-ow-ow-ow-oo'. This rather suggests a triphthongal variant, a type with which I am unacquainted (but cf. a similar interpretation of J. Franklyn's description p. 88 n. 1). So do the spellings 'ao' ('aold' old, *JB*), 'aoh' ('aoh' oh, *CBC*), 'aow' ('knaow' know, *CBC*), and 'aou' ('shaoulders' shoulders, *MB*). However, they may also indicate an open, front starting-point (3.63). On the other hand, 'ow' is simply another common spelling for /əw/, but used by Shaw in words which are normally spelled otherwise, e.g. 'wrowt' wrote, 'agow' ago, 'downt' do not, 'howver' over (all from *CBC*). It is difficult to interpret these spellings, especially since there is some inconsistency, e.g. 'downt' and 'daownt', i.e. do not, both from *CBC*.

Shaw has various ways of indicating unstressed /ə/ (for the wider use of /ə/ in unstressed syllables, see 3.642), and there is little consistency in their use. Most of these pronunciations are not exclusively Cockney. The following are some examples:

> 'er': 'feller' (fellow, *C*), 'oughter andle' (ought to handle, *C*),
>   'f'yer' (for you, *P*), 'stetcher' (statue, *CBC*);
> 'u': 'missus' (Mrs., *P*), 'wottud she' (what would she, *MB*),
>   'a bad un' (a bad one, *MB*), 'awlus' (always, *CBC*);
> 'o': 'enaff o this' (enough of this, *MB*).

Consonants. Features of the Cockney consonant system are indicated more sporadically, but then there is not such a great difference from RP in this area.

An 'excrescent' stop consonant (4.165) is sometimes found, e.g. 'twyct' (twice, *C*), 'acrost' (across, *MB* and *CBC*), 'fembly' (family, *CBC*), 'nothink' (nothing, *C*, *MB*, and *CBC*).

There are several indications of /v/ for /ð/ (4.222), e.g. 'wiv' (with, *MB* and *CBC*), 'wevver' (whether, *MB*).

Unstressed /in/ paralleling RP /iŋ/ (4.332) is indicated quite frequently, e.g. 'gawdnin' (gardening), 'bawn' (buying), 'Noontn' (Newington) (all from *CBC*); but there are also cases of inverted spellings, 'gording' (garden, *C*), 'awskink' (asking, *CBC*), pronunciations which I have never come across.

The particular variants of the syllable peaks found before 'dark l' are sometimes suggested (3.0510), but only where /e/ is concerned: 'eol' ('eolth' health, 'teoll' tell, both from *CBC*) or 'yol' ('s'yollin' selling, *P*, 'yolth' health, *CBC*). In the latter spelling the function of 'y' is difficult to interpret, but otherwise both 'eol' and 'yol' suggest a retracted variant of /e/, possibly with a back vocoid off-glide.

Intrusive /r/ (4.4221) is occasionally indicated after /oh/ ('sor em' saw them, 'striteforard' straightforward, 'jawrin' jawing, all from *CBC*) and /aw/ ('nar aw' now I, 'naradys' nowadays, both from *CBC*). But it is difficult to see what is meant by the second 'r' of 'Victawriar Pawrk' (Victoria Park, *C*): there can be no intrusive or linking /r/ before a consonant.

The inconsistent use of /h/ in Cockney (4.432) is indicated very frequently, e.g. in *CBC* 'awt' (heart), 'eah' (here), 'awgher' (higher) vs. 'Hingland' (England), 'hinfluence' (influence), 'hownly' (only). The occurrence of /h/ has apparently nothing to do with stress or prominence: intrusive /h/ is found in syllables which have no stress or only secondary stress, e.g. 'hee-quipped' (equipped), 'hexcursion' (excursion), 'hinterrapted' (interrupted), 'Hetlantic Howcean' (Atlantic Ocean), 'hacquitted' (acquitted), 'hattecked' (attacked). I doubt whether this represents a common type of Cockney.

The lack of /j/ before /uw/ where RP has /Cjuw-/ (4.442) is indicated occasionally, e.g. 'hinterdooce' (introduce, *C*), 'dooty' (duty, *C*), 'pnoomownia' (pneumonia, *JB*), 'noos' (news, *CBC*). But it is difficult to see what is meant by the spelling 'incloodin' (including, *CBC*), which has no /j/ in RP either. And I do not think that 'hooman' (human, *CBC*), 'hoonawted' (united, *CBC*), presumably /húwmən/, /huwnájtid/, represent common Cockney forms.

Conclusion. One may pick out a number of other spelling peculiarities which are probably meant to suggest Cockney forms. But there is little consistency, and we can draw no clear conclusions, apart from the material which is presented above. We have found that if one knows something about Cockney beforehand one may be able to interpret many of Shaw's spellings in a way which seems to fit the phonetic facts. However, these are of course our *interpretations* only. A normal orthography can never unambiguously represent the pronunciation, unless the phonetic value of the letters is indicated.

In addition, there are inconsistencies and ambiguities. Thus, the spellings 'gorden' and 'gording' (i.e. garden, *C*) occur three lines apart, and 'gowin' and 'gowing' (going, *MB*) are found in the same paragraph. We must assume that both 'ow' and 'aow' are meant to suggest /əw/ in 'gow an shaow' (go and show, *MB*), and that 'oi' and 'aw' both indicate /aj/ in 'Oi should lawk' (I should like, *JB*).

The most notable instance of ambiguity is the spelling 'aw', which may represent /a/ ('smawshin' smashing), /ah/ ('Pawk' park), /aj/ ('rawt' right), /oj/ ('chawce' choice), and /oh/ or /ow/ ('sawdid' sordid) (all from *CBC*). The ambiguity emerges clearly from spellings like 'Awd Pawk' (presumably /ájd+páhk/ Hyde Park, *CBC*), 'Victawriar Pawrk' (/viktóhriə+páhk/ Victoria Park, *C*), 'aw rawt' (/ów+rájt/ all right, *P*).

The spelling 'or' may indicate /ah/ ('gordon' garden, *C*), /o/ ('storp' stop, *CBC*), and /ow/ ('dorter' daughter, *MB*), whereas 'y' suggests /ej/ ('sy' say, *JB*) or /aj/ ('Kyzer' Kaiser, *JB*).

These inconsistencies and ambiguities in Shaw's works are probably no greater than those we find with other writers. I am inclined to believe that Shaw is a rather better observer than most other literary men.

7. Problems in English Phonology

7.1. GENERAL PROBLEMS

7.10. This study of Cockney is incomplete without a discussion of the principles underlying the analysis, and of some of the problems raised by it. I have found it convenient in my description of Cockney to take the conceptual framework for granted. I now want to justify it.

7.11. What is a Phonemic Analysis?

What is a phonemic analysis? Is it merely 'a technique for reducing languages to writing'?[1] Pike may be using the phrase literally, having in mind the analysis of languages which have no written traditions and for which one wants to set up practical orthographies. Taken in a wider sense, however, this definition may be said to apply to much that has been done in phonemic analysis since the 1930's, and to the description of the 'sounds' of languages before that time, provided that what we have in mind is not only the written product, i.e. the transcription or the alphabet, but also the analysis from which it results.

E. Haugen and W. Freeman Twaddell, criticizing Trager and Bloch's analysis of English, say that analysing *bear*, *balm*, etc., as /behr/, /bahm/, etc., is only 'a statement of orthographical

---

[1] Cf. the sub-title of K. L. Pike's publication, *Phonemics: a Technique for Reducing Languages to Writing.*

preference, not a contribution to linguistic knowledge'. 'We know nothing after such manipulation of symbols that we didn't know before.'[1] It is hardly fair to say that it is a question of *orthographical* preference only, and that it is only the *symbols* which are manipulated: the 'orthography' adopted by the analyst parallels a certain *analysis*, an interpretation of the *system*, and it is in the choice of analysis that personal preferences are of some importance. However, there is something to be said for the view expressed in the latter part of the statement quoted above, but then it applies to any new description of a language which is well known, such as the numerous attempts at a phonemic analysis of English: they do not add to our knowledge of the data, they only order the facts for us.[2]

These analyses of English are in part widely different, apparently even conflicting. Is only one (perhaps none of the analyses presented so far) correct, all the others being wrong? We cannot, at least in the present state of linguistic research, consider an analysis *wrong* if it accounts for all the language material, since there is no general agreement about the principles of linguistic analysis, particularly about some of the less fundamental ones. By what generally accepted criteria could we call, for instance, Trager and Bloch's analysis of English wrong and D. Jones's correct? There may be alternative interpretations of the phonology of a language, which may all describe and account for the facts of the language adequately; they are simply different ways of expressing the same thing. If clearly stated they should all be convertible, translatable, into one another. This is so because they all deal with the same language material, which is structured in a certain way.

Many, perhaps most, linguists are of the opinion that linguistic analysis should be an attempt to discover a system inherent in the language in question. At first blush, this view seems to imply

---

[1] 'Facts and Phonemics' p. 236.

[2] The statement may apply to other branches of science, in so far as they do not actually present new data.

that only one analysis can be correct. However, this is not necessarily so. True, every language is structured in a certain way: it has certain contrasts, and there is a characteristic distribution of certain items. But there is not an inherent system of, say, six vowel phonemes, twenty-two consonant phonemes, etc.: these are units postulated by the linguist. He may set up larger units (for example, the syllable) or smaller ones (for example, distinctive features) as his basic units, and his choice will depend on a number of factors, including personal preferences and prejudices.

An example of the rôle played by orthography and literary traditions is found in the languages of the Sino-Tibetan family: many linguists, steeped in the literary traditions of these cultures, are loath to analyse, for example, Chinese into smaller units than the syllable. They are able to account for all the facts of the language without resort to the concept of the phoneme. The argument that it is possible to analyse the syllable into smaller units, which we may call phonemes, does not invalidate the syllable-type analysis, any more than the possibility of considering English phonemes as combinations of distinctive features makes nonsense of the analysis into phonemes.

Hockett rightly points out[1] that such differences in interpretation are only apparent: the difference of opinion may simply be due to a difference in the level of analysis, for example, in the IC level at which the term 'phoneme' is introduced. The utterance chunks between 'b' and 't' in *beat, boot, bite*, etc., i.e. the syllabics, clearly form units of some kind, at a certain level of analysis, and some analysts may prefer to call them phonemes. One cannot avoid having to account for the complexity of the material at some level of analysis. 'The worker who sets up a larger number of "phonemes" has to present more information of this kind [i.e. specification of the constituent elements of the phonemes themselves], and less at the "superphonemic" level (clusters etc.); the worker who sets up fewer "phonemes"

---

[1] *A Manual of Phonology*, especially pp. 160, 161.

must cover less "subphonemically" but correspondingly more "superphonemically." Quite obviously, equally accurate descriptions can be presented either way, and there is no way to show that one way is any more economic than the other.'[1]

This study is, in the wider sense suggested above, an attempt to reduce Cockney to writing, with the descriptions necessary to make the writing intelligible. I am fully aware that there are alternative analyses which will also account for the data, in general or on particular points. I shall discuss below (7.2—7.4) my reasons for adopting this or that phonemic solution in special areas of the phonology; here we are concerned with the general approach only.

7.12. General Principles

In general, it may be stated that my guiding principle has *not* been a pedagogical one: I have not been concerned with making an analysis which would result in a transcription easy to read and suitable for teaching and learning purposes. For such purposes my system of transcription, if not the analysis itself, would probably have to be modified in several respects.

I have, however, been concerned with *simplicity, economy,* and *symmetry,*[2] with *neatness* and *elegance* of description. In my interpretation this means that I want to state the phonology of a language in terms of a system with few units which have wide combinatory possibilities, a system where a general distributional statement applies to many units, a system where as many pigeon-holes as possible are filled, and where few gaps are left.

In practice, in any one situation one will often be faced with conflicting principles. Thus, if we want a reduction in the

---

[1] *Op.cit.* p. 160.

[2] Cf. K. L. Pike on 'the premises of practical phonemics', *Phonemics* pp. 57–66.

number of phonological units we must accept a greater number of allophonic variants of these units: the complexity is removed from the phonemic level, but is re-introduced on the subphonemic one. In general, this is the solution preferred in the present study, provided that the allophonic variation is statable in simple terms.

I agree with K. L. Pike[1] as to the usefulness of setting up several parallel and interlocking hierarchies for the structure of language,[2] and of describing, as far as possible, the units within each hierarchy independently of the other hierarchies.[3] This is the reason why I have stated the distribution of phonemes within higher *phonological* units — syllable peak and margin, syllable, microsegment, macrosegment — instead of within *words*. But it does not mean that there are not close ties between the phonological category and the morphological and grammatical ones, or that I deny the psychological reality of the word: the contrast between the postulated /oh/ and /ow/ peaks could probably largely be explained by morphological conditioning (3.451), and there is an obvious correlation with word boundaries when *feel it* may be /fílit/ (besides /fíjlit/), in analogy with /fílðat/ *feel that*, whereas *feeling* is only /fíjlin/ (3.141). Likewise, there is a close correlation between morphological, especially word, boundary and phonological juncture; but juncture is also used for other purposes than to set off a morphological boundary: it is simply an element of the phonological system which may be exploited by the morphological system. Juncture and morphological boundary should therefore be clearly distinguished.

[1] K. L. Pike, *Language*.

[2] A 'behavioral system', thus also language, is 'hierarchically and trimodally structured' (*Language* § 5.1).

[3] *Op.cit.* § 8.443. Cf. also C. F. Hockett on the phonological hierarchy: 'the phonologic structure of an utterance shows a *hierarchic* organization, involving units of various size-levels: the units at any size-level save the smallest consist of arrangements of units of the next smaller size-level.' (*A Manual of Phonology* p. 43.).

7.13. Special Criteria

7.130

To be more specific, one may mention a number of factors which might be taken into consideration in establishing the phoneme inventory.

7.131. Phonetic (Articulatory-Acoustical) Facts

Are the allophones of the postulated phoneme phonetically similar? When phonetic *similarity* is not adequate, one may use the phonetic *relationship* between members of several sets in order to group segments into phonemes.[1] Is there any phonetic *overlapping* between the phonemes? Can one sound type belong to different phonemes in different environments? Cockney [ʔ] is an extrasystemic prosodic feature when used for emphasis, but an allophone of the /t/ phoneme in other contexts.[2] Cockney /e/ has generally a more open allophone in /ej/ than the usual allophone of /a/ in /CaC/, though /e/ in /CeC/ is closer than /a/ in /CaC/. There is nothing extraordinary about such a situation, and we account for it in terms of the phonetic relationship between, for example, the second segment of /CeC/ and /CaC/, and between /Cej/ and /Caj/.

7.132. Distinctive Features[3]

Is it possible to set up distinctive features which apply to all variants of the postulated phoneme? It may be difficult to set up

---

[1] G. L. Trager and B. Bloch, in 'The Syllabic Phonemes of English', did so for the second segment in the series *bit, bet, bat*, etc., *beat, bait, bite*, etc., *mirror, merry, marry*, etc., and *beer, bear, bar*, etc. E. Haugen and W. F. Twaddell ('Facts and Phonemics') take exception to this criterion.

[2] According to another interpretation, the glottal stop may even be an allophone of several consonants in the same type of environment: § 7.32.

[3] For an elaboration of the concept of distinctive features, in articulatory and acoustical terms, see R. Jakobson, C. G. M. Fant, and M. Halle, *Preliminaries to Speech Analysis*.

such distinctive features as positive, additive features, the same
for a particular phoneme in all contexts. Hans Kurath[1] refuses to
analyse e.g. *calm, law* as /kahm loh/ and to group this /h/ together
with pre-vocalic [h] into one phoneme, because in his opinion they
share no distinctive features. I believe that it is possible to set up
such distinctive features in this case (3.02, 4.04), but we have en-
countered other difficulties: how can we justify the interpretation of the syllabicity of a contoid as a member of the /ə/
phoneme (3.612), of the nasality of a vocoid as a member of
a nasal consonant phoneme (4.32), of the voiced flap [ṭ] and the
glottal stop [ʔ] as members of the /t/ phoneme (4.13, 4.14),
and of the back vocoid glide [ɤ̆] as a member of the /l/ phoneme
(4.412, 4.413)?[2]

For the present analysis of the Cockney segmental phonemes
into distinctive features, see 3.02 and 4.04. I have not solved
all the relevant problems there,[3] and I suspect that the view
of distinctive features as positive, additive, constant features
may be irreconcilable with a system consisting of *few* phonological units. It is probably more fruitful to assign *relative*
values to the distinctive features. G. L. Trager and B. Bloch
use phonetic relationships as a criterion in the setting up of
phonemes, and K. L. Pike's 'identificational-contrastive features' are also relative, not constant.[4] Our description of the
phonemes may have to be phrased as follows: '/e/ in the frame
C–C is . . . ; in the frame C–h it is . . ., and in C–j it is . . .'.

It may also be convenient to postulate *zero* as a distinctive
feature, or, in other words, to define a phoneme negatively.
Such a label might perhaps be given to /h/ in English: it is a
zero dorsal sonorant, i.e. within the dorsal sonorant category

[1] 'The Binary Interpretation of English Vowels. A Critique.'
[2] B. Bloch and G. L. Trager (*Outline of Linguistic Analysis* § 3.4)
consider lateral opening as 'the characterizing phonetic feature' of [l]
and [ɤ̆]. I am not too sure that [ɤ̆] has more markedly lateral opening
than, for example, the [ʊ] allophone of /u/.
[3] As far as the vowels are concerned, see 7.23.
[4] *Language* § 8.33.

it has no special resonance or articulation of its own: its 'position' is simply that it depends on the contiguous vowels (4.04). A similar definition might perhaps be given to /ə/, which would be a vowel with zero feature, i.e. it would be negatively defined as being none of the other five vowels (3.02).

7.133. Distribution

Are two segments in complementary distribution? If this is so, this is one reason, but not a sufficient one, for grouping them into one phoneme.

Is it possible to find minimal or near-minimal contrasts for a pair of segments? If not, should they be grouped into one phoneme? In my opinion, the impossibility of finding any (near-) minimal contrasts has no bearing on the interpretation of two segments as phonologically same or different, since the existence of such minimal pairs may be largely fortuitous; our phonemic solution may be just as valid if it results from a long chain of argument.

Membership in distributional classes is another criterion which, in my opinion, is a valuable clue for the phonemic interpretation of a segment. If, for instance, the sound complex in *I* is considered a combination of two phonemes, but we are uncertain whether to group the last segment with [ɪ] of [bɪt] *bit* or with [j] of [jɑ·d] *yard*, one may ask, does the final element of *I* belong to the same distributional class as vowels or consonants (assuming that we have already set up such a distinction)?

7.134. Pattern Symmetry

In the tentative analysis adopted, do we find symmetry or near-symmetry in the combinatory possibilities of the several members of a class of phonemes? Finding such symmetry may be one reason, but not a sufficient one, for analysing the English syllable peak system in terms of V, Vh, Vj, and Vw, whereby one achieves a neat system with nearly all the pigeon-holes filled.

Is there any parallelism between the allophonic memberships of different phonemes in our tentative system? There is a clear parallelism in such aspects as the length, the diphthongization, the variants before /l/, etc., of the syllable peaks (3.05) and the voicing, the glottalization, the aspiration and the affrication of groups of consonants (4.05, 4.12). But it might be difficult to find any parallel to the phonetic relationship between [h] and [ŋ] of RP [hæŋ] *hang*, if one wanted to group these segments into one phoneme, or to the phonetic relationship between [ʔ] and [tˢ] and between [ɣ̆] and [l] (4.14, 4.412 sq.).

7.135. Considerations of Other Systems

Should we let our phonemic analysis be influenced by considerations of the morphological system to be established? Simplicity of the morphological description is obviously an advantage, and if, for instance, we interpret any occurrence of [ʔ] in Cockney, except in post-junctural position, as a member of the /t/ phoneme, our morphological description might become somewhat complicated (4.14, 7.32). In my opinion, such morphological considerations may be of value, but they should not be given too much weight when they are in conflict with important phonological facts.

To what extent should we let considerations of historical phonology, dialectology, and stylistics play any part? Can we find a type of analysis which would make it possible to describe different stages of the same language, different dialects, and different styles in terms of the same system? I believe that these are considerations which should be given some weight, along with other factors. This is not the same, however, as the 'overall pattern' approach of G. L. Trager and H. L. Smith, C. F. Hockett, and H. A. Gleason,[1] to which I object (7.211).

---

[1] G. L. Trager and H. L. Smith, *An Outline of English Structure;* C. F. Hockett, *A Course in Modern Linguistics;* H. A. Gleason, *An Introduction to Descriptive Linguistics.*

7.136. *Native Reaction*

Is our tentative analysis supported by comments and reactions observable in the informants? E. Sapir has used this criterion, and discussed it in his writings,[1] and most analysts try at least to elicit opinions about 'same or different' from their informants. A. C. Gimson has tried to find what is most important for the distinction between the syllable peaks of RP *bit* and *beat* by studying the reaction of some informants to utterances like [bɪ•t] and [bit].[2] There is no doubt that a study of informants' reaction may throw light on the way language functions, and that it may give us valuable clues for our phonemic analysis.[3]

7.137. *Conclusion*

All the factors mentioned in 7.131—7.136 are facts which are relevant for a phonemic analysis. When objections are raised against phonemic analyses of the type presented in this study on the ground that it violates the facts of the language, the critics seem to be having certain specific facts only in mind, viz. the articulatory ones, neglecting other equally relevant data. Characteristic in this respect are the following statements by Malone.

(1) 'The limits of movement in these glides [viz. the syllable peaks of *spite* and *spout*] are ill defined and variable; indeed, in some allophones the glide moves within limits so narrow that it is hard to tell from a simple vowel. Moreover, since the movement is gradual, without division into two sharply distinguished parts by means of a shift, the usual symbolization with two characters, as [ai] or [aj] and [au] or [aw], does violence

[1] See e.g. E. Sapir, 'The Psychological Reality of Phonemes'. Cf. also K. L. Pike, *Phonemics* pp. 64 b and 160 b.

[2] A. C. Gimson, 'Implications of the Phonemic/Chronemic Grouping of English Vowels'.

[3] For a general discussion of the problem of native reaction as a criterion in linguistic analysis, see *Proceedings of the Eighth International Congress of Linguists* pp. 573–91.

to the phonetic facts and falsifies the phonemic picture.'[1]

On the other hand, Malone considers /oə yə iə ǫı/ in /boə/ boa, /lyən/ lion, /ydiə/ idea, /kǫın/ coin biphonematic sequences.[2] The reasons for this difference in treatment are not clearly stated, but one seems to be that the 'allophonic range [of the semivowel /ə/] is slight by comparison with the other tectals: it has no allophones that can be called truly velar or truly palatal, and in making it one must keep pretty close to the intermediate position.'[3]

Malone apparently considers irrelevant for phonemic analysis the fact that in distribution the syllable peaks of spite and spout parallel those of the stressed syllables of idea and mayor rather than those of pit and pat (cf. 7.2121). In this case he even disregards certain phonetic facts. (a) The syllable peaks of spite and spout parallel those of idea and mayor even in length and in syllabification of the following consonant or consonants (7.2211). (b) It is true for the syllable peaks of idea and mayor, just as well as for the peaks of spite and spout, that 'the movement is gradual, without division into two sharply distinguished parts by means of a shift'. (c) 'ea', 'ayo', 'a', 'oo', and 'oi' of idea, mayor, mare, floor, and coin, which Malone analyses as /ydiə meər mæər floər kǫın/, represent single syllables only,[4] whereas 'oa', 'io', 'owe', and 'ohe' of boa, lion, towel, and Cohen, which Malone analyses as /boə lyən twəl koın/, are disyllabic, which appears clearly, for example, from the distribution of stress and intonation over these utterances; it 'does violence to the phonetic facts' to analyse these two series in the same way.

(2) 'In spite of the unshakable phonetic evidence for sonantal liquids and nasals in the weak syllables of English, many ana-

---

[1] 'The Phonemes of Current English', 1959 edition p. 238.

[2] Malone calls them diphthongs, and defines a diphthong as a mono-syllabic sequence of a vowel or a glide and a semivowel. Op.cit. p. 244.

[3] Op.cit. p. 240.

[4] At least in British RP and in Cockney, where mayor and mare are homonyms.

lysts ignore this evidence and write the weak syllable of words like *bottle* and *button* with a fictitious vowel, set before the liquid or nasal sign. I was myself guilty of this practice in my paper of 1940, though I mended my ways in 1942, bringing my phonemic theories into harmony with the phonetic facts. It is indeed a falsification of the facts to write, say, *isn't* as /izʌnt/; that is, to insert a phoneme /ʌ/ that is not actually there. And such a transcription may lead the unwary astray, inducing foreigners and even native speakers to try to pronounce the fictitious vowel. How much better it would be for the analysts to base their theories, and accordingly their transcriptions, on the facts, instead of distorting the facts to make them fit the theories!'[1]

Malone here disregards the distributional fact that unstressed [Ç] and [əC] are in free or complementary distribution in such contexts (3.612), and that the difference between them cannot be used to differentiate meanings. Further, he leaves out of account the psychological fact that the naive speaker is wholly unaware of not pronouncing any 'vowel' for instance in the last syllable of ['dʌzn̩t] *does not*. Moreover, the author seems to be mixing up his phonemics and his phonetics when he calls /ʌ/ (in my analysis, /ə/) 'a fictitious vowel' and asserts that the 'phoneme /ʌ/ ... is not actually there': there is no *vocoid* there, but there may well be a *vowel* occurring (1.6).

It is obvious that the linguist must base his analysis on the facts of the language. However, he must take *all* the facts into account, and not arbitrarily select a certain type of facts only.

7.14. Is a Synchronic Structural Analysis Possible?

Is a purely synchronic structural description, in phonemic terms, possible at all? What are we to do with problems like *feel* vs. *fill*, *fool* vs. *full*, *salt* vs. *sort*, *board* vs. *bored* (3.141, 3.541, 3.452, 3.451), where there is obviously vacillation among

[1] *Op.cit.* p. 264.

the speakers? Sometimes these word pairs are identical, sometimes they are different.[1] A linguistic system is subject to change;
it is, to some extent, always in the process of development.
At certain periods a language changes more rapidly than at
other periods: some contrasts within the system may be dying
out, while new ones are arising. Cockney seems to be in such a
period now, and the result is fuzziness and erratic forms.[2] If
our ideal is neatness and compactness of description this may
be deplorable, but it does not invalidate the description. One
cannot expect to be able to set up, at any one point in the history
of a language, a completely neat and finished description in
terms of categories which never overlap, with no fuzzy borders.
If this were so, there would be no change, no development in
the language. When we find fuzziness at a certain point, it
may be a sign that change is going on in the system at that
point, and at that point a completely synchronic description
is then impossible: one may have to refer to certain *trends* and
changes. Such points in the phonology of Cockney are the contrast between the syllable peaks /oh/ and /ow/ (3.451), the
syllable peaks before pre-junctural and pre-consonantal /l/
(4.414 and 7.2224), and the phonemic status of the glottal
stop (7.32).[3]

---

[1] For similar vacillations, both in phonology and morphology, with
overlap between units which may otherwise, with other speakers or in
other contexts, be distinct, see Magne Oftedal, *The Gaelic of Leurbost*,
especially §§ 34, 51, 54, 63, 66, 69, 77, 249.

[2] Cf. M. Oftedal, *op.cit.* § 249, on the present state of the Celtic
dialect of Leurbost: 'The case system is, from the historical point of
view, in the process of breaking down. This has resulted in a very complicated distribution of forms with a large amount of vacillation.'

[3] I have borrowed the term 'fuzzy' from K. L. Pike, who is himself
prepared to incorporate fuzziness, or indeterminacy, in the linguistic
system. See his *Language* e.g. §§ 3.25, 6.91, 7.324.

7.2. THE SYLLABLE PEAK SYSTEM

7.21. Alternative Analyses

7.210

The English syllable peak system has been analysed in several ways. These differences reflect not only differences in language material, i.e. different dialects, but also differences in the approach and the preferences of the analysing linguist.[1]

7.211. The Overall Pattern

There is an interesting attempt to account for differences in dialect in terms of an overall pattern or grid. The idea was first elaborated by G. L. Trager and H. L. Smith,[2] and it has been adopted by H. A. Gleason[3] and C. F. Hockett.[4] Nine vowels, occurring as peak nuclei, and three peak satellites are postulated, making a total of thirty-six combinations for syllable peaks, including the combination of vowel and zero peak satellite. All combinations are possible, and occur in some dialect or other, but no dialect has them all.

The advantage of such an approach is that it gives a frame of reference for the comparison of dialects. However, it seems to me that a comparison on this basis is *phonetic* rather than *structural* or systemic. When analysing a particular dialect the analyst takes his grid, and fills the relevant boxes on the basis of phonetic similarity; no mention is made of distributional criteria. Thus, according to Gleason,[5] *house* in one dialect has the peak /aw/, in another /æw/, in still another /ew/ or /əw/; *boat* is sometimes /ow/, sometimes /əw/, and the two forms may be found with the same speaker. Here there is obviously no

---

[1] Surveys of various interpretations are found in A. Cohen, *The Phonemes of English* p. 75 sqq.; H. A. Gleason, *An Introduction to Descriptive Linguistics* p. 226 sqq.; K. L. Pike, *Language* § 9.73.

[2] *An Outline of English Structure.*

[3] *An Introduction to Descriptive Linguistics* pp. 27–39 and 230 sqq.

[4] *A Course in Modern Linguistics* pp. 339–349.

[5] *Op.cit.* § 3.11.

question of *contrast*, a criterion which so far has been considered essential for linguistic analysis. The phonological system of a dialect is not analysed according to its own internal laws and structure; extra-systemic considerations are imposed on the analysis. Structural linguists all agree in condemning many older grammarians for doing violence to the grammatical system of a modern language by describing it in terms of Latin grammar, i.e. of another system. Are not the overall-pattern linguists doing something similar in phonology? Is it not a revival of the much-decried IPA approach to the description of a sound system, i.e. in terms of boxes to be filled on a generalized phonetic chart?[1]

The following is an attempt at an analysis of the Cockney syllable peaks in terms of the Smith—Gleason—Hockett overall pattern. Within each set, the appropriate boxes have been filled on the basis of phonetic similarity. There is a contrast of no more than six vowels within each set, but in one case seven boxes have been filled, since stressed [ʌ] and unstressed [ə], in our analysis both /ə/, are phonetically too dissimilar for inclusion in the same box. Out of the nine vowels only one, i, does not occur in any syllable peak. Alternative analyses are put in parentheses.

G. L. Trager and B. Bloch[2] also aim at an overall system for all dialects of English. They are on somewhat safer ground than most of the overall-pattern linguists when they assert that for each dialect one must 'take account of the *phonetic data* (including *facts of distribution*) and of the consequent *pattern relationships*' (italics mine).

M. Swadesh[3] has elaborated another overall vowel system for

---

[1] For a more detailed criticism of the overall pattern approach, see the review by the present writer of H. A. Gleason, *An Introduction to Descriptive Linguistics*, to appear in *Norsk Tidsskrift for Sprogvidenskap* vol. 19.

[2] 'The Syllabic Phonemes of English' p. 245.

[3] 'On the Analysis of English Syllabics'.

i bit	i	u · put
e bet	ə about	o
	(unstressed)	
æ bat	a but	ɔ pot
	(stressed)	

Simple peaks

ih beer	ih	uh tour
eh bear	əh bird	oh (bored)
æh	ah bar	ɔh bored

Vh peaks

ij bee	ïj	uj
ej	əj ⹀	oj (boy)
æj bay	aj buy	ɔj boy

Vj peaks

iw	ïw	uw boot
ew (bound)	əw boat	ow board
æw bound	aw	ɔw (board)

Vw peaks

Fig. 10

*The Cockney syllable peak system in terms of the overall
pattern of Gleason, Hockett, and Trager-Smith*

the description of any English dialect. It differs from the Smith—
Gleason—Hockett analysis mainly in that it identifies the last
element of the complex syllable peaks with various *vowels*
(cf. 7.21222).

7.212. Main Types of Analysis

7.2121. *Survey.* The various interpretations of the syllable
peaks in English can be divided into two categories.

(1) The syllable peaks are all interpreted as unit phonemes,
or vowels (some of which may well be *written* with diagraphs).

(2) Some of the syllable peaks are interpreted as complex, consisting of one of the elements making up the simple peaks plus another unit.

The first analysis gives a relatively large number of minimum phonemic units, twenty-one or even more for RP. Some linguists find strong support in historical and comparative linguistics for such an interpretation. H. Kurath[1] says that with a complex syllable peak analysis, at least of the Bloch and Trager type, phonemic change becomes unintelligible, and there is created a barrier between structural linguistics and historical and area linguistics.

The unit-phoneme analysis seems to be the solution adopted by A. Cohen,[2] J. S. Kenyon,[3] A. C. Lawrenson,[4] A. C. S. Ross and J. Josephs,[5] M. Swadesh,[6] N. S. Trubetzkoy,[7] and J. Vachek,[8]

[1] 'The Binary Interpretation of English Vowels. A Critique' p. 120 sq.

[2] *The Phonemes of English*. Some of Cohen's syllable peaks are considered phonetically complex, but apparently phonemically simple.

Cohen makes an exception of the so-called centring diphthongs: some, but not all, of their occurrences he considers phoneme sequences of /V/ plus /ə/. This part of his analysis is particularly unsatisfactory, because of the inconsistency in the treatment of phonetically identical forms; thus, *sear* is /si(r)/, with a monophonematic peak, but *seer* is /siər/, with a biphonematic one; *fear* is /fi(r)/, but *fierce* is /fiəs/. Grammatical considerations and potentiality for occurrence ('potential [r]' is a phoneme to Cohen, apparently differing from other [r]'s) are Cohen's main criteria on this point.

[3] J. S. Kenyon and T. A. Knott, *A Pronouncing Dictionary of American English;* J. S. Kenyon, *American Pronunciation*.

[4] 'Some Observations on the Phonology of English Vowels'. However, the peaks of *beer, bare, tour,* i.e. the so-called centring diphthongs, are considered biphonematic units.

[5] 'Triangular Tables for the Phonemes of English'.

[6] 'The Vowels of Chicago English'. Swadesh has a rather unusual classification of the vowels into the categories of 'sharp' and 'blunt'. For a later interpretation by Swadesh, see p. 183 n. 4.

[7] *Grundzüge der Phonologie* p. 108 sqq.

[8] 'Über die phonologische Interpretation der Diphthonge mit besonderer Berücksichtigung des Englischen'. Both Trubetzkoy and Vachek make an exception of the segment(s) following [b] in *boy:* this is a biphonematic unit.

and it may be one of the analyses implied in the transcription system used by D. Jones.[1] B. Trnka considers all the 'long vowels' and all the 'diphthongs' except [ɔɪ̯] 'simple phonemes'.[2] K. Malone[3] adopts a monophonemic interpretation for most of the syllable peaks, but has a biphonematic interpretation of the peaks of *boy, peer, pair, pour, moor.*

The second type of analysis is an application of the concept of immediate constituents, IC's, to phonological analysis: there are segments which, on one level of analysis, can be considered complex, but which, in a higher structural layer, act as single units.[4] This analysis has the advantage of resulting in a system of few minimum phonemic units, and of taking into account phonetic and distributional characteristics of groups of syllable peaks, viz. the fact that the 'long vowels' and 'diphthongs' may occur before a syllable cut, before a juncture, or even as a macrosegment in itself, whereas the 'short vowels' never so occur when stressed: they occur only in checked syllables (cf. 2.4).[5]

---

[1] *An Outline of English Phonetics* and *The Pronunciation of English.* Jones seems to favour an analysis in terms of chronemes for the so-called long vowels (cf. 7.21221), though he thinks that recent trends may rather lead to an analysis in terms of unit phonemes only; cf. *The Phoneme* pp. 166–70, especially §§ 515, 519, and n. 11.

[2] *A Phonological Analysis of Present-Day Standard English.*

[3] 'Phonemes and Phonemic Correlations in Current English', 'The Phonemes of Current English', and 'The Phonemic Structure of English Monosyllables'.

[4] A number of linguists have stressed the usefulness of the concept of immediate constituents in linguistic analysis, e.g. L. Bloomfield, *Language* pp. 1 58–69, 184–97, 227–46; Z. S. Harris, 'From Morpheme to Utterance'; C. F. Hockett, *A Manual of Phonology* p. 150 sqq. and *A Course in Modern Linguistics* pp. 147–56; E. A. Nida, 'The Analysis of Grammatical Constituents'; K. L. Pike, 'Taxemes and Immediate Constituents'; R. S. Wells, 'Immediate Constituents'.

[5] Cf. C. Hj. Borgstrøm's 'fullstendige' (complete) and 'ufullstendige' (incomplete) vowels, *Innføring i sprogvidenskap* p. 43 sqq. Similarly, Trubetzkoy distinguishes between 'vollablaufende Vokalphoneme' and 'Vokalphoneme mit unterbrochenem Ablauf' (*Grundzüge der Phonologie* p. 108), or, in the French version, between 'phonèmes vocaliques à

7.2122. IC Analysis. The IC analysis may take several forms.
(1) The 'long vowels' are considered combinations of short vowels and a phoneme of length, /V·/ (7.21221).
(2) The 'long vowels' and 'diphthongs' are considered combinations of vowels, /VV/ (7.21222).
(3) The 'long vowels' and 'diphthongs' are considered combinations of vowels and consonants, /VC/ (or /VS/) (7.21223).

7.21221. Chronemes. The so-called 'long vowels' are considered combinations of 'short vowels' plus a phoneme of length, a 'chroneme'. In such a type of analysis the 'diphthongs' are interpreted as unit phonemes. Daniel Jones represents this line of approach.[1] In my opinion this kind of analysis suffers under the fact that it takes into account certain *phonetic* facts only, viz. the difference in length between certain groups of syllable peaks, without paying due regard to the fact that the 'long vowels' share certain distributional features with the 'diphthongs'. Besides, even phonetic facts may be violated by such a classification of the peaks: there is often no neat distinction between long and short vowels.[2]

7.21222. Complex Peaks = /VV/. The 'long vowels' and 'diphthongs' are considered combinations of vowels, e.g. /biit/ *beat*, /beit/ *bait*, /bout/ *boat*, /buut/ *boot*, /paa/ *pa*. This view is represented by W. Merlingen,[3] M. Swadesh,[4] and H. J. Uldall.[5] K. L. Pike favours a similar solution for some of the 'diphthongs', though not for the 'long vowels'.[6]

déroulement complet' and 'phonèmes vocaliques à déroulement interrompu' (*Principes de phonologie* p. 128).

  [1] 'Chronemes and Tonemes' and *The Phoneme* § 515.

  [2] See 3.04 and notes.

  [3] 'Zur Phonologie der englischen Diphthonge und langen Vokale'.

  [4] 'On the Analysis of English Syllabics'. For an earlier interpretation by Swadesh, see p. 181 n. 6.

  [5] 'On the Structural Interpretation of Diphthongs'.

  [6] 'On the Phonemic Status of English Diphthongs', *Phonemics* p. 45 sqq., and *Language* § 9.223.

Uldall's analysis is made on the basis of 'exchangeability': in deciding whether the long vowels and diphthongs are monophonematic or biphonematic, 'the question whether the substance is uniform or not has no bearing whatever on the structural interpretation'.[1] If the emphasis on *commutation* rather than on *phonetic similarity* as a criterion is accepted, such an analysis has much to recommend it.

One might argue, however, that there is no other combination of vowels in English, and considerations of analogy would therefore lead us to another kind of solution. Still, this would be a circular argument, an appeal to a system which we are setting up. If we accept Uldall's analysis there *are* combinations of vowels in English.

Such an analysis gives an even better basis than is possible, for example, according to the analysis adopted in this study for a simple distinction between the distributional classes of vowels and consonants: the syllable peaks consist of vowels only, the syllable margins of consonants only.

But how are we to distinguish between a monosyllabic VV sequence and a disyllabic one? Are we to postulate a phoneme of syllabicity? There may perhaps be few instances of transcriptional ambiguity: if we analyse the peaks of *beat, bait, bite, boy, boot, boat, bout, pa, law, bird* as /ii ei ai oi uu ou au aa oo əə/ we shall find that only a few of these are possible disyllabic vowel sequences, at least in Cockney,[2] so that, for example, the transcriptions /ei/ and /ou/ will always have to be considered single syllables. However, there are some cases of disyllabic VV sequences, which contrast with a VV sequence interrupted by juncture,[3] and how should we then show the difference between [iˑ], [ii], and [i+i]? We shall find still greater difficulties of this

---

[1] *Op.cit.* p. 275.

[2] Of the 'short' vowels only /i u ə/ occur before the syllable cut; cf. 2.4 and 3.01.

[3] E.g. /stə́diin/ *studying* vs. /stə́di+in/ *study in*, p. 15 n. 1.

kind in the analysis of sequences which are here analysed as VSV and VSSV (2.52, 2.53).[1]

Moreover, even if the practical problems of *transcription* could be solved satisfactorily, so that the transcription itself was unambiguous, this would not mean that we had solved the problems of the underlying analysis. Our theory would still have to account for the fact that there is a contrast between monosyllabic VV sequences (my complex peak, /VS/), disyllabic VV sequences (in my analysis, microsegment with zero interlude, /VV/), and disyllabic VV sequences interrupted by juncture (in this analysis, two microsegments, /V+V/).

Finally, Uldall makes an exception of the centring diphthongs, which he interprets, at least alternatively, as /Vr/ because of the 'latency' criterion: [hɪə] *here* is /hir/ because of its parallel with utterances like ['hɪərənd'ðɛə] *here and there*. However, the fact that words like *here* have variant forms is better dealt with in the morphology, or in the morphophonemic section: [hɪə] and [hɪər] are allomorphs of the same morpheme.[2] Such an analysis is all the more justified in view of the fact that the 'latency' criterion does not apply to words like [aɪ'dɪə] *idea* except in those idiolects where 'intrusive r' (4.4221) consistently occurs, and in no dialect is there any alternation between [ɪə] and [ɪər] in words like ['θɪətə] *theatre* and ['rɪəl] *real*. One might adduce considerations of the history of the language and of other dialects (7.135) as an argument for interpreting [Və] as /Vr/: for example, [ɪə] has developed from [ɪr], which form still exists in many dialects. However, the argument does not apply to *idea, theatre, real*, etc., and it hardly seems satisfactory to analyse identical segments in similar phonological environments in different ways: [ɪə] in *dear* would be /ir/, whereas it would be /iə/ in *idea*. Nor should one disregard the fact that the centring diphthongs

---

[1] S = semiconsonant.

[2] Cf. 7.12 on the desirability of keeping the phonological and the morphological analyses separate.

have a distribution paralleling that of the other complex peaks: they ought to be analysed in the same way.

Similar objections may be raised against Merlingen's and Swadesh's analyses.

7.21223. Complex Peaks = */VS/*. The 'long vowels' and 'diphthongs' are considered combinations of vowels and some consonants of a special nature. The latter are often called 'semi-vowels' or 'semiconsonants'.[1] This view is shared by a number of linguists, particularly American linguists, such as B. Bloch, L. Bloomfield, H. A. Gleason, C. F. Hockett, E. A. Nida, H. L. Smith, G. L. Trager, and B. L. Whorf, and it is suggested by a few Europeans like C. Hj. Borgstrøm and W. Jassem.[2] It is also the analysis adopted in the present study.

The number of simple syllable peaks, i.e. of vowel phonemes,

---

[1] C. F. Hockett distinguishes between semivowels and semiconsonants; according to his definition the English peak satellites are semiconsonants (*A Manual of Phonology* p. 75 sq. and *A Course in Modern Linguistics* p. 94). I have adopted this terminology.

[2] See e.g. B. Bloch and G. L. Trager, *Outline of Linguistic Analysis* § 3.7.

L. Bloomfield, *Language* pp. 90 sq. and 124. Bloomfield distinguishes between 'simple phonemes' and 'compound phonemes': '*Compound phonemes* are combinations of simple phonemes which act as units so far as meaning and word-structure are concerned.' (p. 90). This clearly parallels our simple vs. complex peaks.

L. Bloomfield, 'The Stressed Vowels of American English'.

C. Hj. Borgstrøm, *Innføring i sprogvidenskap* p. 45.

H. A. Gleason, *An Introduction to Descriptive Linguistics* pp. 27–39.

C. F. Hockett, *A Manual of Phonology* p. 80.

C. F. Hockett, *A Course in Modern Linguistics* pp. 339–50.

W. Jassem, *Fonetyka języka angielskiego*. I have not had access to this work. It is reviewed by P. L. Garvin in *Language* 33 (1957) pp. 253–6.

E. A. Nida, *Morphology* pp. VI and 332.

H. L. Smith, *Linguistic Science and the Teaching of English* p. 28 sqq.

G. L. Trager and B. Bloch, 'The Syllabic Phonemes of English'.

G. L. Trager and H. L. Smith, *An Outline of English Structure* p. 22.

B. L. Whorf, 'Linguistics as an Exact Science' p. 4.

varies somewhat with these analysts: Bloomfield, Gleason, Hockett, and Trager and Smith all postulate nine vowels. In the dialect under consideration there are only six: only six peaks have the distributional characteristic that they never occur stressed before a syllable cut or a juncture (2.4).

7.22. The Present Analysis

7.221. *General Considerations*

7.2210. An analysis in accordance with 7.21223 accounts for the phonetic and distributional facts, and it does so in a fairly neat way.

7.2211. *Two-way rather than Three-way Classification.* A two-way classification of the syllable peaks is, in many ways, more in accordance with phonetic facts than a three-way one: there is no neat distinction between short vowels, long vowels, and diphthongs, since the so-called pure vowels may be diphthongized, the 'diphthongs' may be monophthongal, and the 'short vowels' are not always short. However, there is some phonetic justification for the setting up of *two* classes: before a consonant interlude the simple peaks are shorter than the complex ones, and, more important, the syllable cut falls later after a simple peak than after a complex one (2.5, 3.04). Such a bipartite grouping is certainly more in accordance with distributional facts (7.2121).

One might argue that even if the syllable peaks, on phonetic and distributional grounds, fall into two categories, it is not necessary to regard one of the classes as *complex*: we may simply distinguish between *complete* and *incomplete* vowels (7.2121, especially p. 182 n. 5). This is certainly possible. There are several reasons why such a view is not adopted here.

(1) An IC analysis results in fewer minimum phonemic units (7.2121).

(2) Since a clearly defined group of syllable peaks, our V class, needs 'support' and can never occur alone as a macrosegment, it is tempting to consider this a characteristic of the vowels in general. In the present analysis such a support is provided by the second element of the complex peaks.

(3) One should also bear in mind the correlation between the place of the non-phonemic syllable cut and the nature of the preceding syllable peak (2.5): the cut falls in the middle of VSSV and VSCV, just as it falls between the consonants in VCCV, and it falls one place earlier in a consonant cluster when the cluster is preceded by a semiconsonant than when it is preceded by a simple peak. Thus, what is here analysed as a peak satellite seems to fill the place of one segment.

(4) Finally, it is interesting to note the tendency to replace /ih/ and /ij/ by /i/, /uh/ and /uw/ by /u/, etc., before 'dark l' (4.414): if the syllable peaks of *beer, bee, boor, boot* are regarded as complex it is easy to understand why they should be simplified before 'dark l', which seems itself to be developing into a peak satellite (7.2224).

7.2212. Identification of the Final Element. It is possible to identify the last element of the complex peaks with the onset consonants /h j w/, on phonetic and distributional grounds: §§ 3.02 and 4.04 show that it is possible to give /h j w/ a phonetic definition which covers both their pre-peak and post-nuclear variants,[1] and the peak satellites are clearly in complementary distribution with [h j w].

Objections have been raised against this phonetic identification. Thus, M. Swadesh maintains that the second part of Bloomfield's /aj aw/ are dissimilar to pre-vocalic /j w/.[2] However, this is interpreting 'phonetic similarity' too narrowly: there is

---

[1] For the definition of /h j w/ I am much indebted to B. Bloch, H. A. Gleason, C. F. Hockett, H. L. Smith, and G. L. Trager (cf. the Bibliography).

[2] 'The Vowels of Chicago English'.

the same phonetic *relationship* between the high front dorsal consonant /j/ and the labial back dorsal consonant /w/, on the one hand, and between the glide towards high front tongue position in /aj/ and the glide towards high back tongue position in /aw/ on the other. Cf. also H. A. Gleason: 'The differences between initial and final /y/, or initial and final /w/, must be taken as the consequences of their position rather than as any significant differences in their function in the language.'[1]

More linguists have been unwilling to identify pre-peak [h] with the last element of the peaks in *beer, bear*, etc. Even Gleason does not identify them, but sets up an extra phoneme, /н/, as peak satellite in words like *pa*. H. Kurath objects to the identification because, like Gleason (§§ 2.14, 2.20), he classifies pre-peak /h/ as a fricative, a label which obviously does not fit the peak satellite.[2] In this study /h/ is classified in another way, viz. as a sonorant (4.04). There is doubt about the phonetic justification for calling pre-peak [h] a fricative,[3] and its distribution parallels that of sonorants rather than that of fricatives: like all the other sonorants it occurs only immediately before the syllable peak (there is one exception: [h] occurs, in many dialects, before /j/, e.g. in *huge*), and like /j w/ it never occurs as a coda consonant.

H. Kurath maintains that it is not possible to set up any distinctive feature for the postulated peak satellite /h/: it varies with the preceding vowel; besides, though it is, in its manifestation, completely dependent on the preceding vowel, it determines the allophones of this vowel, and this fact is in conflict with the principle that 'allophonic variants are produced ... by the (partial) anticipation or prolongation of an articulatory

---

[1] *An Introduction to Descriptive Linguistics* p. 38. Gleason's /y/ equals my /j/.

[2] 'The Binary Interpretation of English Vowels. A Critique'.

[3] K. L. Pike considers it a voiceless vocoid (*Phonetics* pp. 71 sq., 76 sq., 140 sqq., *Phonemics* p. 5 b). Cf. also E. Dieth, *Vademekum der Phonetik* pp. 91, 100 sq.; E. Fischer-Jørgensen, *Almen Fonetik* p. 76 sq.

(hence acoustic) feature of a following or preceding sound'.[1] In my opinion this variability with and dependence on the preceding or following vowel can be considered the distinctive feature, or at least characteristic of, /h/, and the definition of /h/ can be based on it. Even Malone, who generally hugs the phonetic ground fairly closely, sees no difficulty in this variability of /h/, at least as far as the onset consonant is concerned: 'The breathing /h/ ... always agrees in tongue and lip position with the phoneme that follows it.'[2] As to the last part of Kurath's argument, if the principle quoted were to be considered binding for phonemic analysis, we should find ourselves in difficulty on more than one point, and we should have to rewrite the phonemic description of many languages, for many segments which today are commonly grouped together as allophones of the same phoneme cannot be so explained. This applies to the distribution of [l] and [ɫ] in many English dialects; for [ɫ] can hardly be considered an anticipation of silence or of consonants, and [l] can hardly be an anticipation of vowels, including the back ones. How could one explain phonetically the occurrence of the palatalized dental lateral finally after short vowels, and of the retroflex flap after long vowels, and of the unpalatalized dental lateral initially before vowels — all three considered manifestations of one phoneme, /l/ — in the Trondheim dialect of Norwegian? If [ʔ] is a manifestation of /t/ in Cockney, and in many other English dialects, of what is it an anticipation or prolongation?

The elements occurring as peak satellites are a special subclass of the consonants, set apart by certain phonetic and distributional facts; Hockett calls them semiconsonants. We cannot expect them to pattern like any other consonant. Therefore, Swadesh's argument is beside the point when he says that the last element of a complex peak cannot be considered a consonant, because a consonant, in syllabification between an unstressed

---

[1] *Op.cit.* p. 114.
[2] 'The Phonemes of Current English', 1959 edition p. 239.

and a stressed vowel, always goes with the following syllable, whereas our semiconsonant goes with the preceding syllable or remains ambisyllabic.[1] It must obviously go with the preceding vowel, since it forms a close-knit structural unit with this vowel, the syllable peak, one of the IC's of the phonological hierarchy.

For the same reason one cannot expect the semiconsonants of the complex peaks, VS, to be commutable with other consonants, in Cohen's sense.[2] On a certain level of analysis he is correct in saying that it is the *whole* 'diphthong' which is commutable with simple vowels, viz. as syllable peaks in the frame C–C (but not in the frame C–). However, on a lower level of analysis S of VS is commutable, not with C, but with other S's: /j/ is commutable with /h/ and /w/.

7.2213. Identification of the Initial Element. It is more difficult to identify the first element of the complex peaks with the vowels occurring as simple peaks, and strong criticism has been made of such attempts.[3] The phonemic grouping is said to be arbitrary.[4]

There may be some justification for the complaint of arbitrariness: the personal preferences and prejudices of the analysing linguist may influence his analysis. However, this influence may be kept at a minimum if the analyst lets himself be guided by certain principles.

Instead of expecting more or less complete phonetic *identity* between segments which are to be grouped into phonemes, one

---

[1] 'The Vowels of Chicago English' and 'On the Analysis of English Syllabics'.

[2] A. Cohen, *The Phonemes of English* e.g. pp. 20 sqq., 94, 97, 99.

[3] See in particular E. Haugen and W. F. Twaddell, 'Facts and Phonemics'.

[4] Cf. C. Hj. Borgstrøm, *Innføring i sprogvidenskap* p. 44: 'Efterpå kan man jo identifisere så langt det går', which almost seems to imply that one way is as good as another.

should look for identical phonetic *relationships* between sets of segments, i.e. between the sets occurring in the frames C–C, C–h, C–j, C–w in stressed position. Gleason and Hockett, in analysing different dialects within the general framework of an overall pattern, have neglected this criterion of phonetic relationships, as well as the criterion of structural relationships. Thus, Hockett states that *road* in some dialects has the peak /ow/, in others /əw/, or /ew/, or /o/,[1] without making it clear whether the phonetic and structural relationships to other peaks in the dialect in question justifies such an interpretation.

Obviously, each of the vowel phonemes will cover quite an area on the conventional vocoid chart if their variants in all peaks are taken into account. But though /e/ in /ej/ in Cockney is between half-open and open it is closer than /a/ in /aj/, so that the relationship /e/ = mid and /a/ = low still holds good. Likewise, though /a/ in /aj/ is certainly not so front as /a/ as a simple peak it is more front than /o/ in /oj/, and /a/ can therefore still be classified as front in relation to the back /o/.[2]

It is likely that such an analysis will result in partial phonetic overlapping between the allophones of different phonemes. At least it does so in Cockney: /e/ in /ej/ is commonly more open than /a/ is as a simple peak, but it is closer than /a/ is in the complex peak /aj/; the initial element of the strongly glided variants of /ij/ and /uw/, [ši] and [šü], may be perceptually identical with an unstressed variant of the simple peak /ə/, but /ə/ never occurs in a complex peak */əj/, and in /əw/ it is manifested by a fronter, more open variant than /u/ in /uw/: thus, the phonetic relationship between /ə/ and a closer, more back /u/ obtains for the context Vw as well as for VC. Within each context — CVC, CVh, CVj, and CVw — the same phonetic relationships between the six vowel phonemes obtain.

Besides, such a phonetic overlapping between phonemes is found even if one considers a single set of syllable peaks, e.g.

---

[1] *A Course in Modern Linguistics* p. 344 sq.
[2] On the classification of Cockney vowels, see 3.02.

the simple peaks. There are markedly different allophones before pre-junctural and pre-consonantal /l/ (3.051), so that e.g. /e/ in this context (e.g. in *belt*) may be as open as the simple peak /a/ in other contexts (e.g. in *bad*), and it may be centralized so that it resembles the stressed simple peak /ə/ in other contexts (e.g. in *bud*); however, the allophones of the three phonemes are clearly distinct in the same context, i.e. in Vl (e.g. in *belt*, *pal*, *bulb*).

Figures 1—5 (3.03) are a measure of the amount of phonetic overlapping between syllable peaks one must be prepared for in any dialect.

7.222. *Special Problems*

7.2221. *The Peak of 'boat'.* The identification of the peak nucleus in *boat* with a simple peak is a point about which there is some disagreement. The identification with the peak of *cut* may seem somewhat surprising at first blush, but this may be due to orthographical conventions, and to the fact that the phonetic symbols [ou] and [o] are commonly used for it. Phonetic considerations bear out such an analysis for several dialects. American linguists, e.g. Bloomfield, Bloch and Trager, Gleason, Hockett, Trager and Smith, are justified in analysing the peak of *boat* as /ow/ for many American dialects, because [o] and [oŭ], both manifestations of this peak, are vocoids in the mid back area, and /o/ of /ow/ stands in the same phonetic relationship to other V's in Vw as the simple peak /o/ does to other simple peaks. In Cockney, on the other hand, the first element of the peak of *boat* is in the half-open to open, front to central area, and so are the stressed simple peak of *cut* and the syllable peak in *bird*: there is obvious phonetic similarity between the syllable peaks of *cut*, *bird*, and *boat* (/ə/, /əh/, and /əw/). The phonetic similarity is not, perhaps, quite so striking in RP, but the phonetic relationships among the peak nuclei of each set (V, Vh, Vj, and Vw) remain the same: /ə/ is the central vowel *par excellence*, a vowel which is neither quite front nor quite back, neither quite close nor quite open; for Cockney we have to add: but rather front and open than back and close.

Moreover, for Cockney the /ow/ pigeon-hole is already taken by another syllable peak, viz. the peak of *board*, which, since it is not the same as *bored*, and also for obvious phonetic reasons, must be /bówd/.

7.2222. [ə] Ever Stressed? [ə] occasionally seems to occur stressed, viz. in a few words which frequently occur in unstressed position where [ə] /ə/ might be expected. D. Jones has observed it for RP in *because, just* (adverb), *such*;[1] I believe that I have heard it in *because* and *just* in Cockney. Because the occurrence of stressed [ə] is rare, and confined to these words only, it is better to leave it outside the phonological system and to assign an extra-phonological, expressive value to it; it cannot be dealt with on the same level of analysis as other phonemes.

The alternative would be to set up an extra phoneme, /ə/, with [ə] as the phonemic norm, and with a very limited distribution: it occurs only in unstressed position plus, very rarely, in stressed position in two or three morphemes as an alternant to [ʌ]. The peak of *bud*, on the other hand, /ʌ/, with [ʌ] as the phonemic norm, also has a limited distribution: it occurs only under primary or secondary stress, never unstressed. The first part of the complex syllable peaks in *bird, boat* could then be interpreted as either /ə/ or /ʌ/, for reasons of phonetic similarity perhaps rather the latter.

There is a similar problem in American English. The unrounded close central vocoid [ɨ] occurs mainly in unstressed syllables, where it could presumably be considered an allophone of the /i/ phoneme[2]. However, it also occurs stressed in a limited number of words, some, but not all, of which commonly

[1] *The Pronunciation of English* § 136.
[2] If it is not simply an unstressed allophone of /ə/.

appear in unstressed position. Several American linguists[1] have set it up as a separate phoneme. There may be greater justification for such an interpretation in this case, since stressed [ɪ] seems to be of more common occurrence than stressed [ə] in Cockney and in RP.

However, even for American [ɪ] the data presented as evidence for setting up an /i/ phoneme do not appear wholly convincing. Gleason admits that its functional load is very low. Most occurrences of [ɪ] seem to be phonologically conditioned (the following categories are Gleason's and Hockett's): in unstressed position it is an unstressed allophone of /i/ (Hockett's /háwziz/ *houses*); before /lC/ (as in *children, milk, silver*) it is also an allophone of /i/, whose central quality is predictable from the following velarized lateral ('dark l'). Where it occurs stressed in words which often appear without stress (*his, if, is, this, with; could, should, would; pretty* (adverb), *just,* (adverb)), it may perhaps be considered an extra-phonological expressive variant of /i/. The only occurrences which cannot be accounted for in these ways are in a few disyllabic words (*dinner, sister*) in the South; these should then be more closely scrutinized as regards the contrastiveness of [ɪ] to other syllable peaks *in those dialects,* and *not* considered in relation to an overall phonemic pattern of all (American) English dialects.

7.2223. Rising Diphthongs? In the 1956 edition of his *Outline of English Phonetics* D. Jones postulates a number of additional diphthongs for RP. He admits that some of them are 'unessential'[2] and that there are variant forms in several cases.

---

[1] E.g. H. A. Gleason, *An Introduction to Descriptive Linguistics* pp. 32 sq. and 231 sq.; C. F. Hockett, *A Course in Modern Linguistics* p. 339 sqq.; H. L. Smith, *Linguistic Science and the Teaching of English* p. 24; M. Swadesh, 'On the Analysis of English Syllabics' p. 142 sq.; Swadesh marks this sound [ə] /ə/ (differing from [ʌ] /ʌ/ in, e.g., the adjective *just*); G. L. Trager and H. L. Smith, *An Outline of English Structure.*

[2] *Op.cit.* § 378 b.

B. S. Andrésen has carried out a little phonemic experiment on one of Jones's contrasting diphthong pairs, viz. the peaks of (*rein*)*deer* and (*win*)*dier* (Jones: [iə] vs. [ĭə]); the listeners could not distinguish between the two.[1]

There is no reason to doubt that there actually is a difference between such pairs in many cases: when the need is felt for distinguishing between them a difference *is* made, a difference which is noticeable not only to the speaker, as suggested by Andrésen, but also to the listener; i.e. (*win*)*dier* will have two variant forms, one of which is homophonous with (*rein*)*deer*.

However, neither in Cockney nor in any form of RP with which I am familiar do we have to postulate an extra syllable peak to account for the difference. In the following paragraphs I shall give my own interpretation of Jones's new diphthongs. Some of these interpretations are suggested by Jones himself.

The 'rising diphthongs' [ĭə and ŭə],[2] in so far as they are different from Jones's 'falling diphthongs' [iə] and [uə], may be manifested in several ways. The difference may be due to the fact that the 'rising diphthongs' are always unstressed,[3] whereas the 'falling' ones may have secondary stress; this situation may well apply to unstressed (*win*)*dier*, /wíndih/, vs. (*rein*)*deer* with secondary stress, /réjndìh/. The presence of juncture may explain some differences, e.g. /kówn+ih/ (or /kówn+ìh/) *corn-ear* vs. /kównih/ *cornea*. The difference may also be one of the number of syllables: (*win*)*dier* [dɪə] is disyllabic, /diə/, whereas (*rein*)*deer* [dɪə̆] is monosyllabic, /dih/. Or the 'rising diphthong' may be a sequence of a semiconsonant and a vowel: /wíndjə/ *windier* vs. /réjndih/ *reindeer*.

In the same way, Jones's [ŭə] may either be unstressed /uh/, or disyllabic /uə/, or /wə/, e.g. *rescuer* vs. *rest-cure*: /réskjuh/ vs. /rés(t)kjùh/, or /réskjuə/ vs. /rés(t)kjuh/; *influence* may possibly be /ínflwəns/.

---

[1] '-*dier* ənd -*deer*'; ən iksperimənt'.
[2] *Op.cit.* §§ 466a – 466u.
[3] *Op.cit.* § 466b

Jones's [ŭi] vs. [ui]:[1] Neither is, in my opinion, a diphthong, but a disyllabic sequence. [ui] has always stress, primary or secondary, whereas [ŭi] is always unstressed, and there is therefore no contrast. Cf. *Outline* § 466v: [ŭi] 'is always replaceable by the disyllabic sequence **u-i**, which is difficult to distinguish from it.' Therefore, *ruin* is /rúin/, *valuing* is /váljuiŋ/. Alternant forms with /uwi/ are found both in stressed and unstressed position.

Nor are [ŏi] and [oi], [ŏə] and [oə], [ĕə] and [eə] diphthongs,[2] but disyllabic sequences, [ŏi], [ŏə], and [ĕə] being the unstressed variants. The first part of these sequences is a monophthongal variant of /əw/ and /ej/ respectively; such monophthongal variants are common before zero interlude.[3] There is certainly no contrast between a glided and a non-glided variant of the first peak in such disyllabic sequences. Thus, in my interpretation:

[ŏi] /jéləwiʃ/ *yellowish*, [oi] /gə́wiŋ/ *going*;
[ŏə] /fóləwə/ *follower*, [oə] /slə́wə/ *slower*;
[ĕə] /fórejə/ *forayer*, [eə] /pléjə/ *player*.[4]

The 'levelled' 'triphthongs' /ajə/ and /awə/ — Jones's [aə] or [a:], and [a̲ə] or [a̲:][5] — are not additional syllable peaks either. [aə] is a disyllabic variant of /ajə/, and [a̲ə] is a similar variant of /awə/. For those speakers who distinguish between the long monophthongs [a:], [a̲:], and [ɑ:] in *fire, power*, and *pa* respectively, the first two are probably actually disyllabic, with a pressure dip in the middle, and therefore simply variants of /ajə/ and /awə/ respectively.

7.2224. Vl Peaks? There is another set of diphthongs in Cockney not paralleled in RP, viz. the vocoid glides manifesting the sequence syllable peak plus pre-consonantal or pre-junctural

---

[1] *Op.cit.* §§ 327a, 466v – 466w.
[2] *Op.cit.* §§ 392a, 403, 466x.
[3] As far as Cockney is concerned, see 3.054.
[4] It is possible that some speakers use variants with /ehə/ instead of /ejə/.
[5] *Op.cit.* §§ 414–6, 430–2.

/l/ (4.4122, 4.412). There might be some justification for considering these diphthongs a new set of complex peaks, with /l/ as the peak satellite. Like three of the other four sonorants, /h j w/, /l/ would then be a semiconsonant, a peak satellite in post-vocalic position and a marginal element pre-vocalically.

However, it is preferable to call V in pre-junctural and pre-consonantal Vl a simple peak, and to consider /l/ part of the margin both pre- and post-vocalically for the following reasons:

(1) /l/ is not invariably a vocoid; it may also be a lateral contoid.

(2) The vocoid allophone of /l/ occurs not only after simple peaks but also after complex ones, and there is no other instance of more than one peak satellite in a syllable.

The dialect is in a state of flux, however. After some decades — or centuries? — it may be preferable to classify [y̆] as a peak satellite, on a par with /h j w/, which also, it should be noted, like /l/ may have contoid allophones in pre-vocalic position. Already we notice a tendency to simplification of the complex peaks before pre-junctural /l/, to 'neutralization' of several peaks, to weakening of their functional load; among the complex peaks only /oj əh əw/ remain quite intact (4.414). It is also of importance to note that the vowels have markedly different allophones before pre-junctural and pre-consonantal /l/ (3.051), just as they show different allophones for each syllable peak type, V, Vh, Vj, and Vw. It would not be the first time in the history of English, any more than of other languages, that a change has taken place in the vowel system before /l/.

This is another instance of what is here called 'fuzziness' (7.14): at this point a change is going on in the Cockney phonological system.

7.23. Vowel Classification and Definition

In 3.02 we attempted a classification of the vowels in terms of a phonological (not a phonetic) vowel chart, of the type elaborated by N. S. Trubetzkoy[1] and recently further developed by C. F. Hockett.[2] A limited set of contrastive features are set up, and the vowels are classified in terms of a vertical dimension (the position of the tongue at the point of constriction relative to the roof of the mouth) and a horizontal one (the position of this constriction relative to the opening (the front) of the mouth). There may also be other dimensions.

However, this type of analysis lends itself to different solutions and arbitrary decisions. One reason for our difficulty, as far as English is concerned, is that the vowels occur in different types of peaks. For each of these separately it might perhaps be easier to set up a classification on which linguists might agree. Thus, I suggest for Cockney:

Simple peaks: i   u
              e   ə
              a   o

Even this is rather arbitrary: /ə/ differs from /o/ rather in being fronter; neither /ə/ nor /o/ are quite open. A phonologically more justified, but less symmetrical chart would be:

i	u		i		u
e		or	e	ə	o
a	ə o		a		

       Vh: ih   uh
            eh   əh   oh
               ah

There would be little phonetic justification for making a more symmetrical chart

       ih   əh   uh
       eh   ah   oh

since /əh/ is definitely *not* close.

---

[1] *Grundzüge der Phonologie* pp. 86–114.

[2] *A Manual of Phonology* pp. 82–91. See also L. Bloomfield, *Language* pp. 102–8.

Vj: ij   oj
      ej   aj

This neat, symmetrical chart agrees well with the phonetic data.

Vw: uw

      aw   əw   ow

We have had to classify some vowels in different ways in these different frames. This is clearly undesirable. The classification suggested in 3.02 is meant to cover all the occurrences of vowels, in all syllable peaks:

i   u

e   ə

a   o

The vowels are defined as combinations of the following distinctive features: high, mid, low, front, central, back. One vowel has one distinctive feature only: /ə/ is central.

A few explanations are necessary:

(1) 'Front' is used in the sense of 'non-back'; for /a/ in /ah/ and especially in /aj/ is central to back, but it is not so back as /o/ in the same context.

(2) /e/ may be called 'mid' even in /ej/, for though, phonetically speaking, /e/ in this complex peak is between half-open and open, nevertheless /a/ in /aj/ is still more open even if it is also more back.

(3) 'Low' as applied to back vowels actually means 'non-high'; but since we need three categories for the front vowels, high, mid, and low, /o/ is arbitrarily assigned to one of these three categories; we might as well have chosen 'mid'.

(4) /ə/ falls outside the dimensions set up (front vs. back, high vs. mid vs. low). It might be defined as non-high non-back, but we cannot call it low front, because this phonetic label does not quite cover it, and because this category is already taken by /a/. It might be described negatively as being none

of the other vowels occurring in those contexts where /ə/ is found, in other words, an extended use of the schwa concept. However, it seems preferable to define the vowel positively, and to give it a distinctive feature of its own, central. This definition allows for rather widely differing phonetic manifestations of the phoneme.

But there are alternative ways of classifying the vowels:

(1)	i		u	(2)	i		u	(3)	i		u
	e	ə	o		e	ə			e		o
		a				a	o			a	ə

(1) /a/ should be defined as having one distinctive feature only, viz. low; for it is phonetically front in CaC and Caw, but non-front (central or back) in Cah and Caj. /ə/, too, can only be given one distinctive feature, because of the relationship between /ə/ and /a/ in CVC and CVw: /ə/ is *not* closer than /a/ here. The chart then hardly gives an adequate picture of our classification; but the difficulty of devising any visual presentation of the classification need not prevent us from retaining this classification.

If the initial element of the syllable peak of *now* is interpreted as /e/ instead of /a/, the classification suggested by chart (1) may be more appropriate for the contexts CVh, CVj, and CVw, since in these contexts /ə/ is then always closer than /a/ (/a/ and /ə/ would actually *contrast* in only one of these contexts, viz. CVh). However, this relationship does not apply to the context CVC; and *pat* cannot be interpreted as /pet/, since *pet* must be analysed in this way. Besides, interpreting *now* as /new/ makes a comparison with other dialects more difficult, since this interpretation would not be possible for RP and for a great number of other English dialects.

(2) Such a classification is not in agreement with phonetic facts; for /ə/ is phonetically front rather than back, and /ə/ is not closer than /o/.

(3) In this classification /ə/ is again a problem: phonetically speaking, it would be nonsense to call it a low back vowel.

Many of our problems will be solved if we postulate *seven* rather than *six* vowels: /i e æ a o u ə/ as in *pit, pet, pat, part* (the first part of the peak, /ah/), *pot, put, putt.* /e/ occurs as a simple peak (*pet*) and as part of the complex peak /eh/ (*pair*); /æ/ occurs as a simple peak (*pat*) and as part of the complex peak /æw/ (*now*); /a/ occurs only as part of the complex peaks /ah/ (*part*) and /aj/ (*bite*). The other peaks are interpreted as in 3.01. The system is fairly symmetrical:

i		u
e	ə	o
æ		a

/i/ = high front, /e/ = mid front, /æ/ = low front, /u/ = high back, /o/ = mid back, /a/ = low back, /ə/ = central.

Such a classification is more in accordance with the facts of articulation than any other classification suggested in this study, including the analysis of 3.02, and it applies equally well to all types of syllable peaks, V, Vh, Vj, and Vw.

The disadvantages are that we have an additional phonemic unit, and that a number of the potential vowel+semiconsonant combinations do not occur as syllable peaks. One vowel never occurs as a simple peak. The following do occur (cf. the table given 3.03):

V	Vh	Vj	Vw
i	ih	ij	—
e	eh	—	—
æ	—	æj	æw
—	ah	aj	—
o	oh	oj	ow
u	uh	—	uw
ə	əh	—	əw

Because the basis of my phonological analysis is the distributional fact that a limited set of syllable peaks, viz. the six so-called short vowels, never occur stressed before juncture, and because there is a contrast of not more than six in any type of syllable peak (V, Vh, Vj, Vw), I think that an analysis in terms of six vowels parallels the phonological facts more closely, and I reject this vowel chart, neat as it may be.

I have stated elsewhere (7.13) the difficulties involved in setting up distinctive features as positive, additive characteristics. Such attempts have sometimes the character of *manipulations* with the data rather than *interpretations* of them. The attempts in 7.23 are such manipulations.

But if the distinctive features postulated in 3.02 are interpreted strictly in a relative sense in terms of each of the sub-systems of syllable peaks, V, Vh, Vj, and Vw, they will be found to furnish an adequate set of descriptive terms for the vowels.

7.3. THE SYLLABLE MARGIN SYSTEM

7.30. There is less disagreement among linguists about the analysis of the syllable margin system in English. Only a few points are worth mentioning.

7.31. Affricates

7.310

A set of additional consonant phonemes are postulated by many linguists, viz. the affricates. As many as six have been set up, viz. [ts dz tʃ dʒ tr dr],[1] but most analysts are satisfied with two, [tʃ dʒ].[2]

---

[1] D. Jones, *An Outline of English Phonetics* §§ 600–36.

[2] E.g. H. A. Gleason, *An Introduction to Descriptive Linguistics* § 2.18; C. F. Hockett, *A Course in Modern Linguistics* p. 109 sq.; J. S. Kenyon and T. A. Knott, *A Pronouncing Dictionary of American English* p. XVI sq.; K. Malone, 'The Phonemic Structure of English Monosyllables', 'Phonemes and Phonemic Correlations in Current English', and 'The Phonemes of Current English'; G. L. Trager and B. Bloch, 'The Syllabic Phonemes of English' p. 229; L. Bloomfield, *Language* p. 91; I.. G. Jones, 'English Consonantal Distribution'.

7.311. [ts dz tr dr]

The main reason why D. Jones considers [ts dz tr dr] unit phonemes is probably that they are phonetically rather close-knit groups. However, there is no question of a contrast between, for example, a close-knit cluster [ts] and a sequence [t] + [s]. As an onset before a stressed vowel ([dz] never occurs in such a position, and [ts] hardly ever) the stop + fricative/ sonorant combination has a very close transition, whereas the two segments may be more loosely linked as a coda ([tr] and [dr] never occur in this position);[1] if there is a contrast between a stop + fricative/sonorant combination with phonetically close transition and a similar combination with open transition utterance-medially, the difference is explainable in terms of juncture and/or stress. In *tsetse(-fly)* and *curtsey* /ts/ constitutes an interlude, /tsétsi/, /kə́htsi/, whereas there is a juncture present in /áwt+sájd/ *outside*, /áwt+sèt/ or /áwt+set/ *outset*. Likewise, [tr] and [dr] are interludes in /méjtrən/ *matron*, /símitri/ *symmetry*, /bédrum/ *bedroom*, /hə́ndrid/ *hundred*, but there is an internal juncture present in /awt+réjdʒəs/ *outrageous*, /rést+rùm/ or /rést+rum/ *rest-room*, /béd+ròk/ or /béd+rok/ *bed-rock*, /hánd+ràjtiŋ/ *hand-writing*.

Further, these sequences are paralleled by other consonant clusters which are analysed biphonematically. This applies particularly to /tr dr/, which parallel /pr br kr gr/ both as onsets and interludes, and alongside of /str/ we find /spr skr/:

/tŕ j/ *try*, /drájf/ *dry*, /prájf/ *pry*, /bréd/ *bread*, /krájf/ *cry*, /gréj/ *grey*; /stréj/ *stray*, /spréj/ *spray*, /skríj/ *scree*; /méjtrən/ *matron*, /hə́ndrəd/ *hundred*, /éjprən/ *apron*, /débri/ *debris*, /séjkrid/ *sacred*, /áŋgri/ *angry*.

7.312. [tʃ dʒ]

As far as [tʃ dʒ] are concerned, the argument does not hinge on any contrast between a biphonematic and a monophonematic sequence. Just as in the case of the other affricates,

[1] Cf. D. Jones, *Outline* § 623.

any difference can be accounted for in terms of juncture: /hátʃit/ *hatchet* vs. /hát+ʃop/ (or /hát+ʃòp/) *hat-shop*, /wáj+tʃúwz/ *why choose* vs. /wájt+ʃúwz/ *white shoes*. C. F. Hockett finds a contrast in some dialects between [č] in *pitcher* and [tʃ] in *hit you*.[1] In the dialects with which I am familiar there would either be no difference in the intervocalic consonant sequence, /pítʃə/ as well as /hítʃə/, or there might, perhaps, be a juncture in /hít+ʃə/. Alternant forms have, of course, /tj/ or /t+j/: /hít+ju(w)/, /hítju(w)/.

Distributional criteria have been used in support of either theory. Hockett considers these affricates unit phonemes in order to achieve 'neatness of pattern': there are no other onset clusters in English consisting of stop + fricative. This may be true, for we can safely disregard the apparently only example of /ts-/ found to date, /tsétsi+flàj/ *tsetse-fly*: it hardly belongs to the vocabulary of most speakers. Besides, it is doubtful whether /tsétsi/ is in fact the most common pronunciation even among those speakers who are familiar with the word.[2] However, the affricates are paralleled by many clusters of stop + sonorant: /tr dr tj dj tw dw pl pr pj bl br bj kl kr kj kw gl gr gj gw/.[3] /tʃ dʒ/ do not parallel these clusters in every way, though: some of the Cl Cr Cj Cw clusters may be preceded by /s/, viz. /spl spr str skr spj stj skj skw/, but /tʃ dʒ/ are never so combined in onsets. However, since /l r j w/ form a separate class, distributionally as well as in terms of distinctive features, one cannot expect complete parallelism. Again, if the affricates are clusters /ʃ ʒ/ differ from /l r j w/ in only occurring after /t d/, never after other stops; but this limitation applies to onsets only: other combinations of stops and /ʃ/ occur as interludes:

---

[1] *A Course in Modern Linguistics* p. 110.

[2] Paul Christophersen informs me that during his years in West Africa (Nigeria) he observed no other form than /tétsi/. The speakers from whom he heard the word were mostly from Great Britain, partly also from other English-speaking countries like Canada and New Zealand.

[3] /tj dj stj/ do not occur in all dialects of English.

/hámpʃə/ *Hampshire*, /fíkʃən/ *fiction*, /áŋkʃəs/ *anxious*.

As interludes there are also combinations of stops and other fricatives:

/tópsi+təhvi/ *topsyturvy*, /bétsi/ *Betsy*, /bóksiz/ *boxes*, /tówdzə/ *towards a* ..., /détfəd/ *Deptford*, /brékfəst/ *breakfast*, /éjtθəv/ *(the) eighth of (July)*.

Similar combinations are found as codas:

/éjtθ/ *eighth*, /tóps/ *tops*, /lóts/ *lots*, /bóks/ *box*.

If the affricates are considered unit phonemes they differ from all other onset consonants[1] in never occurring in a complex onset:[2] they occur neither before /l r j w/ nor after /s/, otherwise the two most common types of onset clusters. But if they are interpreted as clusters they are paralleled, as we have seen, by other consonant clusters.

The same parallelism is found in codas:

/béltʃ/ *belch*, /bélts/ *belts*; /báldʒ/ *bulge*, /bálbz/ *bulbs*; /líntʃ/ *lynch*, /límps/ *limps*, /líŋks/ *links, lynx*.

Another type of argument for interpreting the two affricates in question as clusters is provided by A. Cohen, who uses the criterion of *commutability*.[3] Compare as onsets:

/tʃíp/ *chip*, /tríp/ *trip*, /típ/ *tip*, /ʃíp/ *ship*; /dʒəmp/ *jump*, /drəm/ *drum*, /dəm/ *dumb*;

as codas:

/witʃ/ *witch*, /wiʃt/ *wished*, /wits/ *wits*, /wínʃ/ (or /wíntʃ/) *winch*, /wít/ *wit*, /wíʃ/ *wish*; /réjdʒ/ *rage*, /réjdz/ *raids*, /réjnʒ/ (or /réjndʒ/) *range*, /béjʒ/[4] *beige*, /réjd/ *raid*;

and as interludes:

---

[1] Except /ð/, in some dialects also /z/.

[2] B. Bloch and G. L. Trager (*Outline of Linguistic Analysis* § 3.7) adduce a similar argument for considering them clusters.

[3] *The Phonemes of English* pp. 43–6. The examples quoted are my own.

[4] This form does not occur in all dialects of English.

/néjtʃə/ *nature*, /méjtrən/ *matron*, /léjtə/ *later*, / géjʃə/ *geisha*; /lédʒə/ *ledger*, /léʒə/ *leisure*, /ládə/ *ladder*; cf. other dC clusters: /kídni/ *kidney*, /médlə/ *meddler*, /módrit/ *moderate*.

On the whole, the distributional facts seem to speak more strongly in favour of a biphonematic interpretation of the affricates [tʃ dʒ]. Such an analysis has also the advantage of giving fewer phonemic units.

7.32. The Glottal Stop

I have analysed post-junctural [ʔ] as a feature of the juncture, not as a separate phonemic segment (2.6): [ˈʔʌp] /ə́p↓/ *up*. All other occurrences of the glottal stop are considered manifestations of the phoneme /t/ (4.144):

[ˈbʌʔn̩] /bə́tən/ *button*, [ˈreʔn̩] /rétən/ *reckon*,
[ˈkuʔn̩] /kútən/ *could not*, [ˈpæɪ̆ʔə] /péjtə/ *paper*.

The question might be raised whether one could not consider [ʔ] an allophone of several consonants, for example a variant of /k/ in [ˈreʔn̩], of /d/ in [ˈkuʔn̩], and of /p/ in [ˈpæɪ̆ʔə].

I have let myself be guided by the consideration that identical segments, occurring in phonologically the same type of context, should not be considered manifestations of different phonemes. Only when the context is a different one, viz. in post-junctural position, have I given another interpretation to [ʔ]; but even here I have not considered it a separate segmental phoneme.

Morphological considerations have been disregarded. Some of the words in question may have variant forms: *reckon* may be [ˈrekn̩] /rékən/, *could not* may be [ˈkudn̩] /kúdən/, and *paper* may be [ˈpæɪ̆pə] /péjpə/. But these facts are accounted for in terms of allomorphs: /rékən/ and /rétən/ are allomorphs of the morpheme *reckon*.

The situation seems straightforward, then: [ʔ] is an allophone of /t/, the occurrence of which is partly phonologically, partly stylistically conditioned; sometimes [ʔ] seems to be in free variation with other /t/ allophones (4.14, 4.15).

However, there is one problem which we have not yet solved. When the words *reckon, could not, paper* have allomorphs with /t/, this phoneme is never manifested by any other allophone than [ʔ]. Thus, *reckon, could not, paper* never appear in the forms *['retn̩], *['kʊtn̩], *['pæɪtə], whereas *button* may be ['bʌtn̩] (besides ['bʌʔn̩]). This irreversibility raises interesting theoretical problems.

A somewhat similar situation may perhaps be found in the Norwegian dialect described by H. Vogt.[1] The retroflex contoids [ṭ ḍ ṇ ḷ] are in free or stylistically conditioned variation with the sequences [rt rd rn rl], i.e. with [r] + a dental contoid, and they might therefore be considered manifestations of the phoneme sequences /rt rd rn rl/. However, because of a few cases of irreversibility, i.e. where the retroflex contoid is *not* replaceable by [r] + dental contoid, Vogt rules out this interpretation and considers the retroflex contoids unit phonemes.

One could, of course, set up [ʔ] as a separate phoneme. But it would be a phoneme with a low functional load and an unusual distribution: it is always in free or stylistically conditioned variation with some other consonant, mostly with /t/, sometimes with /k p d/ and a few other consonants and consonant clusters.

If we consider [ʔ] an allophone of /t/ in all its occurrences (except after juncture), we shall find that Cockney has consonant clusters consisting of identical consonants:

[fɛʔt] /fátt/ *fact*,[2] ['dɔʔtə] /dóttə/ *doctor*, ['prɛʔtɪkli] /práttiklij/ *practically*.

---

[1] 'Some Remarks on Norwegian Phonemics'.

[2] [ʔt] differs from glottalized [t'], as it may occor in [fɛt'] /fát/ *fat;* cf. 4.123.

This violates the distributional rule set up for American English at least for monosyllabic utterances.[1]

It is obvious that we have not solved the theoretical problems raised by the use of the glottal stop in Cockney (and in RP). We shall have to consider it a case of 'fuzziness' (7.14), where there is no immediately obvious and completety satisfactory solution in the present stage of the language.

7.4. JUNCTURE, STRESS, INTONATION

7.41. Juncture

As many as three junctures have been postulated for English.[2] Some of these contrasts are here accounted for within the intonation system, as terminal contours, and we need therefore postulate only one internal juncture, /+/.

The internal juncture is, in a way, a fiction. It is characteristically different from other phonemes in that it is manifested by an absence of any segment — by a rhythmic break — or by the phonetic characteristics of the neighbouring phonemes. The segmental phonemes have their characteristic allophones before and after internal juncture (most of these are the same as before or after a terminal contour, cf. 2.6), and in describing juncture we must enumerate all these details: it is not possible to describe it in terms of a few additive distinctive features.

Internal juncture is an *ad hoc* unit which we postulate in order to be able to account for a great number of very varied phonetic phenomena.

But once we have postulated such a unit we find that there are certain characteristics in the distribution of phonemes at the points where it occurs, and that juncture often coincides with a morphological boundary. It seems therefore that these

---

[1] L. G. Jones, 'English Consonantal Distribution' p. 248; B. L. Whorf, 'Linguistics as an Exact Science'.

[2] E.g. by B. Bloch and G. L. Trager, *Outline of Linguistic Analysis* and 'The Syllabic Phonemes of English'.

points are of some importance to the functioning of language, at various levels, and our analysis should account for this.

Juncture is not the same as 'syllable cut'. There will always be a phonetic syllable cut at a juncture,[1] but there is not a juncture at every syllable boundary (cf. 2.5).

Internal juncture is a 'segmental phoneme' in the sense that it occurs at a definite point in the utterance chain, between specific segments. However, it may also be called a supra-segmental phoneme or a prosody, because it characterizes a phonological unit higher than the phoneme, viz. the micro-segment. (A microsegment is an utterance chunk between two junctures: 2.3.)

7.42. Stress

7.421. Various Analyses

Linguists disagree about the number of stress phonemes in English. G. F. Arnold[2] and K. L. Pike[3] think there are two; Stanley S. Newman[4] and C. F. Hockett[5] postulate three; whereas B. Bloch,[6] H. A. Gleason,[7] H. L. Smith,[8] and G. L. Trager[9] find it necessary to set up four contrastive stresses. H. Sweet appears to have vacillated: his *Elementarbuch des gesprochenen English* and *A New English Grammar* postulate three degrees

---

[1] In my data, but apparently not in Hockett's material. Cf. *A Course in Modern Linguistics* p. 85.

[2] 'Stress in English Words'.

[3] *Phonemics* p. 45, and *The Intonation of American English;* his 'emphatic stress' and 'sentence stress' (*Phonemics* p. 45) seem to be phenomena belonging to another level of analysis, particularly to intonation.

[4] 'On the Stress System of English'.

[5] *A Manual of Phonology* p. 66 sq., and *A Course in Modern Linguistics* pp. 47–53.

[6] B. Bloch and G. L. Trager, *Outline of Linguistic Analysis* § 3.7.

[7] *An Introduction to Descriptive Linguistics* §§ 4.2–4.10.

[8] *Linguistic Science and the Teaching of English* p. 36 sqq.

[9] G. L. Trager and B. Bloch, 'The Syllabic Phonemes of English' pp. 226–9.

of stress, whereas *A Primer of Spoken English* and *The Sounds of English* have four stresses.

To some extent their differences are only apparent: what one accounts for in the stress system is taken care of under the heading of intonation by another. The close link with intonation and with other, perhaps non-systemic, aspects of the language is one of the reasons why stress analysis is difficult. Therefore Newman avoids testing compared items for stress when they occur at the intonation centre or have emphasis: he wants to eliminate 'the intensity phenomena superimposed by intonation and emphasis'; for 'the blast effect of nuclear heavy stresses in the compared items is apt to drown out the more delicate differences of intensity between stresses'.[1] Arnold goes one step further: as one of his procedures for getting at the stress categories he pronounces the test items on a monotone.[2]

Within the present framework of analysis it does not seem necessary to postulate as many as four stresses. Those who have done so have not placed the test items in the same context as far as intonation and juncture are concerned. If we do so it will be impossible to find contrasts for more than three stresses. E. Haugen and W. F. Twaddell have criticized Trager and Bloch's analysis in this respect,[3] and there is little to add. We can find no support in their data for the contrast between the reduced loud (ˆ) and the medial (´) stress postulated. The reduced loud stress occurs apparently only in words with internal open juncture (–); therefore *if* there is any difference between *syntax* and *tin-tax*, it is not *sýntàx* vs. *tín-tâx*, but *sýntax* vs. *tín-tax* (or *sýntàx* vs. *tín-tàx*).[4] Nor can the contrast be demonstrated by such pairs as *àuditórium* vs. *móvie-àuditórium*: the

[1] *Op.cit.* p. 179.

[2] 'Stress in English Words' pp. 225, 227.

[3] 'Facts and Phonemics'.

[4] The examples quoted from Trager and Bloch and from Gleason in this section are given in normal orthography but with their phonemic symbols of stress and juncture.

stress pattern is rather *àuditórium* vs. *móvie-auditòrium*, with no stress on *au* in the latter utterance.

Gleason's distinction between primary (´) and secondary (ˆ) (vs. tertiary (`) and weak (˘)) stress seems in most cases to be a difference in intonation. Thus, in Gleason's *I'm góing hóme* vs. *I'm góing hôme* the difference probably lies in the position of the intonation centre: it is on *home* in the former, and on *go* in the latter. In most utterances of this construction both *go* and *home* have the strongest out of a system of three stress categories. The difference between the two utterances can therefore be accounted for in the following way: /²ajm+³gə́wiŋ+³hə́wm¹↓/ vs. /²ajm+³gə́wiŋ+hə́wm¹↓/. There are alternative pronunciations: /²ajm+gə́wiŋ+³hə́wm¹↓/ for the former, and /²ajm+³gə́wiŋ+hə̀wm¹↓/ for the latter.

Hockett gives a good account of the stress system of English. The contrasts are well documented. He points out that a stronger variant of the primary stress occurs at the centre of the macrosegment (the intonation centre) as a conditioned variant.

Newman gives an interesting, detailed account of the stress system of English. He distinguishes between 'expressive stress accents' and 'phonemic stress' (or stress in a more narrow sense). He postulates three contrastive phonemic stresses, each of which has two conditioned variants, heavy and light. He ties his description of stress to the word, and shows in some detail how the different stresses are utilized in grammatical constructions.

Some analysts find that only one or two or three syllable peaks occur in unstressed position in English.[1] Newman thinks that all syllable peaks occur unstressed; but /ə/ is associated with a special, 'pepet weak', allophone of the weak stress (New-

---

[1] E. g. K. Malone, 'The Phonemes of Current English'; Carl Hj. Borgstrøm, *Innføring i Sprogvidenskap* p. 43 sqq. B. Trnka, in *A Phonological Analysis of Present-Day Standard English* (pp. 16–7), states that only two vowels occur unstressed, viz. [ɪ] and [ə], but later admits that 'full' vowels and diphthongs may occur in this position in 'the cultivated pronunciation of some words', in 'literary words', and in 'words of foreign origin'.

man's weak stress equals our no stress). The Cockney data agree with Newman's analysis in this respect.

Within the present framework of analysis it is not possible to account for the data in terms of two stresses, stress and no stress, only. What we have called 'secondary stress' can in no way be considered an allophonic variant of absence of stress: apart from the contrasts observable in 'loudness' there are differences in vocoid quality which we explain in terms of the presence of secondary stress; thus, the distribution of [ʌ] and [ə], both of which are considered allophones of the /ə/ phoneme (p. 84 n. 2), cannot be stated unless we postulate a secondary stress. Nor would we be able to state the point of the phonetic syllable cut as phonologically conditioned, especially in VSV and VCV (2.5), since the statements are based on the presence of primary or secondary stress.

However, it might also be possible to arrive at a system of only two stress categories by considering our secondary stress an allophonic variant of our primary stress. This is precisely what Arnold has done.

7.422. Arnold's Analysis

Arnold arrives at a system of two stress categories only, viz. strong stress and weak stress, by eliminating all pitch phenomena, considering these relevant to the intonation system only. Primary stress is, according to Arnold, always accompanied by 'prominent pitch' (prominent pitch apparently being defined as either a relatively high level before the intonation centre, or the intonation centre itself), whereas secondary stress never is; therefore the two stress types are allophones of the same phoneme. If the words are said on a monotone there is no difference between primary and secondary stress.[1]

I am not completely convinced that this is actually so. For one thing, saying words on a monotone is not the same as speaking naturally. We cannot be sure that other phonetic

[1] 'Stress in English Words' p. 225.

aspects of the utterance remain the same if we change the pitch pattern in this way; we cannot expect to find the same contrasts and differences. The validity of such a procedure therefore seems doubtful.[1]

In addition, is it quite true that there is no difference between syllables with primary and secondary stress when the utterance is said on a monotone? Are there not other differences, for example in length and in articulatory force, which are still present? Is there not such a difference between the first and the fourth syllable in *stabilization* (according to Arnold, p. 248: ᴼᵛᵛᴼᵛ, where ᴼ denotes strong stress and ᵛ indicates weak stress; in terms of the present analysis: /stèjbilajzéjʃən/)? The same applies to, for example, *unsatisfactory* (Arnold p. 241: ᴼᴼᵛᴼᵛᴼ; my analysis: /ə́n+sàtisfáktəri/) and *inadmissibility* (Arnold p. 255: ᴼᵛᴼᵛᴼᵛᴼ; my analysis: /ìnədmisəbíliti/, or, more slowly, /ín+ədmìsəbíliti/). Only instrumental research and listening tests can answer the question.

However, even if we are prepared to admit the possibility of postulating two degrees of stress only, viz. stress and no stress, the following points should be noted.

(1) If we consider for instance *ambulance, advantages* as having the stress patterns /ámbjuláns/, /ədváhntidʒíz/, as Arnold does,[2] we shall have to rework our analysis of the syllable peak system and have to consider [ə] a vowel phoneme contrasting

---

[1] Arnold also uses another procedure for discovering the stress categories: he tries to 'neutralize the effects of pitch phenomena by seeking to identify our stress degrees by, and to correlate them with, other speech phenomena that have as close a relation to stress and produce as strong a linguistic effect as does pitch.' This phenomenon which he uses for reference is 'the rhythm pattern that accompanies the word or utterance' (p. 227). Since Arnold does not define what rhythm is, i.e. its physical and/or physiological correlates, and since it does not emerge how he actually compares the syllable which carries the intonation centre with other syllables, it is impossible to evaluate this procedure.

[2] *Op.cit.* p. 397. The phonemic transcription is mine. Arnold bases his stress analysis on the phonemic analysis which is reflected in D. Jones's *English Pronouncing Dictionary*.

with [ʌ], since the basis for considering them allophonic variants of the same phoneme has been the fact that [ʌ] always occurs under (primary or secondary) stress, whereas [ə] is never stressed (p. 84 n. 2). However, it does not seem necessary to postulate any occurrence of stress on [ləns] or [ɪz]. If the English-speaking linguist feels that there is a greater 'push' on this syllable, it is because of the prevailing rhythmic pattern of English, which avoids two successive rhythmically weak syllables (or two successive strong ones) utterance-finally.[1] Between the points of stress incidence every other syllable may, to an English ear, but not necessarily to the ears of people with a different linguistic background, have some greater prominence. This prominence is, however, a sub-phonemic feature of the utterance, not comparable to the greater prominence of the last syllable of *reading-room*. The stress difference between the last syllables of *reading-room* and *ambulance* or *advantages* (all have, according to Arnold, the same stress pattern: *réading-róom, ámbulánce, advántagés*) is just as great as the stress difference between the last syllables of *ball-room* or *bullfinch* and *silence* or *office* (according to Arnold, apparently *báll-róom, búllfinch* vs. *sílence, óffice*: p. 400). It seems better to analyse the stress patterns of these words in the following way, accepting the postulation of two degrees of stress only: *réading-róom, ámbulance, advántages, báll-róom, búllfinch, sílence, óffice*.[2]

Thus, if Arnold's analysis of the stress system is to be retained, it seems better to modify it as suggested above.

(2) If pitch is not regarded as one of the features in the manifestation of the stress phonemes, our intonation analysis may be somewhat complicated. It was possible, by taking into account variations conditioned by the intonation pattern, to reduce the number of stress categories from four (Trager and Bloch, Gleason) to three (Hockett, Newman) without such complications (7.421), but any further reduction is more diffi-

---

[1] *Op.cit.* pp. 399–400. I have, of course, left 'rhythm' undefined.
[2] *Báll-room, búllfinch* are possible alternative forms.

cult. In the analysis adopted for this study it is possible to predict the pitch behaviour of the syllables between the occurrence of any phonemic pitch level (PL), but only if the difference between primary and secondary stress is considered contrastive: the pitch pattern is conditioned by the occurrence of *primary* stresses (2.8).

Thus, between two PL's (exclusive of the last PL of an intonation) both of which occur on a syllable with primary stress there is a gradual fall in pitch; but if there are any syllables with primary stress between the two PL's, the gradual fall takes the form of a definite stepping-down on to the stressed syllables. We are therefore able to distinguish between the following utterances of *Mary's run out*:[1]

/³méhriz+rɔ́n+²áwt¹↓/ (i.e., of the room)

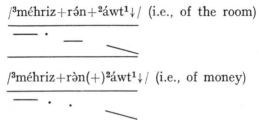

/³méhriz+rɔ̀n(+)²áwt¹↓/ (i.e., of money)

The pitch pattern between the centre PL and the end PL of a macrosegment is also predictable in terms of any primary stresses. For example, in a rising intonation — rising either because the centre PL is lower than the end PL, or because the terminal contour is /↑/ — the pitch remains low till the last primary stress, from which point it rises. There is a contrast between the following utterances:

/³wózitə+¹blák+bə̀hd²↑/ *Was it a black bird?*

/³wózitə+¹blák+bə̀hd²↑/ *Was it a blackbird?*

---

[1] Cf. C. F. Hockett, *A Course in Modern Linguistics* p. 52.

If it is argued that *blackbird* may be /blákbəhd/ here, with no stress on the last syllable, one should notice that *Did John come?* may be said with the same intonation patterns, /³díd+¹dʒón+kə́m²↑/ and /³díd+¹dʒón+kə̀m²↑/, the [ʌ] allophone of /ə/ showing that *come* is not unstressed. Similarly, there is a difference between the two utterances of *I can't make it without eggs*:

(a) /²aj+³káhnt+méjkit+wiðáwt+égz¹↑/

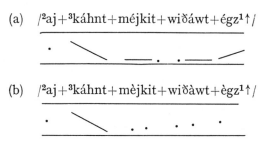

(b) /²aj+³káhnt+mèjkit+wiðàwt+ègz¹↑/

Now, if only *one* stress is postulated, we shall have to account for these differences in pitch behaviour in our *intonation* analysis. We may have to postulate the occurrence of a PL on every syllable which, in the present analysis, is considered to have primary stress. Thus, the difference indicated above might be: (a) /²aj+³káhnt+¹méjkit+wi¹ðáwt+¹égz¹↑/ vs. (b) /²aj+³káhnt+méjkit+wiðáwt+égz¹↑/. However, then we should not be able to define the place of the intonation centre as the last but one PL in a macrosegment, and our description of sub-phonemic, phonologically conditioned pitch behaviour between the PL's would be very complicated. Moreover, this solution is not suited for the explanation of the pitch behaviour *before* the intonation centre: there may be any number of steps down in pitch between two PL's — in terms of the present analysis, any number of primary stresses — and we might have to postulate many more than four contrastive PL's. How, for instance, should we analyse the following utterance?[1]

[1] The example is quoted from L. E. Armstrong and I. C. Ward, *A Handbook of English Intonation* p. 24.

Does this train stop at Clapham Junction?[1]
['dʌz ðɪs 'treɪn 'stɒp ət 'klæpəm 'dʒʌŋkʃn̩]

― · ― ― · ― · ―

(3) If Arnold's analysis is adopted, we shall have to re-interpret the term intonation.

So far, intonation has generally been considered characteristic of the utterance, or phrase, as a whole, not of the lexical items; it has been supposed to suggest the attitude of the speaker, or the relative importance of the various parts of the utterance, or grammatical categories. *Lexically* significant pitch has been dealt with under 'tone' or accentual systems. Cf. K. L. Pike: 'The two most deep-seated characteristics of intonation are (a) the distribution of its contours over phrases, and (b) the addition of shades of meaning to phrases rather than the giving of lexical meaning to words.'[2] 'A tone language may be defined as a language having lexically significant, contrastive, but relative pitch on each syllable ... Pitch is also significant in English, but in English the semantic differential applies to the phrase as a whole, constituting a shade of meaning rather than a dictionary or lexical meaning.'[3]

However, some of the phenomena which Arnold wants to include in the intonation system are characteristic of the lexical units called words.[4] *Blackbird* can only be ['blæk͵bɜ•d];

---

[1] The objections raised in (2) apply at least to RP and to Cockney. They are probably also valid, in part at least, for other dialects of English. For the gradual stepping down between two PL's, see K.L. Pike, *The Intonation of American English* p. 70.

[2] *The Intonation of American English* p. 24 sq.

[3] *Tone Languages* p. 3. According to an oral communication (of 1954) Pike may reconsider his view regarding the tone as tied to the *syllable* rather than the *word*, in order to include languages like Swedish and Norwegian among the tone languages.

[4] The following remarks apply to the words when uttered as isolates, thus as complete utterances with an intonation pattern. However, the different pitch patterns observable in these words in longer utterances

['blæk'bɜ·d] would give another lexical meaning. The particular intonation pattern used may vary, but the intonation centre will always fall on the first syllable of *blackbird* and on the second syllable of *black bird*. Thus, *blackbird* may be

$/^3$blák+bə̀hd^1↓/ or /^{1}blák+bə̀hd^2↑/ or /^{3}blák+bə̀hd^1↑/,

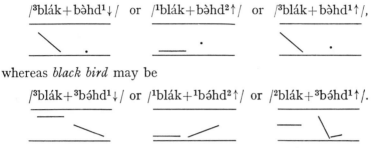

whereas *black bird* may be

$/^3$blák+^{3}bə́hd^1↓/ or /^{1}blák+^{1}bə́hd^2↑/ or /^{2}blák+^{3}bə́hd^1↑/.

In the same way, in *inadmissibility*, which, according to Arnold, is /ínədmísəbílətí/,[1] the intonation centre can fall only on the fifth syllable (except for rare cases of emphatic contrast, for instance, *I said inadmissibility*).

In actual fact, Arnold finds it necessary, for 'purely practical' reasons, to distinguish between two types of strong stress in the discussion of English words, viz. 'tonic strong' and 'nontonic strong'; 'tonic' indicates a stress which coincides with the intonation centre.[2]

may partly be regarded as morphophonemic phenomena, and the difference between such word pairs is retained. Thus, the potential stress on the second syllable of *blackbird* may be absent in longer utterances, but the stress on the last syllable of *black bird* is hardly ever missing.

[1] Cf. particularly *op.cit.* p. 255. In my opinion there is no stress on the last syllable.

[2] *Op.cit.* p. 228. Arnold agrees that the 'tonic strong stress' in English words is 'free', i.e. its position is not phonologically conditioned but is characteristic of each word (*op.cit.* p. 232). We find support for this view in Newman, who declares that 'In English every lexical, derivational and inflective element has stress characteristics as an essential part of its phonetic form. These stress characteristics may vary according to the combinations, morphologic or syntactic, in which the elements occur; nevertheless, it is possible to define the stress patterns applicable to each element and to state the situation in which each pattern appears.' (*op.cit.* p. 171).

(4) It is not the opinion of the present writer that, on the basis of the material presented in (3), English should be classified as a tone language. However, pitch phenomena may well be considered one of the factors which serve to distinguish between three degrees of stress. Other such factors are articulatory force, loudness, and length. Thus, in *unsatisfactory* /ə́n+sàtisfáktəri/, /á/ differs from /à/ in these three respects. Pitch phenomena are of importance in two sub-systems of the English phonemic system, viz. in the stress system as well as in the intonation system. In other parts of our phonemic analysis, too, do we find that one type of phonetic phenomena may have different functions. For example, length is one of the factors which help to distinguish between the syllable peaks of *bit* and *beat*, and it is also a characteristic of certain parts of the intonation pattern (3.052). Hockett's definition of stress, 'an accentual system in which the differences are *largely* in relative loudness or prominence is called a stress system' (italics mine),[1] does not preclude pitch as one of the factors.[2]

(5) In such contrastive differences as those indicated above a bundle of various phonetic phenomena are involved, closely interwoven, such as vocoid quality, length, loudness, pitch, and juncture. There is more than one way of sorting these factors out. Thus, if more vowel contrasts are postulated we may perhaps do with fewer stress contrasts (cf. particularly the distribution of [ʌ] and [ə]). And if many contrastive degrees of stress are postulated our intonation analysis may be simplified. In fact, R. Kingdon refuses to distinguish clearly between a stress

---

[1] *A Course in Modern Linguistics* p. 47.

[2] Although Arnold rejects using only articulatory force as a criterion for determining the stress categories (*op.cit.* pp. 224–8), this seems, in Arnold's view, after all to be the only physical/physiological correlate to stress, apart from the undefined 'rhythm', for he deplores that 'most times recognition of any stress type results, not from an accurate assessment of articulatory force alone, but from the interplay of this force and other, non-stress factors.' As examples of such 'non-stress criteria' he mentions 'pitch and vowel quality' (*op.cit.* p. 227).

system and an intonation system; he suggests how closely interwoven they are by using one set of symbols to indicate both.[1]

When this is the situation, it seems impossible, and useless, to go hunting for any one 'correct' phonemic analysis. Our choice of analysis will, among other things, depend on our general approach and personal preferences. For the reasons suggested above the present analysis has adopted a system of three contrastive degrees of stress.[2]

7.423. Definition

No rigorous definition of stress is attempted for the purposes of this analysis. It is assumed that there is such a phonological phenomenon, and that it is paralleled by certain features of the articulatory, auditory, and acoustical aspects of speech in terms of which it can be defined. These physical/physiological correlates are a bundle of various phonetic phenomena. Articulatory force and loudness are two important factors in the manifestation of stress; others are length, pitch, and vocoid quality.

7.43. Intonation

The Hockett—Gleason—Smith type of intonation analysis, which I have adopted for this study (2.8), is not incompatible with the description of English intonation made by other phoneticians.

K. L. Pike's analysis in *The Intonation of American English* is very similar to Hockett's. At least as far as his 'simple rhythm unit' is concerned, his 'total contour' covers Hockett's macrosegment, his 'primary contour' corresponds to the utterance

---

[1] *The Groundwork of English Stress* and *The Groundwork of English Intonation.*

[2] For the possibility of several different phonemic analyses of a language, see 7.11.

chunk between the centre and the end of the intonation, and his 'precontour' covers the syllables before the centre. However, there are also 'complex rhythm units', containing several total contours. Hockett probably accounts for the same material partly by means of his fourth PL occurring between the beginning and the centre, partly by means of the TC / | /, which seems to have no parallel in Pike's system. Pike's two 'pauses', 'tentative' and 'final', which occur at the end of a rhythm unit, parallel Hockett's TC's /↑/ and /↓/. In his *Language* § 9.32 Pike modifies his analysis somewhat. The 'emic stress group' or 'abdomineme' parallels rather closely Hockett's macrosegment.

The traditional analysis of RP intonation in terms of different 'tunes'[1] is also convertible to a Hockett-type analysis. The 'fall' (Armstrong and Ward's 'Tune I') is a falling centre pitch level (PL_c) and end PL (PL_e) sequence followed by /↓/ or / | /, or a sequence of identical PL's followed by /↓/. The 'rise' ('Tune II') is a rising PL_c PL_e sequence followed by /↑/ or / | /, or a sequence of identical PL's followed by /↑/. The 'fall-rise' ('Tune II with emphasis') is a falling PL_c PL_e sequence followed by /↑/. Kingdon's contrast, in 'The Teaching of English Intonation', between 'high prehead' and 'low prehead' is accounted for in terms of the PL at the beginning of the macrosegment, and his 'head' is the second PL of an intonation of four (or more) PL's. The intonation analysis adopted for teaching purposes at the Department of Phonetics, University College London, in terms of five tunes, the low fall, the high fall, the low rise, the high rise, and the fall-rise, plus various kinds of 'prehead', 'head', and 'body', is still more easily reducible to a system of a limited number of PL's and TC's, and so is Kingdon's more elaborate analysis in

---

[1] See especially L. E. Armstrong and I. C. Ward, *A Handbook of English Intonation;* W. S. Allen, *Living English Speech;* R. Kingdon, 'The Teaching of English Intonation' and *The Groundwork of English Intonation;* H. E. Palmer, *English Intonation with Systematic Exercises.*

The Groundwork of English Intonation. For teaching purposes the University College—Kingdon approach may be preferable.[1]

The University College—Kingdon analysis seems to be an adaptation and a further development of H. E. Palmer's theory: there are four 'nucleus tones' (falling, high-rising, falling-rising, and low-rising) and four kinds of 'heads' (inferior, superior, scandent, and heterogeneous). It may be somewhat difficult to accommodate the 'scandent head' in a system of PL's and TC's. However, it is possible that the scandent head is not contrastively different from the superior head: Palmer states that 'The significative difference between a superior and a scandent head is not great.'[2]

---

[1] The University College material is available only in mimeographed form as handouts to the students.

[2] *English Intonation* p. 18.

Bibliography

The following is a list of the publications referred to in this study:

Allen, W. Stannard, *Living English Speech*, Longmans, Green and Co., London—New York—Toronto 1954.

Andrésen, Bjørn Stålhane, '*-dier* and *-deer;* ən iksperimənt', *Le Maître Phonétique* 3rd series No. 108 (1957) pp. 35–7.

— 'The Glottal Stop in the Received Pronunciation of English', *Universitetet i Bergen, Årbok 1958*, Historisk-Antikvarisk Rekke, No. 5, Bergen 1958.

Armstrong, Lilias E., and Ward, Ida C., *A Handbook of English Intonation*, 2nd ed., W. Heffer and Sons, Cambridge 1949.

Arnold, G. F., 'Stress in English Words', *Lingua* 6 (1957) pp. 221—67, 397—441.

Bloch, Bernard, and Trager, George L., *Outline of Linguistic Analysis*, Linguistic Society of America, Baltimore 1942; *see also* Trager, George L.

Bloomfield, Leonard, *Language*, Henry Holt and Co., New York 1933.

— 'The Stressed Vowels of American English', *Language* 11 (1936) pp. 97–116.

Borgstrøm, Carl Hj., *Innføring i sprogvidenskap*, Oslo University Press, Oslo 1958.

Christophersen, Paul, 'The Glottal Stop in English', *English Studies* 33 (1952) pp. 156–63.

Cohen, A., *The Phonemes of English*, Martinus Nijhoff, The Hague 1952.

Dieth, Eugen, *Vademekum der Phonetik*, A. Francke A. G. Verlag, Berne 1950.

Fant, C. Gunnar M.: *see* Jakobson, Roman.

Fischer-Jørgensen, Eli. *Almen Fonetik*, Copenhagen 1951 (1954), mimeographed.

Franklyn, Julian, *The Cockney. A Survey of London Life and Language*, Andre Deutsch, London 1953.

Gimson, A. C., 'Implications of the Phonemic/Chronemic Grouping of English Vowels', *Acta Linguistica* 5 (1945–9) pp. 94–100.

Gleason, H. A., Jr., *An Introduction to Descriptive Linguistics*, Henry Holt and Co., New York 1956.

Green, Harriet C.: *see* Potter, Ralph K.

Halle, Morris: *see* Jakobson, Roman.

Harris, Zellig S., 'From Morpheme to Utterance', *Language* 22 (1946) pp. 161–83.

— *Methods in Structural Linguistics*, The University of Chicago Press, Chicago 1951.

Haugen, Einar, and Twaddell, W. Freeman, 'Facts and Phonemics', *Language* 18 (1942) pp. 228–37.

Heffner, R-M. S., *et al.*, 'Notes on the Length of Vowels', *American Speech* 12 (1937) pp. 128–34, 15 (1940) pp. 74–9 and 377–80, 16 (1941) pp. 204–7, 17 (1942) pp. 42–8, 18 (1943) pp. 208–15.

Heffner, R-M. S., 'A Note on Vowel Length in American Speech', *Language* 16 (1940) pp. 33–47.

Hockett, Charles F., *A Manual of Phonology*, Memoir 11 of the *International Journal of American Linguistics* 21 (1955) No. 4.

— *A Course in Modern Linguistics*, The Macmillan Company, New York 1958.

International Phonetic Association, *The Principles of the International Phonetic Association*, University College, London 1949.

Jakobson, Roman, Fant, C. Gunnar M., and Halle, Morris, *Preliminaries to Speech Analysis*, Technical Report No. 13, Acoustics Laboratory, Massachusetts Institute of Technology, Cambridge, Mass. 1952.

Jassem, W., *Fonetyka języka angielskiego*, Warszawa Pánstowow Wydawnietwo Naukowe, Warsaw 1954.

Jones, Daniel. 'Chronemes and Tonemes', *Acta Linguistica* 4 (1944) pp. 1–10.

— *The Phoneme. Its Nature and Use*, W. Heffer and Sons, Cambridge 1950.

— *An English Pronouncing Dictionary*, 11th ed., Everyman's Reference Library, J. M. Dent and Sons, London 1956.

— *An Outline of English Phonetics*, 8th ed., W. Heffer and Sons, Cambridge 1956.

— *The Pronunciation of English*, 4th ed., Cambridge University Press, Cambridge 1956.

Jones, Lawrence Gaylord, 'English Consonantal Distribution', *For Roman Jakobson*, Mouton and Co., The Hague 1956, pp. 245–53.

Joos, Martin, *Acoustic Phonetics*, Supplement to *Language* 24 (1948) No. 2.

Josephs, J.: *see* Ross, A. S. C.

Kenyon, John S., *American Pronunciation*, 9th ed., Wahr, Ann Arbor 1945.

Kenyon, John S., and Knott, T. A., *A Pronouncing Dictionary of American English*, Merriam Company, Springfield, Mass. 1944.

Kingdon, Roger, 'The Teaching of English Intonation', *English Language Teaching* 2 (1948) pp. 85—91, 113—21, 141—7; 3 (1948) pp. 11—9.

— *The Groundwork of English Intonation*, Longmans, Green and Co., London—New York—Toronto 1958.

— *The Groundwork of English Stress*, Longmans, Green and Co., London—New York—Toronto 1958.

Knott, T. A.: *see* Kenyon, John S.

Kopp, George A.: *see* Potter, Ralph K.

Kurath, Hans, 'Mourning and Morning', *Studies for William A. Read*, Louisiana State University Press, Louisiana 1940, pp. 166–72.

— 'The Binary Interpretation of English Vowels. A Critique', *Language* 33 (1957) pp. 111–22.

Lawrenson, A. C., 'Some Observations on the Phonology of the English Vowels', *Proceedings of the 2nd International Congress of Phonetic Sciences*, Cambridge University Press, Cambridge 1936, pp. 131–4.

Malone, Kemp, 'The Phonemic Structure of English Monosyllables', *American Speech* 11 (1936) pp. 205–18.

— 'Phonemes and Phonemic Correlations in Current English', *English Studies* 18 (1936) pp. 159–64.

— 'The Phonemes of Current English', *Studies for William A. Read*, Louisiana State University Press, Louisiana 1940, pp. 133–65. A revised edition appeared in K. Malone, *Studies in Heroic Legend and in Current Speech*, ed. by Stefán Einarsson and Norman E. Eliason, Rosenkilde and Bagger, Copenhagen 1959, pp. 226–67.[1]

Matthews, William, *Cockney Past and Present*, George Routledge and Sons, London 1938.

Merlingen, W., 'Zur Phonologie der englischen Diphthonge und langen Vokale', *Acta Linguistica* 6 (1950–1) pp. 87–93.

Newman, Stanley S., 'On the Stress System of English', *Word* 2 (1946) pp. 171–87.

Nida, Eugen A., 'The Analysis of Grammatical Constituents', *Language* 24 (1948) pp. 168–77.

— *Morphology*, 2nd ed., University of Michigan Press, Ann Arbor 1949.

[1] According to the editors, the author had revised the article 'rather drastically' for the 1959 edition. It came into my hands too late for a careful comparison with the original edition. However, unless otherwise specified the references to this article apply to both editions.

O'Connor, J. D., *New Phonetic Readings from Modern English Literature*, Bibliotheca Anglicana, A. Francke A. G. Verlag, Berne 1948.
— 'RP and the Reinforcing Glottal Stop', *English Studies* 33 (1952) pp. 214–8.
— and Trim, L. J. M., 'Vowel, Consonant, and Syllable — a Phonological Definition', *Word* 9 (1953) pp. 103–22.
Oftedal, Magne, *The Gaelic of Leurbost*, Supplement 4 of *Norsk Tidsskrift for Sprogvidenskap*, Oslo 1956.
Palmer, Harold E., *English Intonation with Systematic Exercises*, 2nd ed., W. Heffer and Sons, Cambridge 1924.
Pike, Kenneth L., *Phonetics; a Critical Analysis of Phonetic Theory and Technic for the Practical Description of Sounds*, University of Michigan Press, Ann Arbor 1943.
— 'Taxemes and Immediate Constituents', *Language* 19 (1943) pp. 65–82.
— *The Intonation of American English*, University of Michigan Press, Ann Arbor 1945.
— 'On the Phonemic Status of English Diphthongs', *Language* 23 (1947) pp. 151–9.
— *Phonemics; a Technique for Reducing Languages to Writing*, University of Michigan Press, Ann Arbor 1947.
— *Tone Languages*, University of Michigan Press, Ann Arbor 1948.
— *Language in Relation to a Unified Theory of the Structure of Human Behavior*, Parts I–II, Preliminary Edition, Summer Institute of Linguistics, Glendale, California 1954.
Potter, Ralph K., Kopp, George A., and Green, Harriet C., *Visible Speech*, D. Van Nostrand Company, New York 1947.
Proceedings of the Eighth International Congress of Linguists, Oslo University Press, Oslo 1958.
Ross, A. S. C., and Josephs, J., 'Triangular Tables for the Phonemes of English', *Archivum Linguisticum* 1 (1949) pp. 41–3.
Sapir, Edward, 'The Psychological Reality of Phonemes', *Selected Writings of Edward Sapir in Language, Culture and Personality*, ed. David G. Mandelbaum, University of California Press, Berkeley and Los Angeles 1951, pp. 46–60.
Shaw, George Bernhard, *Works*, Standard edition, Constable and Company, London 1931.
Smith, Henry Lee, Jr., *Linguistic Science and the Teaching of English*, Harvard University Press, Cambridge, Mass. 1956; *see also* Trager, George L.
Swadesh, Morris, 'The Vowels of Chicago English', *Language* 11 (1935) pp. 148–51.

Swadesh, Morris, 'On the Analysis of English Syllabics', *Language* 23 (1947) pp. 137–50.

Sweet, Henry, *A New English Grammar Logical and Historical*, Part I, Clarendon Press, Oxford 1891.

— *Elementarbuch des gesprochenen Englisch*, 3rd ed., Clarendon Press, Oxford 1904.

— *A Primer of Spoken English*, 4th ed., Clarendon Press, Oxford 1911.

— *The Sounds of English*, 2nd ed., Clarendon Press, Oxford 1929.

Trager, George ¦L., and Bloch, Bernard. 'The Syllabic Phonemes of English', *Language* 17 (1941) pp. 223–46; *see also* Bloch, Bernard.

Trager, George L., and Smith, Henry Lee, Jr., *An Outline of English Structure* (= *Studies in Linguistics*, Occasional Papers No. 3), Battenburg Press, Norman, Oklahoma 1951.

Trim, L. J. M.: *see* O'Connor, J. D.

Trnka, B., *A Phonological Analysis of Present-Day Standard English*, *Studies in English* 5, Facultas Philosophica Universitatis Carolinae Pragensis, Prague 1935.

Troubetzkoy, N. S., *Principes de phonologie*, Librairie C. Klincksieck, Paris 1949.

Trubetzkoy, N. S., *Grundzüge der Phonologie*, *Travaux du Cercle Linguistique de Prague* 7, Prague 1939.

Twaddell, W. Freeman: *see* Haugen, Einar.

Uldall, Hans Jørgen, 'On the Structural Interpretation of Diphthongs', *Proceedings of the 3rd International Congress of Phonetic Sciences*, Ghent 1939, pp. 272–6.

Vachek, J., 'Über die phonologische Interpretation der Diphthonge mit besonderer Berücksichtigung des Englischen', *Studies in English* 4 (1933) pp. 87–170.

Vogt, Hans, 'Some Remarks on Norwegian Phonemics', *Norsk Tidsskrift for Sprogvidenskap* 11 (1939) pp. 136–44.

Ward, Ida C., *The Phonetics of English*, 4th ed., W. Heffer and Sons, Cambridge 1948; *see also* Armstrong, Lilias E.

Weinreich, Uriel, *Languages in Contact*, Publications of the Linguistic Circle of New York, No. 1, New York 1953.

Wells, Rulon S., 'Immediate Constituents', *Language* 23 (1947) pp. 81–117.

Whorf, Benjamin Lee, 'Linguistics as an Exact Science', *The Technology Review* 43 (1940), Massachusetts Institute of Technology, Cambridge, Mass. 1940.

Wyld, Henry Cecil, *A History of Modern Colloquial English*, 3rd ed., Basil Blackwell, Oxford 1936.

Appendix: Texts

With the exception of 'Memories of the War', the following texts were transcribed from tape recordings made in the homes of the informants and at the social settlement. Pp. 233—40 were transcribed from a disc recording made in the laboratory of the Department of Phonetics, University College London; the informant did not seem to be too much embarrassed by the unusual surroundings.

The texts appear with the grammatical inconsistencies and discontinuities observable in the recordings. Only a few repetitions, short interrupted sentences, and hesitation noises are left out, as well as a few short passages where the voice is drowned by extraneous noise.

The first line of every triplet gives the utterance in normal orthography, the second line is a phonetic transcription, and the third line is a phonemic interpretation of the material.

Phonetic Transcription

In order to facilitate the reading and the understanding of these transcribed texts I have listed below the phonetic symbols used for the allophonic variants of the syllable peaks and of a few consonants. The vocoid variants of the sequence syllable peak + pre-junctural or pre-consonantal /l/ are also added; it is to be understood that /l/ may also be manifested by a lateral.

/i/	[ɪ]		/oj/	[ɔĭ ɔ°ĭ]
/il/	[ĭɤ̆]		/ojl/	[ɔɜ̆ɤ̆ ɔĭɤ̆]
/ih/	[ɪɜ̆]		/ow/	[ɒʊ̆ ɒ·]
/ihl/	[ĭ·ɤ̆]		/owl/	[ɔŏ]
/ij/	[ɜ̆i ĭi i·]			
/ijl/	[i·ɤ̆]		/u/	[ʊ ü]
			/ul/	[ʊ̰ŭ ʊ̰·]
/e/	[e eə eⁱ]		/uh/	[ʊɜ̆ üɜ̆]
/el/	[ĕɤ̆]		/uw/	[ɜ̆ü ʊ̆ü ü· u·]
/eh/	[eɜ̆]		/uwl/	[ʊ̰·ŭ ɜ̆ʊ̰ŭ]
/ej/	[æĭ ɛĭ ęĭ æ·]			
/ejl/	[æ̆ɜ̆ɤ̆ æ̆ĭɤ̆]		/ə/	[ʌ ə]
/a/	[ɛ æ ɛᵉ ɛⁱ]		/əl/	[ʌɤ̆]] ̱ ɤ̆]
/al/	[æ̆ɤ̆ ä̆ɤ̆]		/əh/	[ɜ· ɜɜ̆]
/ah/	[ɑ· ɑɜ̆]		/əhl/	[ɜ̱ɤ̆]
/ahl/	[ɑɤ̆]		/əw/	[œʊ̆ œ̈ʊ̆ œ̈]
/aj/	[ɑĭ ɑ°ĭ ɑə ɑ·]		/əwl/	[ɔ̰ŏ ɔ̆ŏ]
/ajl/	[ɑɜ̆ɤ̆ ɑĭɤ̆]			
/aw/	[ɛ̰ɜ̆ ɛʊ̆ ɛ·]		/p/	[p p']
/awl/	[aɔ̆]		/t/	[t t' tʰ tˢ t̪ ?]
			/k/	[k k' kˣ]
/o/	[ɔ ɔə ɔ°]		/d/	[d dᶻ]
/ol/	[ɒɔ̆]		/l/	[l ɫ ɤ̆ ŭ ŏ ŭ]
/oh/	[ɔɜ̆ ɔ· ɔ°ɜ̆]		/r/	[r ɾ]

/h/   pre-vocalically [h], post-vocalically [ɜ̆ ·]
/j/   pre-vocalically [j ç], post-vocalically [ĭ ɜ̆ ·]
/w/   pre-vocalically [w], post-vocalically [ʊ̆ ɜ̱̆ ü ·]

Only one phonetic symbol is used for each of the other consonant phonemes, and this symbol is the same as the phonemic one: /b g f θ s ʃ v ð z ʒ m n ŋ/. However, /ð/ may be manifested in the dental quality of the preceding segment, for example [n̪] = /nð/, and a nasal consonant may be manifested in the nasality of the preceding segment, for instance [ĩ] =

/in/. The unstressed vowel /ə/ may be manifested in the syllabicity of the following segment, for example [n̩] = /ən/, and [ɤ] = /əl/.

The length mark, [·], may be added to or omitted from any symbol for the peak variants.

Not all of these variants occur in the particular texts transcribed here.

For an understanding of the exact value of these symbols the reader is referred to the detailed description of syllable peaks and margins in §§ 3 and 4.

There is no indication in the phonetic transcription of minor variations of the syllable peaks such as labialization and centralization (see e.g. 3.11 for /i/), nor of the voicelessness of phonemically voiced consonants in certain contexts (4.051) or of the particularly open quality of unstressed /ə/ before a pause (3.612).

A raised vocoid symbol is used (1) for the slight off-glide observable in some simple peaks, e.g. [eⁱ] = /e/, [ɛᵉ] = /a/, and (2) to indicate a slight hesitation noise when the informant pauses in the middle of a macrosegment, for example [ɛndᵊ] = /and+/. The more prominent on- or off-glide which forms part of a complex peak, or of the sequence peak + pre-junctural /l/, on the other hand, is indicated by a letter written on the line, but with the mark of non-syllabicity above it; thus, [æɪ̯] = /ej/, [ɜ̃i̯] = /ij/.

In the sequence VCV the consonant is ambi-syllabic. When there is a stress on the second vowel, I have adopted the convention of placing the stress or intonation mark *before* the consonant, since it would be awkward to put it *above* the letter. Thus, [ˈʃʌˈt̯ʌp] /ʃə́təp/ *shut up*, [fɪˈlʌp] /filə́p/ *fill up*, [əˈrḛ̃nd] /əráwnd/ *around*. Such a transcription should not be interpreted as showing a syllable cut after the vowel, however (cf. 2.4, 2.5). The same argument applies to the placement of /l/ and /r/ after the terminal contour / | / (cf. 4.4221).

A question mark, ? , in the phonemic transcription suggests that the author is unable to make a phonemic interpretation, or that the sounds observed cannot be considered manifestations of phonemes on this level of analysis.

Intonation Transcription

In the *phonetic* transcription, the intonation and the stress pattern is indicated by one set of symbols. This is, in a slightly simplified and modified form, the system used by R. Kingdon.[1] Only five 'tunes' (Kingdon: 'tones') are indicated, viz. high-falling ['], low-falling [ˌ], high-rising ['], low-rising [ˌ], and falling-rising [ˇ]. These symbols occur at the intonation centre only. The fall-rise may be 'divided' [' ˌ].[2] ['] is put before any other syllable with primary stress, and secondary stress is indicated by means of the mark [ˌ].

Thus, the high-placed stress-mark ['] does not always suggest high pitch: it may be low-pitched in the tail of an intonation ([ɪts ə'blɛk 'bɜ·d] /its+ə³blák+bə́hd¹↓/ *It is a black bird*) or in a low head ([ˈwɔts ðə ˈmɛtʰə] /¹wóts+ðə⁴mátə¹↓/ *What is the matter*) or between the two parts of a divided fall-rise. In this respect the transcription given here differs from Kingdon's.

The symbol [⁻] suggests a high prehead, and [↑] denotes a stepping up in pitch, instead of the customary stepping down, in the body of the intonation. A vertical line, [|], shows the end of an intonation (macrosegment). The interruption of an intonation is marked by a raised *.

For the meaning of the terms prehead, head, body, and tail, see R. Kingdon, *op.cit.* Kingdon uses the term nucleus for that part of the intonation which is here called intonation centre.

In the *phonemic* transcription an attempt is made to interpret the material in terms of four pitch levels and three terminal contours. As pointed out in 2.8, this is a tentative interpretation only. Four PL's and three TC's do account for all the contrastive intonation patterns I have come across. However, I am not in a position to rule out the possibility of describing the data in terms of fewer units.

---

[1] *The Groundwork of English Intonation.*
[2] *Op.cit.* p. 10.

Memories of the War

(EE in conversation with ES)

Well,	*Eva,*	*there is*	*one*	*thing*	*stands*	*out in*	*my*
[ˈwɛɫ	ˈi•və|	ðəz	ˈwʌn	ˈθɪŋ	ˈstɛ•nz	ˈɛ̠ə̆ʔn̩	ˈmɑ•
/³wél+	íjvə¹↓	²ðəz+	³wə́n+	θíŋ+	stánz+	áwtən+	máj+

memory.	*Er* —	*it was on a*	*Sunday*	*night.*	*I can*
ˌmemrɪ|	ərə•	ɪtwəzɔnə	ˈsʌndɪ	ˌnɑ•ə̆ʔ|	ɑ•kən
¹mémri²↑	?	²itwəzonə+	³sə́ndi+	²nájt¹↓	²ajkən+

remember	*it*	*as*	*plain*	*as*	*anything.*	*Er* —	*suddenly*
rəˈmembrɪtəz		↑ˈplæɪ̆nəz	ˌenɪθɪŋk|			ərə•	ˈsʌdn̩lɪ
rə³mémbritəz+		³pléjnəz+	²éniθiŋk¹↓			?	³sə́dənli+

the warning	*went,*	*and* —	*no*	*sooner*	*the warning*
ðəˌwɒŭnɪn	ˌwentˢ|	ˌɛnd	ˈnœŭ	ˈsü•nə	ðə↑ᵛwɒŭnɪn
ðə¹wównin+	wènt²↑	²ànd+	³nə́w+	súwnə+	ðə³wównin+

went,	*so*	*the bombs*	*started*	*dropping.*	*Well,*	*I* —
ˌwent|	ˌsœŭ	ðəˈbɔmz	ˈstɑ•ʈɪd	ˈdrɔpɪn|	ˌwɛɫ|	ˈɑ•ĭ
wènt¹↑	²sə̀w+	ðə³bómz+	stáhtid+	drópin¹↓	²wél¹↓	³áj+

I	*turned the*	*light*	*out,*	*and*	*I*	*pulled*	*the curtain*
ˈɑĭ	ˈtˢɜ•ndðə	ˌlɑɪtʰ	ˌɛ̠ə̆tʰ|	ˌɛnd	ɑĭ	ˈpu̠ɫd	ðəˈkɜ•ʔn̩
³áj+	tə́hndðə+	¹lájt+	àwt²↑	²ànd+	aj+	³púld+	ðəkə́htən+

aside	*and*	*looked*	*out*	*the back*	*window.*	*So*	*I*
əˌsɑ•ĭd|	ən	ˌlʊkt	ˌɛ̠ə̆t|	ðəˈbɛk	↑ˈwɪndə|	ˌsœŭ	ˈɑĭ
ə¹sájd¹↑	²ən+	¹lúkt+	àwt²|	²ðə²bák+	³wíndə¹↓	²sə̀w+	³áj+

turned   *round,*   *and I said*   *to my*   *husband,*   *'Oh,*
‚tˢɜ·nd   ‚re̯ə̯n| ŋɑ·   'sed   tʰʊmɑ̯ĭ   ‚ʌzbənd| 'ɔ·
¹tə́hnd+   ràwn²| ²ənaj+   ³séd+   tumaj+   ¹ə́zbənd²| ³óh+

Jack,'   *I said,*   *'it is raining fire.'*   *So — so he said,*
‚dʒæk   ɑ̯ĭ‚sed| ɪts   'ræɪnɪn   ↑'fɑ·ĭə| ‚sœʊ   ‚sœʊi·   ‚sedᵓ
²dʒák+   ajsèd¹| ²its+   ²réjnin+   ³fájə¹↓   ²sə̀w+   sə̀wij+   sèd+

What is wrong with you?   *Gone*   *mad?'*   *So I said,*   *'Yes*
'wɒts   ‚rɒŋ   wɪðjü· | 'gɒ̯ʊn   ‚me·ᵉdᶻ| ‚sœʊɑ̯·sed   'jes|
³wóts+   ²róŋ+   wɪðjuw¹| ³gówn+   ¹mád²↑   ²sə̀wajsed+   ³jés¹|

come and have a look,   *quick!'*   *So he looked.*   *He did not*
'kʌmən   'ɛvə   ‚lʊk| ‚kwɪk| 'sœʊi·   ‚lʊktʰ| hi·'dɪdn̩
³kə́mən+   ávə+   ²lúk¹↓   ²kwík¹↓   ³sə́wij+   ¹lúkt²↑   ²hij³dídən+

say nothing.   *So*   *I*   *opened† the front door and*
‚sæĭ   ‚nʌθɪŋ| ‚sœʊ   'ɑ̯ĭ   ‚œʊpn̩ə   ‚frʌnt   ‚dɔ·| ən
sèj+   ¹nə́θiŋ²↑   ²sə̀w+   ³áj+   əwpənðə+   ¹frə́nt+   dòh²| ²ən+

running up the street.   *So I said,*   *'Look, quick!*
'rʌnɪn   'ʌp   ðə‚strĭitʰ| ‚sœʊɑ̯·‚sedᶻ   'lʊk   'kwɪk|
³rə́nin+   ə́p+   ðə¹stríjt²↑   ²sə̀wajsèd+   ⁴lúk+   ⁴kwík¹↓

The streets are alight.   *The houses are alight.'*   *So*
ðə'stri·ts   ərə'lɑ̯ĭt| ðĭ'e̯ə̯zɪz   ərə'lɑ̯ĭtʰ| ‚sœʊ
²ðə⁴stríjts+   ərəlájt¹| ²ði³áwziz+   ərəlájt¹↓   ²sə̀w+

I said,   *'Isn't it terrible!'*   *So he come in, and*
ɑsed   'ɪnɪt   ‚tʰerəbɤ| sœʊ   i·   'kʌm   ‚ɪn| ən
ajsed+   ³ínit+   ²térəbəl¹↓   ¹səw+   ij+   ³kə́m+   ¹ín²↑   ²ən+

just as he come in I saw one fall right
'dʒʌstəz   'i·   kə‚mɪn| 'ɑ̯ĭ   ‚sɔ·   ‚wʌn| ‚fɒ̯ʊ   ‚rɑ̯ĭt|
³dʒə́stəz+   íj+   kə¹mín²| ³áj+   ¹sóh+   wə̀n²| ¹fów+   ràjt²|

down,   *right*   *the side of our window.*   *Right*
'de̯ə̯n| 'rɑ·t   ðə'sɑ̯ĭdə‚ve̯ʊ̯ə   ↑'wɪndə| 'rɑ·ʔ
⁴dáwn¹↓   ³rájt+   ðəsájdəvàwə+   ⁴wíndə¹↓   ³rájt+

† [n̩] is syllabic.

in the corner of the window it was.   *And — the moment it*

ŋðə'kŏŭnərəv   ðə͵wɪndərɪt   ͵wɔz| ənd°   ðə'mœŭmṇtʰɪtʰ

ənðəkównərəv+   ðə¹wíndərit+   wòz²↑   ²ənd+   ðə³máwməntit+

fell,   *the flames*   *shot*   *up,*   *quite*   *six*   *feet*

͵fëɣ̌| ðə'flɛĭmz   ↑'ʃɔtʰ   ͵ʌ•p| 'kwa̰ĭt   'sɪks   'fi•t

¹fél²↑   ¹ðə²fléjmz+   ³ʃót+   ²áp²↑   ³kwájt+   síks+   fíjt+

high.   *My*   *husband*   *and*   *the man*   *next*   *door*

↑ᵛha̰•ĭ| 'ma̰ĭ   ͵ʌzbən| ənd   ðə'mɛn   ͵neks   ͵dɔ•ɔ̌|

³háj¹↑   ³máj+   ¹ázbən²↑   ²ənd+   ðə³mán+   nèks+   ¹dóh²↑

and   *my*   *intended*   *son-in-law*   *rushed*   *round*   *and*

ən   'ma̰ĭ   ɪn'tˢendɪd   ͵sʌnɪn͵lɔ̰ɔ̌| 'rʌʃt   ͵rḛɔ̌nd| ənd°

²ən+   ³máj+   inténdid+   ¹sáninlòh²| ³ráʃt+   ¹ráwnd²↑   ²ənd+

put   *sand*   *on*   *it,*   *and*   *eventually*   *they got it*   *out.*

'pʊt   ͵sɛ•ndɔnɪʔ| ən   'ventʃəli   ðɛĭ'gɔ̰ṭɪt   ↑'ɛ̰ə̰tʰ|

³pút+   ¹sándonit²↑   ²ən+   ³véntʃəlij+   ðejgótit+   ³áwt¹↓

Well,   *he*   *come*   *in,*   *and — he*   *come*   *in,*   *and he*

͵wëɣ̌| 'i•   ͵kʌm   ͵ɪn| ənd°   'i•   ͵kʌm   ͵ɪn| ṇi•

²wél¹↓   ³íj+   kəm+   ¹ín²↑   ²ənd+   ³íj+   kəm+   ¹ín²| ²ənij+

went   *ba —**   *then he went*   *back again,*   *and he said,*

'went   'bɛ| ͵ðeni•   'went   ͵bækə͵gæĭn| ṇi•   ͵sed°

³wént+   bá| ²ðènij+   ³wént+   ¹bákəgèjn²↑   ²ənijsèd+

'I want to make   *sure it is out.'*   *So*   *he*   *bent*

a̰ĭ'wɔnṭə   'mæĭk   'ʃɔ•rɪts   ͵ɛ̰ə̰tʰ| sœŭ   'i•   ͵bentˢ

aj³wóntə+   méjk+   ʃóhrits+   ²áwt¹↓   ²səw+   ³íj+   bènt+

over it —   *Well,*   *just as*   *he went*   *to make*   *sure it*

↑ᵛœŭvərɪt| ͵wëɣ̌| 'dʒʌstəz   i•'went   tə͵meĭk   'ʃɔ•rɪt

³áwvərit¹↑   ²wél¹↓   ³dʒástəz+   ijwént+   təmèjk+   ʃóhrit+

was   *out,*   *so*   *this*   *thing blasted,*   *and*   *he got*

wəz   ͵ɛ̰ə̰ʔ| ͵sœŭ   'ðɪs   ͵θɪŋ   ↑'bla•stɪd| ən   i•͵gɔʔ

wəz+   ²áwt²↑   ²səw+   ³ðís+   θìŋ+   ³bláhstid¹↓   ²ən+   ijgòt+

the whole full blast.   It   was   marvellous   that he
ði'ɔ̆ŏ   'fʊ̆ŭ   ˌblɑ·st| ɪʔ   wəz   'mɑ·vələs   ðəʈi·
ðij³ɔ́wl+   fúl+   ²bláhst¹↓   ²it+   wəz+   ³máhvələs+   ðətij+

was   not   killed   instantly.   Well   anyway,   the two
↑'wɔzən   ↑'kɨ̆ɫd   ↑'ɪnstəntlɔ̆i| we'lenɪˌwæ·ɪ̆| ðə'tˢü·
³wózən+   ³kíld+   ³ínstəntlij¹↓   ²we³léniwèj¹↓   ²ðə³túw+

men   running   round   the Mildmay   for first   aid.
'men   'rʌnɪn   'rḙ̄ə̃n   ðəˌmɑ·ˌmæ·ɪ̆| fə'fɜst   ˌæɪ̆d|
mén+   rə́nin+   ráwn+   ðə¹máhmèj²↑   ²fə²fə́hst+   ¹éjd²↑

And — while   they was round   the Mildmay for first aid —
ənd³   'wɑ̱ɪ̆ɫ   ðɛɪ̆wəz   'rḙ̄ə̃n   ðə'mɑ·mæɪ̆   fə'fɜst   ˌæɪ̆d|
²ənd+   ³wájl+   ðejwəz+   ráwn+   ðəmáhmej+   fəfə́hst+   ¹éjd²↑

of   course   they was dropping the heavy stuff   as well —
əv   'kɒ̆ŭs   ðɛɪ̆wəz   ↑'drɔpɪn   ðɪ'evɪ   'stʌf   əz↑ᵛwëɤ̆|
²əv+   ³kóws+   ðejwəz+   ³drópin+   ðiévi+   stə́f+   əz³wél¹↑

a bang   come   at   the door.   Er — 'All   you   people
ə'bæŋ   'kʌm   ət   ðəˌdɔ·ɔ̆| ərə·   'ɒ̆ŭ   jü   'pi·pɤ
²ə³báŋ+   kə́m+   ət+   ðədóh¹↑   ?   ³ów+   juw+   píjpəl+

get out   within   ten   minutes,   because   there is
ge'ʈḙ̄ə̃ʔ   wɪˌdɪn³   ↑'tʰen   ˌmɪnɪts| bɪˌkɔz   ðəˌrɪz
getáwt+   wiðìn+   ³tén+   ²mínits¹↓   ²bikòz+   ðərìz+

a landmine   dropped on   St. Hilda's.'   St. Hilda's
ə'lɛ·nˌmɑ·ɪ̆n| 'drɔpt   ɔn   sən↑'tʰɪ̆ɤ̆dəz| sən'tʰɨ̆ɫdəz
ə³lán+   màjn¹↑   ²drópt+   on+   sən³tíldəz¹↓   ²sən³tíldəz+

is a — belongs   to Cheltenham   College.   And
'ɪzə   bl̩↑'ɔŋz   tʰʊ't ʃëɤ̆ʔɳəm   ↑'kɔlɪdʒ| ˌɛnd³
ízə+   bə³lóŋz+   tutʃéltənəm+   ³kólidʒ¹↓   ²ànd+

so of course,   they   said,   'If you do not get out   within
ˌsœ̆ŭə'kɒ̆ŭs| ðæɪ̆   ˌsed   ɪfjü'dœ̆ŭn   ge'ʈḙ̄ə̃ʔ   wɪðɪn
səwə³kóws¹| ²ðej+   sèd+   ifju³də́wn+   getáwt+   wiðin+

ten	minutes,	it	might	go	up	and you'll	all†
'tˢen	ˌmɪnɪts|	ɪt	'mɑ͡ɪ?	gœ	'ʌp	ənjü↑'rọ̆ʊ	
tén+	¹mínits²↑	²it+	³májt+	gəw+	ə́p+	ənju³rów+	

go	up.'	So	my	sister	come	running	round,
gœ	'ʌp|	ˌsœŭ³	'mɑ͡ɪ	'sɪstə	'kʌm	ˌrʌnɪn	ˌrẹ̃nd^z|
gəw+	ə́p¹↓	²sə̀w+	³máj+	sístə+	kə́m+	rə̀nin+	¹ráwnd²↑

and	—	we	found	our	bags,	and	our	belongings,
ɛnd³		wɪ	'fẹ̃nˌdẹ·ə̃	ˌbɛ·gz|		ən	ˌɛə̃	bɪˌlɔŋɪnz|
²and+		wi+	³fáwndàw+	¹bágz²↑		²ən+	àw+	bi¹lóŋinz²↑

and	we	all	started	walking	up	Bethnal	Green
ˌɛn	wɪ'ọ̆ʊ	'stɑ·t̬ɪd	'wọ̆ʊkɪn	'ʌp	'beθnɣ	ˌgrĭin	
²àn+	wi³ów+	stáhtid+	wówkin+	ə́p+	béθnəl+	grìjn+	

Road.	I	looked	this	side	and	that	side,	and
ˌrœŭd|	ɑ͡ɪˌlʊkt	ˌðɪs	ˌsɑ·ɪ̆d|	ən	ˌðet	ˌsɑ·ɪ̆d|	ən	
¹rə́wd²↑	¹ajlùkt+	¹ðís+	sàjd²↑	¹ən+	¹ðát+	sàjd²↑	²ən+	

everywhere	you	looked	so	it	was	fires.	But
'evrɪ	'weə̌	jü'lʊkt	sœŭ	ɪ?	wəz	↑'fɑ·ɪ̆əz|	ˌbʌtˢ
³évri+	wéh+	juwlúkt+	səw+	it+	wəz+	³fájəz¹↓	²bə̀t+

the thing	struck	me	most	was	— as	the men	was
ðə'θɪŋ	'strʌk'	mi	ˌmœŭstʰ|	wəz	'ɛz	ðə'men	wəz
ðə³θíŋ+	strə́k+	mij+	¹mə́wst²↑	²wəz+	³áz+	ðəmén+	wəz+

putting	out	the	fires	everything	seemed	so	quiet
'pʊ?n̩	'ẹ̃ə̃?	ðəˌfɑ·əz|		'evrɪθɪŋk	'si·md	↑'sœŭ	ˌkwɑ·ə?|
pútən+	áwt+	ðə¹fájəz²↑		³évriθiŋk+	síjmd+	³sə́w+	¹kwájət²|

and silent.	They	seem(ed)	not††	seem	to be	making	no
n̩'sɑ·ə̌lən|	ðæɪ̆	'si·mn̩		'si·m	tʰəbɪ'mæɪ̆kn̩	↑'nœŭ	
²ən³sájlən¹|	²ðej+	²síjmən+		síjm+	təbiméjkən+	³nə́w+	

noise.	They	was	just	putting	them	out	quite
ˌnɔɪ̆z|	ðɛɪ̆wəz	'dʒʌst	'pʊ?n̩əm	'ẹ̃ə̃t	↑'kwɑ͡ɪt		
¹nójz²|	²ðejwəz+	³dʒə́st+	pútənəm+	áwt+	³kwájt+		

† /r/ instead of /l/: a slip of the tongue? But see also p. 254 n.
†† A slip of the tongue for *did not*?

naturally.   *And — and then — as*   *we was*   *going*

ˌnɛt ʃəlӟi| ɛndᵊ   ɛnˌðen   'ɛz   wiwəz   'gœŭɪn

²nát ʃəlij¹↓   ²and+   anðèn+   ³áz+   wijwəz+   gə́win+

along   *we started*   *singing — well, I started*   *singing,*

əˌlɔŋ| wɪ'stɑ·tɪd   'sɪŋɪn   we↑'lɑ·ĭ 'stɑ·tɪd 'sɪŋɪn

ə¹lóŋ²↑   ²wi²stáhtid+   síŋin+   we³láj+ stáhtid+ síŋin+

'Fire,   *fire,*   *fire!*   *Get a bucket of water!*   *There is a fire*

↑'fɑ̲·ə   'fɑ·ə   ˌfɑ·ə| ⁻get̲ə'bʌkɪt̲əˌwǫŭtʰə| ðəzə'fɑ̲·ə

³fájə+   fájə+   ¹fájə²| ³getə²bə́kitə¹wówtə²| ¹ðəzə²fájə+

down   *below.'*   *We used to sing that round*   *St. Hilda's.*

'de̲̲ə̲n   bɪ↑'lœŭ| wi'jü·stə   ˌsɪŋðɛt| 're̲̲ə̲n   sn̩'ĭ̆ðəz|

dáwn+   bi³lə́w¹↓   ²wij³júwstə+¹síŋðat²| ²ráwn+   sə³níldəz¹↓

So — anyway,   *just at*   *that*   *minute*   *I*   *looked up,*

ˌsœŭ   'enɪˌwæĭ| 'dʒʌstət   'ðɛt   ˌmɪnɪtʰ| 'ɑĭ   ˌlʊkˌtˢʌp'|

²sə̀w+   ³éniwèj¹↓   ³dʒə́stət+   ðát+   ¹mínit²↑   ³áj+   lùk¹tə́p²↑

and I   *give*   *one*   *shriek.*   *So*   *my*   *sister*   *said,*

ə'nɑĭ   'gɪv   'wʌn   ↑'ʃrĭik| ˌsœŭ   'mɑĭ   'sɪstə   'sed

²ə³náj+   gív+   wə́n+   ³ʃríjk¹↓   ²sə̀w+   ³máj+   sístə+   séd+

'What   *is*   *wrong*   *with*   *her?'*   *So*   *I said,*   *'Look!*   *Quick!'*

↑'wɔts   'rɔŋ   wɪˌðɜ·| sæ̈   ɑ̲·ˌsed   'lʊk| 'kwɪk|

³wóts+   róŋ+   wi²ðə́h¹↓   ²səw+ ajsèd+   ³lúk²| ³kwík¹↓

So   *she said,* --- *'That*   *will not hurt you.'*   *So I said,*

ˌsœŭ   ʃɪsed   'ðɛt   ˌwœŭn   ˌə·tçə| ˌsœŭɑ̲·ˌsed

²sə̀w+   ʃised+   ³ðát+   ¹wə́wn+ əhtjə²↑   ²sə̀wajsèd+

'Oh,'   *I said,*   *'it*   *will.'*   *So — I*   *said,*   *'What is it?'*

'ɔ·   ɑ̲·ˌsed| ɪt   ᵛwĭð| ˌsœŭ   ɑ̲·   sed   'wɔˌtɪzɪt|

³óh+   ajsèd¹| ²it+   ³wíl¹↑   ²sə̀w+   aj+   sed+   ³wó²tízit¹↓

So   *she said,*   *'Oh,*   *it is only the*   —'   *The picture*

ˌsœŭ   ʃɪˌsed   'œŭ| ɪt'sœŭni   ˌði·ᵊ   ðə↑'pɪktʃə

²sə̀w+   ʃisèd+   ³ə́w¹| ²it³sə́wnij+   ðìj+   ðə³píkt ʃə+

post had caught fire, and that hoarding right
ˌpœʊ̆st əd ˈkǫʊ̆t ˏfɑ̠•ɪ̆ə| ⁻ɛnðɛˈt̬oʊ̆dɪn ˈrɑ̠ɪ̆ʔ
pə̀wst+ əd+ kówt+ ^{1}fájə^{2}↑ ^{3}anða^{2}tówdin+ rájt+

the top had got loose, and the wind had
ðə↑ᵛt^{s}ɔ•p| ɛd^{zə} ˈgɔʔ ˏlʊ̆üs| ən ðəˈwɪndəd
ðə^{3}tóp^{1}↑ ^{2}ad+ ^{3}gót+ ^{1}lúws^{2}↑ ^{2}ən+ ðə^{3}wíndəd+

carried it† *right up in the air, and it was spinning*
↑ˈkɛrɪdɪdɪt ↑ˈrɑ̠ɪ̆ˈt̬ʌpʼ n̥ði ˎeə̆| rənɪt wəz ˈspɪnɪɪn
^{3}kárididit+ ^{3}rájtəp+ ənðij+ ^{2}éh^{1}| ^{2}rənit+ wəz+ ^{2}spíniin+

round and round and round, and to my
↑ˈrɛ̠ə̠̆ndən ˈrɛ̠ə̠̆ndən ↑ᵛrɛ̠ə̠̆nd| ən t^{h}ʊˈmɑ̠•ɪ̆
^{3}ráwndən+ ráwndən+ ^{3}ráwnd^{1}↑ ^{2}ən+ tu^{3}máj+

*imagination I thought it was a German bomb —**
ɪ↑ᵛmɛdʒɪˌnæɪ̆ʃən| ˈɑ̠ɪ̆ ˈθǫ•t^{h} ɪtwəzə ↑ˈdʒɜ•mən ↑ˋbɔm|
i^{3}mádʒinèjʃən^{1}↑ ^{3}áj+ θówt+ itwəzə+ ^{3}dʒə́hmən+ ^{4}bóm^{1}|

German parachute coming down, and that is
ˈdʒɜ•mən ↑ˋpɛrəˌʃü•t ˌkʌmɪn ˈdɛ̠ə̠̆n| ən ˈðɛts
^{3}dʒə́hmən+ ^{4}párəʃùwt+ kə̀min+ dáwn^{1}↓ ^{2}ən+ ^{3}ðáts+

what terrified me. So of course, they all
ˈwɔt ↑ˋt^{h}erɪˌfɑ̠•ɪ̆d mə̆i| sœʊ̆ əˋkǫʊ̆s| ⁻ðɛɪ̆ ˈǫʊ̆
wót+ ^{4}téri+fàjd+ mij^{1}↓ ^{2}səw+ ə^{3}kóws^{2}| ^{3}ðej+ ^{2}ów+

roared alaughing, and we laughed and laughed till we got
ˈrǫ•d əˏlɑ•fɪn| ɛn ˈwi• ˈlɑ•ft^{h}ən ˈlɑ•ft t^{h}ɪ̈ɤ̆wɪˈgɔʔ
róhd+ ə^{1}láhfin^{2}↑ ^{2}an+ ^{3}wíj+ láhftən+ láhft+ tilwigót+

to the rest centre. Well, the woman in there, I
təðə↑ˋrest ˌsent^{s}ə| ˎwɛ̈ɤ̆| ðəˈwʊmənɪn ↑ᵛðe•ə̆| ˈɑ̠ɪ̆
təðə^{3}rést+ sèntə^{1}↓ ^{2}wél^{1}| ^{2}ðə^{3}wúmənin+ ^{3}ðéh^{1}↑ ^{3}áj+

think she thought we had all gone crackers, because
ˈθɪŋk ↑ˈʃi• ˈθǫʊ̆t ↑ˈwi•d ˈǫʊ̆ ˌgǫʊ̆n ˋ↑krɛkəz| bəkəz
θíŋk+ ^{3}ʃíj+ θówt+ ^{3}wíjd+ ów+ gòwn+ ^{4}krákəz^{1}↓ ^{2}bəkəz+

† A slip of the tongue for /káridit/ ?

240 COCKNEY PHONOLOGY

everybody   else   was   crying,   and all us   lot   laughing.
'evribɔdi   ‚ëɤ̈s   wəz   ‚krɑ·ɪn| ə'nọ·'lʌs   'lɔ?   ↑'lɑ·fɪn|
³évrijbodij+   èls+   wəz+   ¹krájin²| ²ə³nówləs+   lót+   ³láhfin¹↓

So —   well   anyway,   the lady   (took   down)   our   names
‚sœŭ   we'lenɪ‚wæ·ɪ̆| ðə'læɪ̆di↑'   – – – –   ɛ̰ə̰   'næɪ̆mz
²sə̀w+   we³léniwèj¹↓   ²ðə²léjdij+³   – – – –   aw+   néjmz+

and addresses,   and   — and our   —   identification
ənə‚dresɪz| ənd⁹   ə‚nɛ̰ŭə   'ɑ̰ɪ̆‚dentfɪ‚kæɪ̆ʃən
ənə¹drésiz²↑   ²ənd+   ənàwə+   ³áj+dènt+fi¹kéjʃən+

numbers.   So   she said,   'Do   you   want   something   to eat
‚nʌmbəz| ‚sœŭ   ʃɪ‚sed⁹   djü'wɔnt   'sʌmθɪn   tʰʊ'i·?
nəmbəz¹↑   ²sə̀w+   ʃisèd+   djuw³wónt+   sə́mθin+   tuíjt+

and drink?'   So   we said   yes,   but   we did   not.
ŋ‚drɪŋk| ‚sœŭ   wɪ'sed   ‚je·s| bə?   wɪᵛdɪ?ŋ̩|]
ən¹dríŋk²↑   ²sə̀w+   wi³séd+   ¹jés²| ²bət+   wi³dítən¹↑/

A Guide to London

(MM in conversation with ES)

I	*buy*	*books*	*down*	*the*	*lane.*	*We*	*can*	*buy*
[aɪˠbɑɪ	ˌbʊks|	'deːə̯n	ðəↅ'læɪn|			'wiˑ	kən'bɑɪ	
/²aj³báj+	bùks²ↅ	²dáwn+	ðə³léjn¹↓			³wíj+	kənbáj+	

a	*lot*	*of*	*books*	*down*	*Brick*	*Lane.*	- - - -	*Yes.*	*Have*	*you*
əↅˠlɔțə	ˌbʊks	ˌde̱ːə̯n	brɪk	ˌlæɪn|				'jɜˑs|	ˌɛvjü	
ə³lótə+	bùks+	dàwn+	brik+	lèjn¹ↅ				³jə́hs¹↓	²àvjuw+	

been	*down*	*in*	*Brick*	*Lane,*	*Cheshire*	*Street,*	*on*	*a*
'biˑn	'de̱ːə̯nɪn	ˌbrɪk	'læɪn	ˌtʃeʃəstriˑt|			ŋə	
³bíjn+	dáwnin+	brìk+	léjn+	¹tʃéʃəstrìjt²ↅ			²ənə+	

Sunday morning?
'sʌndɪ 'mɔ̝ˑnɪn\|
³sə́ndi+²mównin³ↅ

(ES: I have been to Petticoat Lane, of course.)

No,	*that*	*is*	*not*	*it.*	*No.*	*You*	*go*	*down*
ˌnœ̆ŭ	ˠðets	ˌnɔțɪʔ|			'nœˑŭ|	jü'gœŭ		'de̱ːə̯n
²nə̀w+	³ðáts+	nòtit¹ↅ			³nə́w¹↓	²juw³gə́w+		dáwn+

Brick	*Lane,*	*on*	*a*	*Sunday,*	*and*	*you*	*go*	*the*	*second*
'brɪk	ˌlæˑɪn|	ɔnəˌsʌndɪ|			ənjüˌgœŭ			ðə'sekən	
brík+	¹léjn²ↅ	²onə¹sə́ndij²ↅ			²ənjuwgə̀w+			ðə³sékən+	

turning	*down*	*Brick*	*Lane.*	*Turn*	*left.*	*You*	*see*
't͡ˢɜˑnɪn	'de̱ːə̯n	brɪk	ˌlæɪn|	't͡ˢɜˑn	ˌleftʰ|	jüˌsiˑ	
tə́hnin+	dáwn+	brik+	²léjn¹↓	³tə́hn+	²léft¹↓	²jusìj+	

Will	*Winkle*	*stall*	*on*	*the*	*corner,*	*a*	*Winkle*	*stall.*
wɪˠ	'wɪŋkˠ	'stɔ̝ˑ|	lɔnðəˌkɔ̝ŭnə|			ə'wɪŋkˠ	ˌstɔ̝ŭ|	
wil+	³wíŋkəl+	stów¹|	¹lonðə²kównə¹↓			²ə³wíŋkəl+	stòw¹↓	

You	*go*	*through*	*there,*	*and*	*you*	*see*	*all*	*the*	*hawkers*
jü'gœŭ	'θrüˑ	ˌðeˑə̯|		ənjüˌsi		'ɔ̝ŭði	'ɔ̝ŭkəz		
²ju³gə́w	+θrúw+	¹ðéh²ↅ		²ənjusìj+		³ówðij+	ówkəz+		

selling   their   clothes.   *You   know.*   *Not   only   hawkers,*
↑'selɪnðeə̆   ˌklœŭz| ˉjü ˌnœ•ŭ| 'nɔʔ   œŭnlɪ   ↑'ǫŭkəz|
³sélinðeh+   ²klə́wz¹↓   ³juw¹náw¹↑   ³nót+   əwnli+   ³ówkəz²|

or   cheap   jacks,   and   all   the   rest   of   it.   *Well,   it   is*
ˌǫ•   't∫i•p   'dʒæks   ə↑'nǫ•ɫ   ðəˌrestʰɔvɪʔ| wɪts
²òh+   ³t∫íjp+   dʒáks+   ə³nówl+   ðə²réstovit¹↓   ²wits+

a   real   good   sight   for   you   to   see.
ə'rïš̆   ˌgʊd   'sɑ̤ĭt   fə↑ᵛjü•tʰə•si•|
ə³ríl+   gùd+   sájt+   fə³júwtəsìj¹↑

(ES: I thought the whole thing was one great market, really.)

No,   no,   Petticoat   Lane   is different altogether.
'nœ•ŭ| 'nœ•ŭ| ᵛpeṭɪkœŭʔ   ˌlæĭn| ɪz`dɪfrən| 'ǫ•ɫ   tə↑'geðə|
⁴náw¹↓   ³náw¹↓   ³pétikəwt+   lèjn¹↑   ²iz³dífrən²| ²ówl+tə⁴géðə¹↓

Petticoat   Lane   goes   into — right   into   Aldgate,
'peṭɪkœŭʔ   ˌlæĭn| 'gœŭz   ˌɪntˢü•   ↑'rɑ̤ĭʔ   ˌɪntˢü   ↑ᵛǫŭˌgæĭʔ|
³pétikəwt+   lèjn²| ²gə́wz+   ìntuw+   ²rájt+   ìntuw+   ³ówgèjt²↑

into   Whitechapel.   And then   you   can   turn   right
ɪntˢü•   'wɑ̤ĭt'ˌt∫æpš̆| ən ̦ðen   jükən   ᵛtˢɜ•n   ˌrɑ•ĭʔ|
²intuw+   ²wájtt∫àpəl³↑   ²ənðèn+   juwkən+   ³tə́hn+   ràjt¹↑

and   go   to   Houndsditch,   or   turn   left,   and   go
əŋ ̦gœŭ   tˢʊ'ɛ•ə̠nzdɪt∫| ǫ•   'tˢɜ•n   ˌleftʰ| əŋ ̦gœŭ
²əŋgə̀w+   tu²áwnzdit∫³↑   ²oh+   ³tə́hn+   ¹léft¹↑   ²əŋgə̀w+

into   Mile   End.   See,   you   go   right   into   Mile   End.
ɪntˢʊ   'mɑ̤ə̆↑'lend| ˌsi•   jügœŭ   'rɑ̤ĭt   ɪntˢʊ   ↑'mɑ̤ə̆↑'lend|
intu+   ³máj⁴lénd¹↓   ²sìj+   juwgəw+   ²rájt+   intu+   ³máj⁴lénd¹↓

You   go   into Bow,   and   all   that   way.   That
jü ̦gœŭ   ɪntˢə'bœ•ŭ| ə ̦nǫ•ɫ   'ðæt   ˌwæĭ| 'ðæt
²juwgə̀w+   intə³báw²| ²ənòwl+   ³ðát+   wèj¹↓   ³ðát+

leads you right   to Bow,   on the left.   And on the right
'li•dʒü   ↑'rɑ̤ĭt   tˢü ̦bœ•ŭ| ɔnðəˌleftʰ| ə'nɔn   ðəˌrɑ•ĭʔ|
líjdʒuw+   ⁴rájt+   tuw²báw¹↓   ¹onðə²léft²↑   ²ə³nón+   ðə¹rájt¹↑

will	*take*	*you*	*to*	*Houndsditch,*	*Threadneedle*	*Street,*
ˌ'tˢæĭkjü	tˢü·	ˌe̠̬nzdɪ·tʃ		‑θred,ni·dɫ	ˌstri·tʰ	
²əl+	²téjkju+	tuw+	¹áwnzditʃ²↑	²θred¹níjdəl+	strìjt²↑

the	*Market,*	*Fenchurch*	*Street,*	*down*
ðə,mɑ·kɪ?|		ˌfentʃɝ·tʃ	ˌstri·tʰ|	'de̠̬n
²ðə¹máhkit²↑		²féntʃəhtʃ+	strìjt²↑	²dáwn+

to	*the*	*Monument,*	*from*	*the Monument*	*over*
tˢüðə,mɔnjuməntˢ|			'frɔm	ðə'mɔnjümənt	'œŭvə
tuwðə¹mónjuwmənt²↑			³fróm+	ðəmónjuwmənt+	ɕwvə+

to	*London*	*Bridge;*	*from*	*London*	*Bridge*	*you*
tˢə'lʌndən	'brɪdʒ|		frəm	'lʌndən	'brɪdʒ|	ˌjü·
təlɕndən+	²brídʒ²↑		²frəm+	³lɕndən+	²brídʒ²↑	²jùw+

can	*go*	*right*	*into*	*Deptford,*	*from*	*Deptford*
kŋ,gœŭ	'rɑ̌ʃ?		ɪntˢʊ	'detfəd|	frəm	'detfəd
kəŋgɕw+	²rájt+		intu+	²détfəd²↑	²frəm+	³détfəd+

to	*Lewisham,*	*from*	*Lewisham*	*to*	*Catford,*	*from*
tʰʊ'lü·ɪʃəm|		frəm	'lü·ɪʃəm	tˢü·	'kɛt'fəd|	frəm
tu²lúwiʃəm²↑		²frəm+	³lúwiʃəm+	tuw+	²kátfəd²↑	²frəm+

Catford	*to*	—	*Catford*	*to Bromley,*	*and then*	*Bromley*
'kɛt'fəd	tˢü·	↑'kɛt'fəd	tˢü·'brɔmlɪ|		ənðen	'brɔmlɪ
³kátfəd+	tuw+	³kátfəd+	tuw²brómli²↑		²ənðen+	³brómli+

to Bow.	*Yes,*	*you can go all*	*that*	*way.*	*Oh,*
tˢʊ↑'bœŭ|	'jɝ·s|	jükŋ,gœŭ 'ʊ̣̌	'ðæt	↑ᵛwæ·ĭ|	'œŭ|
tu⁴báw¹↓	³jɕhs¹↓	²jukəŋgɕw+ ³ów+	ðát+	³wéj¹↑	³ɕw¹|

it	*goes*	*a long*	*way*	*round.*
ɪt	ˌgœŭz	ə'lɔŋ	'wæĭ	↑'re̠̬nd|]
²it+	gɕwz+	ə³lóŋ+	wéj+³ráwnd¹↓/	

244 COCKNEY PHONOLOGY

Concerts

(MM in conversation with ES)

When I was twelve years of age,   *I used to*
[we'nɑ̆ĭ wəz ↑'twëÿv 'jɜ•zəv ˌæɪ̆dʒ| ɑ̆ĭ,jü•stə
/¹we²náj+ wəz+ ³twélv+ jə́hzəv+ ²éjdʒ¹↓ ²ajjùwstə+

sing at concerts. – – – –   *That was benefits.*
'sɪŋ ət ↑'kɔnsəts| '∂ætwəz ↑'benəfɪts|
²síŋ+ ət+ ³kónsəts¹↓ ²∂atwəz+ ³bénəfits¹↓

They called them benefits.   *And say, like a woman's*
–∂ɛĭ'kǫ•ɫdəm ˌbenəfɪts| ən 'sæĭ lɑ̆ĭkə ↑'wʊmənz
³∂ej²kówldəm+ ²bénəfits¹↓ ²ən+ ³séj+ lajkə+ ³wúmənz+

husband was to die, or the — wife died.
'Pʌzbən wɔz tʰə̩dɑ•ĭ| ɔ• ∂i• 'wɑ̆ĭf 'dɑ•ĭd|
ə́zbən+ woz+ tə²dáj¹↓ ²oh+ ∂ij+ ³wájf+ dájd¹↓

The man's got some children to bring up.   *Well,*
∂ə'mɛ•nz 'gɔt səm ↑'tʃĭÿdrən tˢə̩brɪŋ 'ʌp| wëÿ
²∂ə³mánz+ gót+ səm+ ³tʃíldrən+ təbrìŋ+ ə́p¹↓ ²wel+

they'd have a concert.   *Costermongers would have a*
∂ɛĭ'dævə ˌkɔnsət| ᵛkɔstə̩mʌŋgəz| wʊ̩dævə
∂ej³dávə+ ²kónsət¹↓ ³kóstəmə̀ŋgəz¹↑ ²wudàvə+

concert. Well, they would have turns,   *you know,*
'kɔnsətʰ| wëÿ ∂ɛĭ̩dæv 't̩ˢɜ•nz| ¬jü̩nœŭ|
³kónsət¹↓ ²wel+ ∂ejdàv+ ³tə́hnz¹↓ ²juw¹náw¹|

to sing and that. Professionals. And I was only
tʰə'sɪŋ ən̩∂ɛt| prə'feʃɳᴙz| ən 'ɑ̆ĭ wə↑'zœŭnlɪ
²tə³síŋ+ ən∂àt¹| ²prə³féʃənəlz²↓ ²ən+ ²áj+ wə³záwnli+

about twelve. And I had a strong voice, and they
ə̩bḛ̄t 'twëÿv| ə̩nɑ̆ĭ ædə 'strɔŋ ˌvɔĭs| ən̩∂æĭ
əbàwt+ twélv¹↓ ²ənàj+ adə+ ³stróŋ+ ²vójs¹↓ ²ən∂èj+

used	*to*	*teach*	*me*	*songs,*	*you*	*know,*	*and*	*I*
jüˑst	tʰə'tʰiˑtʃ	miˑ		ˌsɔŋz|	⁻jüˌnœʊ̆|		əˌnɑ̰ĭ̯
juwst+	tə³tíjtʃ+	mij+		¹sóŋz¹↑	²juw¹nə́w¹↑		²ənàj+

used	*to*	*go*	*there*	*and*	*sing*	*twice.*
jüˑstʰə'gœʊ̆			'ðeə̆rən		'sɪŋ	ˌtwɑ̰ĭ̯s|
juwstə³gə́w+			ðéhrən+		síŋ+	²twájs¹↓

(ES: Where?)

In	*this*	*beer*	*shop,*	*upstairs*	*in*	*the*	*beer*	*shop,*
'ɪnðɪs		ˌbɪə̆ˌʃɔp|		'ʔʌp	'steə̆z	ɪnðə̆ˌbɪə̆ʃɔp|
³índis+		¹bíhʃòp²↑		³ə́p+	stéhz+	inðə¹bíhʃop²↑

in	*a*	*big*	*hall.*	*They*	*call*	*it*	*a*	*'lead'.*	*You*	*know,*
ɪnə'bɪg			ˌo̰ˑʊ̆|	ðɛĭ̯'ko̰ʊ̆lɪt'	ə↑'liˑd|		⁻jü'nœʊ̆
²inə³bíg+			²ów¹↓	¹ðej²kówlit+	ə³líjd¹↓		³juw²nə́w+

a	*benefit,*	*a*	*lead.*	*Well,*	*they*	*have*	*songs.*	*And* —
ə↑'benəfɪt|		əˌliˑd|		wɛ̆ɣ̆	ˌðæĭ̯ev	'sɔŋz|	ɛnə
ə³bénəfit¹↓		²ə²líjd¹↓		²wel+	ðèjav+	³sóŋz¹↓	²an+

people	*pay*	*to*	*go*	*in,*	*nearly*	*half*	*a*	*crown*
'piˑpɣ	↑ᵛpæĭ̯	tˢəˌgœʊ̆		ˌɪn|	'nɪə̆li	'ɑˑfə	'krɛ̰g̰n
³píjpəl+	³péj+	təgə̀w+		ìn¹↑	¹níhlij+	áhfə+	kráwn+

or	*two*	*shillings,*	*whatever*	*it*	*is,*	*you*	*know.*	*At*
ə't'üˑ	'ʃɪlɪnz	wɔʔ	'evərɪʔ	'ɪz|	jüˌnœʊ̆|		ɛt
ətúw+	ʃílinz+	wot+	évərit+	²íz²↑	²juw¹nə́w¹↑		²at+

the	*end*	*of*	*the*	*evening*	*they*	*tell*	*you*	*how*	*much*	*they*
ði'end	əvðɪ↑ᵛiˑvnɪn|			ðeĭ̯	't'eljü	'ɛ̰g̰	'mʌtʃ	ðɛĭ̯
ðɪ³énd+	əvði³íjvnin¹↑			²ðej+	³télju+	áw+	mə́tʃ+	ðej+

collected,	*for*	*you,*	*like,*	*if*	*you*	*was*	*the*	*wife,*
kl̩↑'ektˢɪd|	⁻fəˌjüˑ	ˌlɑ̰ĭ̯k|	⁻ef'jüˑ	wəzðəˌwɑ̰ĭ̯f|
kə³léktid¹↓	³fə²júw+	làjk¹|	³ef²júw+	wəzðə²wájf¹|

or	*the*	*husband.*	*I*	*sing*	*for*	*nothing,*	*and*	*the*	*people*
ˌɔˑ	ðɪ'ʌzbən|	'ɑ̰ĭ̯	'sɪŋ	fəˌnʌθɪŋk|	ənðə'piˑpɣ
²òh+	ði²ə́zbən¹↓	³áj+	síŋ+	fə¹nə́θiŋk²↑	²ənðə³píjpəl+

get	*money.*	*You*	*know*	*what*	*I*	*mean.*	*So*	*that*
ˌget	ˌmʌnĭi	jüˈnœ̆ʊ	wɔt̪a̰ĭ	ˌmi·n‖			ˌsœ̆ʊ̆ðət'
gèt+	²mánij¹↓	²juw³náw+	wotaj+	¹míjn²↑			²sə̀wðət+

the	*benefit*	*goes*	*to*	*the*	*husband,*	*or*	*the*	*wife,*
ðəˈbenəfɪt	ˈgœ̆ʊz	t̪ˢuðɪ↑ˈʌzbən				ɔ·	ðəˈwa̰·ĭf
ðə³bénəfit+	gáwz+	tuði³ázbən+				oh+	ðəwájf+

whatever	*it*	*may*	*be.*	*And*	*that*	*is*	*how*
wɔ?	↑ˈevərɪ?	ˌmɛĭ	ˌbĭi‖	ən	ˈðɛts	ˈhḛʊ̆
wot+	³évərit+	mèj+	²bíj¹↓	²ən+	³ðáts+	háw+

they	*used*	*to*	*be,*	*years*	*ago.*	*They*	*used*	*to*	*call*	*you*	*a*
ðɛĭˈjü·st̪ʰə	↑ᵛbi·	ˌjɜ·zə̩gœ̆ʊ‖				ðɛĭˈjü·st̪ʰə			ˈkɒ·ljərə
ðejjúwstə+	³bíj+	jə̀hzəgə̀w¹↑				²ðej³júwstə+			kówljərə+

club	*turn.*	*See,*	*they*	*call*	*that*	*the*	*club.*	*Yes.*
↑ˈklʌb	ˌt̪ˢɜ·n‖	si·	ðɛĭˈkɒ·ɫ	ˌðɛt	ðə↑ˈklʌb‖	ˈje·ʒ‖
³kláb+	tə̀hn¹↓	²sij+	ðej³kówl+	ðàt+	ðə³kláb¹↓	³jéh¹↓

And	*—*	*they*	*have*	*these*	*here*	*concerts*	*for*	*years*	*and*
ənd³		ðeĭ	ˌɛv	ˌði·z	ˌɪ·ʒ	ˌkɔnsəts‖			fəˈjɜ·zən
²ənd+		ðej+	àv+	ðìjz+	ih+	¹kónsəts¹↑			²fə³jáhzən+

years.	*They*	*do*	*not*	*have*	*them*	*now,*	*because*	*—*
ˌjɜ·z‖	ðɛĭ	ˈdœ̆ʊn	ˌɛvəm	ˌnḛ·ʒ‖	bɪkɒz
²jáhz¹↓	²ðej+	³dáwn+	àvəm+	¹náw¹↑	²bikowz+

They	*are*	*all*	*finished,*	*I*	*think,*	*now.*
ðɛĭəˈrɒ̆ʊ	↑ᵛfɪnɪʃtʰ	a̰ĭ̩θɪŋk	ˌnḛ·ʒ‖]
ðejə²rów+	³fíniʃt+	ajθìŋk+	nàw¹↑/

Life in London in the Good Old Days

(EC and AP in conversation with ES)

AP: *We*   *lived*   *opposite*   *a person*   *that*   *made*
[wɪ   'lɪvd   'ɔpəzɪtʰ| ə‚pɜ·sən| ðət   'mɛĭd
/²wi+   ³lívd+   ²ópəzit³| ²ə¹pə́hsən²↑   ²ðət+   ³méjd+

baskets   *for Leadenhall Market,*   *to go*   *there*
‚bɑ·skɪts| fə'lednɫ   ‚mɑ·kɪtʰ| tʰə'gœŭ   'ðeə̌
²báhskits¹↓   ²fə³lédnəl+   ¹máhkit¹↑   ²tə³gə́w+   ðéh+

Christmas   *and*   *sell them,*   *for the people to bring*
↑'krɪsməs| ən   'seləm| fɔðə'pi·pɫ   tʰə'brɪŋ
³krísməs¹| ²ən+   ³séləm¹| ²fohðə³píjpəl+   təbríŋ+

the poultry   *in.*   *Well,*   *while*   *they was outside*
ðə‚pɔ̌ŏtrɪ   ‚ɪn| ‚wëɤ̌| 'wa̲ĭɫ   ðɛĭwəz   'ɛ̲t   'sa̲ĭd
ðə²pə́wltri+   ìn¹↓   ²wél¹↓   ³wájl+   ðejwəz+   áwt+   sájd+

their   *door,*   *making*   *these*   *great*   *mats*   *for —*
'ðeə̌   ↑'dɔ·| 'mɛĭkɪn   ði·z| 'greĭt   ↑'mɛts| fɔ·
ðéh+   ³dóh²| ³méjkin+   ðijz²| ²gréjt+   ³máts²| ²foh+

come   *from abroad —*   *sugar,*   *sugar-cane*   *mats,*
'kʌm   frəmə↑'brɔ·ŭd| 'ʃʊgə| 'ʃʊgə   ‚keĭn   ‚mɛts|
³kə́m+   frəmə³brówd²| ³ʃúgə¹↓   ³ʃúgə+   kèjn+   màts¹↓

that   *great*   *wide*   *straw —*
'ðɛt   'greĭt   ↑'wa̲·ĭd   'strɔ·ə̌|
³ðát+   gréjt+   ³wájd+   ³stróh¹↓

EC: *Indians.*
‚ɪndɪənz|
²índiənz¹↓

AP: *Yes,*   *Indian*   *mats.*   *Well,*   *they*   *had*
‚jes| 'ɪndɪən   ‚mɛts| 'wëɫ| ðæĭ   ‚ɛd
²jés¹↓   ³índiən+   màts¹↓   ²wél²↑   ²ðej+   àd+

chairs.   *They*   *used*   *to*   *come*   *outside*   *the*   *door*
'tʃe·ăz| ðæĭ   'jü·st   təˌkʌm   'ɛ̱ə̱t   'sɑ̱ĭd   dəˌdɔə̌|
³tʃéhz¹↓   ²ðej+   ³júwst+   təkə̀m+   áwt+   sájd+   ðə¹dóh¹↑

and   *cut*   *them*   *out,*   *hold*   *them*   —   *I*   *seen them.*
ɛn   'kʌtʰəm   ˌɛ̱ə̱tˢ| 'hɔ̆ŏdəm| ⁻ɑ̱ĭ   ˌsi·nəm|
¹an+   ³kə́təm+   ²áwt¹↓   ²hə́wldəm²↑   ²aj+   ¹síjnəm¹↑

I   *used*   *to watch it.*   *Yes.*   *I*   *used*   *to watch them* —
ɑ̱ĭ'jü·st   təˌwɔtʃɪt| ˌjes| ɑ̱ĭ'jü·st   təˌwɔtʃəm|
²aj³júwst+   tə¹wótʃit¹↑   ²jés↓   ²aj³júwst+   tə¹wótʃəm¹↑

EC: *I've*   *done them.*   *In the gutter.*
     ɑ̱ĭv   'dʌnəm| 'mðə   ˌgʌtʰə|
     ²ajv+   ³də́nəm¹↓   ³ĭnðə+   ²gə́tə¹↓

AP: *On*   *the*   *curb.*   *They*   *bring*   *their*   *chair out*
     'ɔn   ðəˌkɜ·b| ðæĭ   'brɪŋ   ðeə̌   ˌtʃe·ə̌ˌrɛ̱ə̱t|
     ³ón+   ðə²kə́hb¹↓   ²ðej+   ³brĭŋ+   ðeh+   ¹tʃéhràwt¹↑

and   *sit*   *there.*   *They*   *worked*   *out*   *in*   *the gutter,*
ən'sɪt   ˌðe·ə̌| ðæĭ   'wɜ·ktˢ   'ɛ̱ə̱tˢ   ↑'ɪn   ðəˌgʌtˢə|
²ən³sít+   ðèh¹↓   ¹ðej+   ³wə́hkt+   áwt+   ³ĭn+   ðə²gə́tə¹↓

in   *these*   —   *in*   *our*   *turning* —
'ɪn   ˌði·z   ↑'ɪn   ˌɛ̱ə̌   ˌtˢɜ·nɪn|
³ĭn+   ðìjz+   ³ĭn+   àw+   ¹tə́hnin¹↑

EC: *All*   *basket*   *makers*   *around*   *these*   *slums* - - -
     'ɔ·ŭ   ˌba·skɪt   ˌmæĭkəz   ə'rɛ̱ə̱n   ˌði·z   'slʌmz|
     ³ów+   ²báhskit+   mèjkəz+   əráwn+   dìjz+   slə́mz¹↓

AP: *I*   *know*   *the*   *name*   *of*   *the*   *old*   *woman:*
     ɑ̱ĭ   ˌnœŭ   ðə'nɛĭm   əvði·   ↑'ɔ̆ŏłd   ˌwumən|
     ²aj+   nə̀w+   ðə³néjm+   əvðij+   ³ə́wld+   ²wúmən¹↓

Harriet   *Buck.*   *That*   *was*   *the woman*   *that*   *made*
'ærɪət   ˌbʌk| ˌðet   wəzðə'wumən| ðət   ˌmæĭd
³áriət+   ²bák¹↓   ¹ðàt+   wəzðə²wúmən²↑   ¹ðət+   mèjd+

all the Chr-* all the baskets, put the handles
'ʊ̆ðə kr| 'ʊ̆ðə ˌbɑ·skɪts| 'pʊt ði· ˌɛ·ndɫz
³ówðə+ kr| ³ówðə+ ¹báhskits²↑ ³pút+ ðij+ ¹ándəlz+

on. And they do them up in dozens, just
ˌɔn| ɛnæɪ̆ 'dü·əm 'ʌpn̥ ˌdʌzənz| 'dʒʌst
òn¹↑ ¹anej+ ³dúwəm+ ə́pən+ ¹də́zənz¹↑ ³dʒə́st+

before Christmas, on the Christmas Eve. They
bɪ'fɔ· ˌkrɪsməs| ɔn ðə'krɪsməs ˌi·v| ðæɪ̆
bifóh+ ¹krísməs¹↑ ¹on+ ðə²krísməs+ ²íjv¹↓ ¹ðej+

put them all on their arm, and they go up to
ˌpʊṭəm 'ʊ̦·lɔn ˌðeə̆ ᵛhɑ·m| ɛn ðæɪ̆ 'gœʊ̆əp tʰə
pùtəm+ ³ówlon+ ðèh+ ²háhm¹↑ ¹an+ ðej+ ²gə́wəp+ tə+

Leadenhall, in Bishopsgate, and sell them, what
↑ᵛledn̥ˌʊ̦·ɫ| 'ɪn ˌbɪʃəpsˌgeɪ̆t| 'ɛnd ˌseləm| 'wɔt
³lédənòwl¹↑ ³ín+ ¹bíʃəps+gèjt²↑ ³ánd+ ¹séləm¹↑ ¹wót+

the people is going to buy the turkeys what was being
ðə'pi·pɫɪz ↑'gœɪn tˢə'bɑɪ̯ ðə't̩ˢɜ·kɪz ↑'wɔt wəz 'bi·ɪn
ðə²píjpəliz+ gə́win+ təbáj+ ðətə́hkiz+ ²wót+ wəz+ bíjin+

auctioneering.† When they found a turkey sold,
'ʊ̆kʃə ↑'nɪ·ə̆rɪn| 'wen ðeɪ̆ 'fe̯g̑nd ə↑ᵛtˢɜ·kɪ ˌsɔ̆ɔ̆d|
ówkʃə+ ⁴níhrin¹↓ ³wén+ ðej+ fáwnd+ ə³tə́hki+ sə̀wld¹↑

they go up and say, 'Want a basket, sir?' Yes.
'ðæɪ̆ gœʊ̆ 'ʌp ən ˌseɪ̆ ˌwonə 'bɑ·skɪt sə| 'je·s|
³déj+ gəw+ ə́p+ ənsèj+ wònə+ ²báhskit+ sə³↑ ³jés¹↓

And that is how it was done, because I've been
ɛn 'ðets ↑ᵛhe̯g̑ ɪtwəz ˌdʌn| bɪˌkʊ̦·z ɑ̆ɪv 'bi·n
²an+ ³ðáts+ ³háw+ itwəz+ dèn¹↑ ²bikòwz+ ajv+ ³bíjn+

† The speaker gets entangled in her long sentence.

up	there	myself		with	my	husband	every
ˌʌp	'ðeˑᵊ	mɑI̯ˏsĕ̌f‖		wɪð	'mɑˑᵊ	ˌʌzbən‖	'evriˑ
əp+	ðéh+	maj+sélf¹↑		¹wɪð+	²máj+	¹ə́zbən¹↑	³évrij+

Christmas	Eve.	And	he's	bought	a	turkey.
'krɪsməs	ˏiˑv‖	ɛn	'iˑz	'bǫˑŭtʰ	ə'tʰᵊˑǩᵊi‖	
krísməs+	²íjv¹↓	²an+	³íjz+	bówt+	ətə́hkij¹↓	

(ES: Where was this?)

EC: *In   that   old   turning.*

'ɪn   ðæt   'ᵓŏd   ↑'tˢᵊ•nɪn‖
³ín+   ðat+   ᵊwld+   ³tə́hnin¹↓

AP: *In   that old   slum.   You   do not   see them*

'ɪn   ðɛ'ʈᵓŏd   ↑'slʌm‖   jüˑ   'dœŭnt   ˏsiˑəm
³ín+   ðatᵊwld+   ⁴slə́m¹↓   ²juw+   ³də́wnt+   sìjəm+

made   now,   girl.

↑'mæĭd   ↑'nḛ̌ᵊ   ˏgᴀˑ̌ᵊ‖
³méjd+   ³náw+   gə́hl¹↑

EC: *Oh,   you do not   see them   now.   No.   Paper*

'œŭ   jü↑'dœŭnt   ˏsiˑəm   ˏnḛ̌ᵊ‖   'nœˑŭ‖   'pæĭpə
³ᵊ́w+   ju³də́wnt+   sìjəm+   ²náw¹↓   ²nə́w¹↓   ³péjpə+

carriers   now,   all   paper   carriers.

ˏkærɪəz   ˏnḛ̌ᵊ‖   'ǫŭ   'pæĭpə   ˏkærɪəz‖
²káriəz+   nàw¹↓   ³ów+   péjpə+   ²káriəz¹↓

AP: *But   these   were   the   proper   baskets.*

bət   'ðiˑz   wəðə   ↑'prɔpə ˏbɑˑskɪts‖
²bət+   ³ðíjz+   wəðə   ³própə ²báhskits¹↓

(ES: Was this round about here?)

EC: *Yes,   where   we   were   born.*

'jeˑs‖   'weᵊ   wɪ   wə   ˏbǫŭn‖
⁴jés¹↓   ³wéh+   wi+   wə+   ²bówn¹↓

AP: – – – *Well,*   *down*   *that*   *turning,*   *right*
'wë̌| 'dɛ̰g̰n   ðet   ↑'tˢɜ•nɪn| 'rɑɪ̆tˢ
³wél²| ¹dáwn+   ðat+   ³tə́hnin¹↓   ³rájt+

at   the   corner.
ət   ðəˌkɒ̆ŭnə|
ət+   ðə²kównə¹↓

EC: *Right   the   bottom   of   St.   Hilda's.   Do   you   know*
'rɑɪ̆t   ðə'bɔṭəməv   sənˌtˢɪ̆łdəz| ⁻djü•   'nœŭ
³rájt+   ðəbótəməv+   sən²tíldəz¹↓   ³djuw+   ²nə́w+

where   —   Do   you   know   there   is   a   court   there,   called*
ˌweǯ| ⁻djü•   'nœŭ   ðəzə↑'kɒ̆ŭt   ˌðeǯ| ˌkɒ•łd
wèh+| ³djuw+   ²nə́w+   ðəzə³kówt+   ðèh¹| ²kòwld+

Bonnet   Box   Court,   right   the   bottom   of   St.
'bɔnɪt   'bɔks   ˌkɒ̆ŭtˢ| 'rɑɪ̆t   ðə'bɔtʰəm   əv   səntʰ
³bónit+   bóks+   ²kówt¹↓   ³rájt+   ðəbótəm+   əv+   sənt+

Hilda's,   and   leading   out   into   Shoreditch.   Well,
ˌɪ̆łdəz| ən   'li•dɪn   'ɛg̰t   n̩tʰəˌʃɒŭdɪtʃ| wë̌
²íldəz¹↓   ²ən+   ³líjdin+   áwt+   əntə²ʃówditʃ¹↓   ²wel+

that   is   where   we   were   born,   just   past   that
'ðets   'weǯ   'wi•   wəˌbɒ̆ŭn| ⁻dʒəst   'pɑ•st   ðet
³ðáts+   wéh+   wíj+   wə²bówn¹↓   ³dʒəst+   ²páhst+   ðat+

public   house.   Well,   we   were   born   there.   They
'pʌblɪk   ˌhɛŭs| wë̌   'wi•   wə↑ᵛbɒŭn   ˌðe•ǯ| ðeɪ̆
pə́blik+   ²háws¹↓   ²wel+   ³wíj+   wə³bówn+   ðèh¹↑   ¹ðej+

were   all   little   pumps.   And —
wə'rɒ•ł   lɪtł   ˌpʌmps| ɛn
wə³rówl+   litəl+   ¹pə́mps²↑   ²an+

AP: *Well,   when   I   was a child   there was a man*
'wëł| wen   ᵛɑɪ̆   wəzəˌtʃɑɪ̆łd| ðəwəzə'mɛ•ᵉn|
³wél¹↓   ²wen+   ³áj+   wəzətʃàjld¹↑   ²ðəwəzə³mán²|

had a coal shop on the corner, opposite our door.

‚ɛdə↑'kŏŏ‚ʃɔp ɔnðə‚kŏŭnə| 'ɔpəzɪt 'ɛ·ə ‚dɔ·ə̌|
²àdə³ḱə́wlʃòp+ onðə¹kównə¹↑ ³ópəzit+ áwə+ ¹dóh²↑

And - - - - over his coals, and emptied them into

'ɛ·nd 'œŭvərɪz ‚kŏŏz| ɛn 'emtˢɪdðəm 'ɪntˢʊ
¹ánd ³ə́wvəriz+ ¹ḱə́wlz²↑ ²an+ ²émtidðəm+ íntu+

the shed. He used to sweep his hut. And

ðə‚ʃeⁱd| ⁻i· 'jü·st tʰə↑'swi·p hɪz ‚hʌtʰ| ɛnd
ðə¹ʃéd²↑ ³ij+ ²júwst+ tə³swíjp+ hiz+ ¹hə́t²↑ ²and+

there he was — gather all the children round him,

'ðeə̌ri· ‚wɔz| ‚geðə'rɔ·ɫ ðə‚tʃïɫdrən ‚rḛ̄ndɪm|
³ðéhrij+ ²wóz¹↓ ²gàðə³rówl+ ðə¹tʃíldrən+ ràwndim²↑

and said,* 'Come on, children. Farthing a ride.'

ɛn ‚sed| ‚kʌm ‚ɔn ‚tʃïɫdrən| 'fɑ·ðɪŋ ə‚rɑ·ĭd|
²an+ sèd+| ³kə̀m+ ²ón+ tʃìldrən¹| ³fáhðiŋ+ ə¹rájd²↑

EC: *Only on a bank holiday.*

'œŭnlɪ ɔnə'beŋk ‚hɔlɪdĭi|
³ə́wnli+ onəbáŋk+ ²hólidij¹↓

AP: *And they went all round Shoreditch. Well,*

ɛnðæĭ wen't'sq·ŭ 'rḛ̄nd ʃoŭdɪtʃ| wëў
²anðej+ wen³tów+ ráwnd+ ²ʃówditʃ¹↓ ²wel+

that is how they got a living.

'ðɛts 'hḛ̄ 'ðɛĭ 'gɔtʰə ‚lɪvɪn|
³ðats+ háw+ ðéj+ gótə+ ²lívin¹↓

EC: *We used to have a lot of callers down*

'wi· 'jü·st tʰü· 'ɛvə ↑'lɔtə ‚kŏŭləz ‚dḛ̄n
³wíj+ júwst+ tuw+ ávə+ ³lótə+ ²kówləz+ dàwn+

our turnings. We had the gypsies coming through,

‚ḛ̄ ‚t'sɜ·nɪnz| ⁻wi 'ɛd ðə↑'dʒɪpsɪz 'kʌmɪn 'θrü·|
àw+ tə́hninz¹↑ ³wij+ ²ád+ ðə³dʒípsiz+ kə́min+ θrúw¹↓

and   *they*   *sold*   *the*   *lavender.*   *You*   *know*   *what*

ɛn   'ðæɪ   'sɔ̆ðd   ðəˌlɛvɪndə| jüˌnœŭ   wɔt

²an+   ³ðéj+   sə́wld+   ðə²lávində¹↓   ¹junəw+   wot+

lavender   *is?*   – – –   *Well,*   *I*   *believe*   *they*   *go*   *up*

ˌlɛvɪndəˌrɪz| ˌwëᴚ| a̤ĭ   bə'liᐧv   ðæɪ   'gœŭ   ˌʌp

¹lávindərìz²↑   ²wél¹| ²aj+   bə³líjv+   ðej+   gə́w+   əp+

the West   *End*   *now,*   *and*   *the Americans*   *give them a lot of*

ðə↑'west   ↑'end   ˌne̤ṳ̌| ɛn   ðəᵛmerɪkənz| ˌgɪvəmə'lɔtə

ðə³wést+   ⁴énd+   náw¹↑   ¹an+   ðə³mérikənz¹↑   ²gìvəmə³lótə+

money,   *going*   *along.*   – – – –   *They*   *pick it*   *from*   *the*

ˌmʌnĭi| 'gœŭɪn   əˌlɔŋ| ðæɪ   'pɪkɪt   frəm   ði·

²mə́nij¹↓   ²gə́win+   ə²lóŋ¹↓   ²ðej+   ³píkit+   frəm+   ðij+

hedgerows.   *Yes.*   *And*   *do you know what,*   *when we*

ˌeⁱdʒˌrœŭz| ˌjeᐧəs| ɛn   'düᐧjünœŭ   'wɔʔ   wen↑'wiᐧ

²édʒrəwz¹↓   ²jéhs¹↓   ²an+   ³dúwjuwnəw+   wót+   wen³wíj+

were little   *girls*   *we used*   *to have*   —*   *there used*

wə↑'lɪʔᵛ   ˌgᴣᵛz| wi'jüᐧst   tʰʊ'ɛv| ðeə̆'jüᐧst

wə³lítəl+   ¹gə́hlz²↑   ¹wij²júwst+   tuáv| ²ðeh³júwst+

to be   *a place just*   *over*   *there by St. Hilda's,*   *let*

tə'biᐧ   ə'plæɪs   dʒəs'tʰœŭvə   'ðeə̆   bɪsn̩ˌtʰïᴚdəz| 'let

təbíj+   əpléjs+   dʒəstə́wvə+   ðéh+   bisən²tíldəz¹↓   ³lét+

out   *perambulators.*   *Penny an hour.*   *And —*   *we used*

ˌe̤ǝ̤t   ↑'preməˌlæɪtəz| 'penɪ   əˌne̤ṳ̌ə| ˌɛᐧn   wɪˌjüᐧst

àwt+   ³práməlèjtəz¹↓   ³péni+   ə²náwə¹↓   ¹àn+   wijùwst+

to all   *go*   *over*   *Victoria*   *Park.*   *You've*

tʰʊ'ǫʊ   gœŭ   'œŭvə   vɪk'tʰǫʊrɪə   ˌpɑᐧk| jüᐧv

tu²ów+   gəw+   ə́wvə+   viktówriə+   ²páhk¹↓   ²juwv+

heard of Victoria   *Park?*   *And we all used to*   *go over*

'ᴣᐧdəv   vɪk'tʰǫʊrɪə   ↑ᵛpɑᐧk| ˌɛn   wɪ'ǫᐧlˌjüᐧstʰə   ˌgœŭ'œŭvə

³ə́hdəv+   viktówriə+   ³páhk¹↑   ¹àn+   wi²ówljùwstə+   gəwə́wvə+

there   when   we   were   kids.   And   we   used   to   say,
ˌðeə̆   ↑'wen   wi•   wə   ↑'kɪdz| ˌɛnd³   wɪˌjü•st   təˌsæĭ
ðèh+   ²wén+   wij+   wə+   ²kídz²↑   ²ànd+   wijùwst+   təsèj+

'Mother,   give   us   a   penny.   We'll†   have   a   perambulator
'mʌðə   ↑ᵛgɪvəs   əˌpenɪ| wɪˌrevə   'præməˌlæĭtʰə
²mə́ðə   ³gívəs+   əpèni¹↑   ²wiràvə+   ³prámələ̀jtə+

ride.' – – – – –
'rɑ̰ĭd|
rájd¹↓

AP: *We   used   to dance   round   the organs   them*
'wi•   'jü•st   tʰʊ'dɑ•ns   ˌrḛŭn   ði↑'o̰ŭgɪnz   ˌðem
³wíj+   júwst+   tudáhns+   ràwn+   ðij³ówginz+   ðèm+

days.   They   all   come   from   Italy.
ˌdɛĭz| –ðɛɪ   'o̰ŭ   'kʌm   frəm   ↑'ɪtˢəli•|
déjz¹↑   ³ðej+   ²ów+   kə́m+   frəm+   ³ítəlij¹↓

EC: *No,   they   did   not.   They   come   from*
'nœ•ŭ   ðæĭ   'dɪdn̦| ðæĭ   'kʌm   frəm
³náw+   ðej+   dídən¹↓   ¹ðej+   ²kə́m+   frəm+

Saffron   Hill.
↑'sæfən   ˌĭɣ|
³sáfən+   ²íl¹↓

AP: *Saffron   Hill,   where   all   the   Italians   live.*
'sæfən   ˌĭɣ| ¬weə̆'ro̰•ł   ði•   ɪ'tˢæljənz   ˌlɪv|
³sáfən+   ¹íl²↑   ³weh³rówl+   ðij+   itáljənz+   ²lív¹↓

EC: *The   Italians,   they   made them.   And it is a shame:*
ði•   ɪ'tʰæljənz| ðæĭ   'mæĭdəm| ænɪᵛtʰɪzəˌʃæĭm|
²ðij+   i³táljənz²| ²ðej+   ³méjdəm¹↓   ²ani³tízəʃèjm¹↑

† /r/ instead of /l/: a slip of the tongue? But see also p. 237 n.

the trade's gone right down. I was listening
ðə'træɪdz 'goʊn ↑'raɪt ˌdēᵍn| aɪwəz 'lɪsn̩ɪn
²ðə³tréjdz+ gówn+ ³rájt+ ²dáwn¹↓ ¹ajwəz+ ³lísənin+

to them, old Italian, on the wireless. He
't͡sü·əm ↑'ɔ̆ɫd ɪˌtʰæljən| 'ɔn ðə'wɑ·ɪəlɪs| i·
túwəm+ ³ə̆wld+ i²táljən¹| ³ón+ ðə²wájəlis¹↓ ²ij+

told me how he made all them barrel organs
't͡sɔ̆dmi· 'ēᵍri· 'mæɪd ↑'ǫ·ɫ ðem 'bærəˌlǫ·gɪnz
³təwldmij+ áwrij+ méjd+ ³ówl+ ðem+ bárəlòwginz+

in Saffron Hill. Clerkenwell. Have you
ɪn ↑'sæfən ˌɪ̆y̆| 'klə·kn̩ ˌwēɫ| 'ævjü
in+ ³sáfən+ ²íl¹↓ ³klɔ́hkən+ ²wél¹↓ ³ávjuw+

heard of it? Well, it is an Italian quarter. Holborn.
ˌə·dɔvɪtʰ| ˌwelɪtsən ɪ't͡sæljən ˌkwǫŭt͡sə| 'œŭbən|
²ə̆hdovit¹↓ ²wèlitsən+ i³táljən+ ²kwówtə¹↓ ³ə̆wbən¹↓

Well, that is it. That is it. I had a sister
wy 'ðæt ˌɪzɪt| ⁻ðætʰ ˌɪzɪt| ˌaɪæd əˌsɪstə
²wəl+ ³ðát+ ²ízit¹↓ ³ðat+ ²ízit¹↓ ²àjad+ əsìstə+

married Italian. That is where they live, Saffron
'mærɪd ɪ't͡sæljən| 'ðæts 'weə̆ 'ðɛɪ ˌlɪv| 'sæfən
³márid+ itáljən¹↓ ³ðáts+ wéh+ ðéj+ ²lív¹↓ ³sáfən+

Hill. 'Bout Holborn. And he made all them
ˌɪ̆y̆| ˌbēᵍt 'œŭbən| ˌæn i·ˌmæɪd 'ǫŭɫðem
²íl¹↓ ²bàwt+ ³ə̆wbən¹↓ ²àn+ ijmèjd+ ³ówlðem+

barrel organs. And I did love them. They used to
ˌbærəˌlǫŭgənz| 'æn aɪ̆ ˌdɪd ˌlʌvəm| ðɛɪ 'jü·stʰə
²bárəlòwgənz¹| ³án+ aj+ dìd+ ²lə́vəm¹| ²ðej+ ³júwstə+

let them out.
↑'letʰəm ˌēᵍt|
³létəm+ ²áwt¹↓

(ES: Do they not make them any more now then?)

EC: *No.*　　*Nobody*　　*wants*　　*them.*　　*All*　　*got*
　　'nœ•ŭ|　　'nœŭbədi　　↑'wɔnts　　ðəm|　　'ǫŭ　　gɔt
　　⁴nə́w²↓　　¹nə́wbədij+　　⁴wónts+　　ðəm²↓　　¹ów+　　gɔt+

wirelesses.　　*Nobody*　　*wants*　　*them.*　　*The*　　*world's*
'wa̱•əlısız|　　'nœŭbədi　　↑'wɔntsəm|　　　　ðə'wa̱ɣ̆dz
⁴wájəlisiz²↓　　¹nə́wbədij+　　⁴wóntsəm²↓　　²ðə²wə́hldz+

changed.　　*That*　　*was*　　*all*　　*old*　　*London.*　　*And*　　*then*
↑'tʃæĭndʒd|　　ˌðæt　　wə'zǫ•↑'lɔ̆ŏ　　↑'lʌndən|　　æn　　'ðen
⁴tʃéjndʒd²↓　　²ðàt+　　wə³zów³lə́wl+　　³lə́ndən¹↓　　¹an+　　²ðén+

there　　*was*　　*the*　　*Italians,*　　*with*　　*all*　　*their*　　*beautiful*
ˌðeə̆wəz　　ði　　ı't̩ˢæljənz|　　wı'vɔŏ　　ðeə̆　　'bjü•t̩ıfɤ
ðèhwəz+　　ðij　　i²táljənz²↑　　²wi³vówl+　　ðeh+　　bjúwtifəl+

costumes　　*on,*　　*with*　　*their*　　*birds,*　　*their*　　*little*
ˌkɔstü•mz　　ˌɔn|　　ˌwıð　　ðeə̆　　'bɜ•dz|　　ðeə̆　　'lıtɬ
¹kóstuwmz+　　òn²↑　　²wìð+　　ðeh+　　³bə́hdz¹↓　　²ðeh+　　³lítəl+

paroquets,　　*selling:*　　*Fortunes*　　*a penny.*　　*Give her a*
'pærə　　↑'ki•ts　　ˌselın|　　'fǫŭtʃənz|　　ə'penǎi|　　ᵛgıvɜ•rə
párə+　　³kíjts+　　sèlin¹↓　　³fówtʃənz¹↓　　²ə³pénij¹↓　　³gívəhrə+

penny,　　*the*　　*bird*　　*would*　　*come*　　*out,*　　*and*　　*they*
ˌpenı|　　ðə'bɜ•d　　wʊd　　↑'kʌm　　ˌḝə?|　　æn　　ðæĭ
pèni²↑　　¹ðə²bə́hd+　　wud+　　³kə́m+　　¹áwt²↑　　²an+　　ðej+

pick　　*a paper up,*　　*with its*　　*beak,*　　*to tell your fortune.*
'pık　　ə'pæĭpəˌrʌp|　　wıðıts　　'bi•k|　　tˢə'tˢeljə　　'fǫŭtʃən|
³pík+　　ə³péjpərəp¹↓　　²wiðits+　　³bíjk¹↓　　²tə³téljə+　　³fówtʃən¹↓

AP:　'*My*　　*little*　　*birds*　　*can*　　*tell.*'
　　'ma̱•ĭ　　lıtɬ　　'bɜ•dz　　kən　　ˌtˢëɬ|
　　³máj+　　litəl+　　bə́hdz+　　kən+　　²tél¹↓

EC: *And there was the old   baked   potato   man.*
    ɛn'ðeə̆   wəzðɪ↑'ɔ̆ŏd   'bæĭkt   pə‚kæĭtˢə   ‚mɛ·n|
    ²an²ðéh+   wəzði³ə́wld+   béjkt+   pə¹kéjtə+   màn²↑

I   say,   there   was   the   old   baked   potato   man.
ɑ̆ĭ‚sǽĭ   ðəwəzðɪ'ɔ̆ŏd   'bæĭkt   pə‚tˢæĭtʰə   ‚mɛ·n|
¹ajsèj+   ðəwəzði²ə́wld+   béjkt+   pə¹téjtə+   màn²↑

'All   hot,   halfpenny!'   Oh,   I   loved   old   London.
'ǫ·'lɔt| 'æĭpm̦ɪ| ‚·ǫ   ɑ̆ĭ'lʌvd   ‚œŭ̆ł   ‚lʌndən|
³ów²lót³↑   ²éjpəmi²↑   ²ŏh+   aj³lə́vd+   əwl+   ²lə́ndən²↓

AP: *'Baked   potatoes,   all   hot!'*
    'bæĭkt   pə't̪ˢæĭtˢəz| 'ǫ·'lɔt|
    ²béjkt+   pə³téjtəz³↑   ³ów²lót³↑

EC: *And   then   there   was   —   (an)   old   girl   used*
    ɛn'ðen   ðeə̆   wəz   ↑'ɔ̆ŏł   'gəł   ‚jü·st
    ²an³ðén+   ðeh+   wəz+   ³ə́wl+   gə́hl+   jùwst+

to   come   down   of   a   night,   selling   meaty   pies.
təkəm   'dɛ̱ə̱n   əvə‚nɑ̆ĭt| 'selɪn   ↑'mi·tʰɪ   ‚pɑ̆ĭz|
təkəm+   dáwn+   əvə²nájt²↑   ²sélin+   ³míjti+   ²pájz¹↓

AP: *Oh   yes.*
    'œŭ̆   ‚jɜ·s|
    ³ə́w+   ¹jə́hs²↑

EC: *She had a basket,   with a beautiful   clean   cloth*
    ʃɪ‚ɛdə   'bɑ·skɪt| wɪðə'bjü·t̪ɪfɤ   'kli·n   ‚klǫŭ̆θ
    ¹ʃiàdə+   ²báhskit²↑   ¹wiðə³bjúwtifəl+   klíjn+   ²klówθ+

over   it.   She   used   to   call   out   (singing)   'Meaty   pies,
‚œŭ̆vrɪt| ʃɪ‚jü·stə   'kǫ·lɛ̱ə̱t   ↑'mi·tʰi·   ‚pɑ̆ĭz
əwvrit¹↓   ²ʃijùwstə+   ²kówlawt+   ³míjtij+   ¹pájz⁖

all   hot!'
ǫ·‚lɔt|]
'owlòt²↑/

A Discussion at the Youth Club: Rock 'n Roll

(A discussion group gathered once a week in the youth club of the social settlement, under the leadership of a club worker. Only four boys were left in the room at the moment of the following discussion. These were among the more vocal members of the group, but even they did not feel quite at ease because of the presence of the stranger (i.e. the present writer) and her tape recorder. The slightly stilted style should probably be ascribed to their embarrassment. However, the style is stilted only as regards grammatical constructions and vocabulary, not in phonology.)

A: *No.*   *Well,*   *I*   *think*   *that*   *'Rocking*   *Round*   *the*
[ˌnœŭ| wəlɑ̰ĭ   ˌθɪŋk   'dɛt   'rɔkən   'rɛ̰ŭnðə
/²nə́w¹↓   ¹wəlaj+   θɪŋk+   ³ðát+   rókən   ráwnðə+

Clock'   *and*   *that*   —   *creates*   *a*   *frenzy*   *in*   *my*   *mind.*
↑ᵛklɔkənˌðɛt| ⁻krɪ'ɛĭtsə   ↑'frenzɪ   ɪnmɑ̰ĭ   'mɑ̰ĭn|
³klókənðàt¹↑   ³kri²éjtsə+   ³frénzi+   inmaj+   májn¹↓

The   *rhythm*   *of*   *the*   *music*   *can*   *create*   *quite*   *a*
ði·   'rɪdəm   əvðəˌmjü·zɪk| 'kæn   krɪ'ɛĭt   ↑'kwɑ̰ĭtə
²ðij+   ³ríðəm+   əvðəmjúwzik¹↑   ³kán+   kriéjt+   ³kwájtə+

frenzy.   *I*   *mean,*   *you*   *get*   —   *in*   *darkest*   *Africa,*   *say,*
'frenzɪ| ɑ̰ĭˌmi·n   jüˌgetˢᵊ   ɪn'dɑ·kɪst   ↑'æfrɪkə   'sæĭ|
³frénzi¹↓   ¹ajmìjn+   juwgèt+   in²dáhkist+   ³áfrikə+   séj¹↓

mere   *beat*   *of*   *a*   *drum . . . .*
'mɪ̆   'bi·tʰəvə   ↑'drʌm|
²míh+   bíjtəvə+   ³drə́m¹↓

B: *I*   *was*   *sitting*   *indoors*   *last*   *night.*   *My*
ˌɑ̰ĭwəz   ˌsɪʔn̩   ɪnᵛdɔ·z   ˌlɑ·st   ˌnɑ̰ĭt| 'mɑ̰ĭ
²àjwəz+   sìtən+   in³dóhz+   làhst+   nàjt¹↑   ³máj+

sister   *can't*   *dance.*   *She was*   *listening*   *to Bill*   *Haley,*
'sɪstə   'kɑ·nt   ˌdɑ·ns| 'ʃi·wəz   'lɪsn̩ɪn   tˢʊbɪ↑'læĭlɪ|
sístə+   káhnt+   ²dáhns¹↓   ³ʃíjwəz+   lísənin+   tubi³léjli¹↓

TEXTS   259

and	I	said	for	a	lark,	'Come	on,	Sis,	let's
ənd³	'aĭ	sed	fərə͵la·k|			ᵛkʌmən	͵sɪs|		'lets
²ənd+	²áj+	sed+	fərə¹láhk¹↑			³kə́mən+	sìs¹↑		³léts+

jive.'	And	she	started!		She	can't	jive.
͵dʒaĭv|	ņ'ʃi·	↑'sta·ʔɪd|		ʃi'ka·nt		'dʒaĭv|	
²dʒájv¹↓	¹ən²ʃíj+	³stáhtid¹↓		²ʃij³káhnt+		³dʒájv¹↓	

She	just	jumps	up	and	off	she	went.	She	was —
ʃi	͵dʒɪst	'dʒʌmps	'ʌp	ņ'ɔf		ʃi	↑'went|		'ʃi·wəz
²ʃij+	dʒìst+	²dʒə́mps+	ə́p+	ənóf+		ʃij³wént¹↓		³ʃíjwəz+	

She	was	just	getting	in	the	frenzy	of	the	music.
'ʃi·wəz	dʒəst	͵geʔņ|		ņðə͵frenzɪəv			ðə↑'mjü·zɪk|		
³ʃíjwəz+	dʒəst+	¹gétən²|		²ənðəfrènziəv+		ðə³mjúwzik¹↓			

C: It is so lively, it makes you feel, well, not

its 'sœŭ ͵laĭvlɪ\| ɪt'mɛĭksjü 'fïy̆ wɤ ↑'nɔt

²its+ ³sə́w+ ²lájvli¹\| ²it²méjksju+ fíl+ wəl+ ³nót+

actually happy, but you — you feel as if you. . . .

'æktʃəli· ↑'hæpi·\| bət jü· jü· ᵛfɪlæzɪfjü·

áktʃəlij+ ³hápij¹\| ²bət+ juw+ juw+ ³fílazifjuw+

(The rest is drowned by noise.)   I   do.

'aĭ ͵dŭü\|
³áj+ dúw¹↑

A: It seems to hypnotize you.

ɪt 'si·mz tʰə ↑'hɪpnə͵ta·ĭzjü·\|

²it+ ²síjmz+ tə+ ³hípnətàjzjuw¹↓

B: You feel like moving around. You can't

jü· 'fïy̆\| ͵laĭk 'mü·vɪn ə↑'re͟g̱n\| jɪ'ka·nt

²juw+ ³fíl²\| ²làjk+ ²múwvin+ ə³ráwn¹↓ ²ji³káhnt+

just sit there and listen to the music. Everyone

dʒəs ↑'sɪt ðeə̌rən ↑'lɪsən tˢəðə'mjü·zɪk\| 'evrɪ͵wʌn\|

dʒəs+ ³sít+ ðehrən+ ³lísən+ təðəmjúwzik¹↓ ³évriwə̀n¹\|

gets	on	moving.	Even	just	sitting	there,
'get's	'ɔn	↑'mŭüvɪn|	'i•vən	dʒəs	↑'sɪʔɳ̊ðeə̌|	
³géts+	ón+	³múwvin¹↓	²íjvən+	dʒəs+	²sítənðeh¹|	

going	like	that,	flicking	your	thumb-nail	or	something.
'gœŭɪn	lɑ̠ə̆k	'dæʔ|	'flɪkɳ	jɔ•↑'θʌm	ˌnæǐlɔ•	ˌsʌmðɪn|	
¹gə́win+	lajk+	²ðát²↑	¹flíkən+	joh³θə́m+	nèjloh+	səmðin¹↓	

You	got	(to)	get	on	the	move	somehow.
jü•	ᵛgɔʔ	ˌgeʔ	ɔnðəˌmŭüv|	'sʌm	ˌɛ̆ŭ|		
²juw+	³gót+	gèt+	onðəmùwv¹↑	³sə́m+àw¹↓			

A:
It	is	just	that	it	goes	a	bit	further	than	that,
ɪts	'dʒʌs	ðət̬ɪt	↑'gœŭzəˌbɪt'	↑ᵛfɜ•ðə	ðənˌðæt|					
²its+	³dʒə́s+	ðətit+	³gə́wzəbìt+	³fə́hðə+	ðənðàt¹↑					

and —
ən³
²ən

B:
And	if	you	sit	there	doing	nothing,	you've	got
ə'nɪf	jü•↑'sɪt'	ˌðeə̌	↑'dü•ɪn	↑'nʌθɪŋ|	jü•v'gɔt'			
¹ə²níf+	juw²sít+	ðèh+	²dúwin+	³nə́θiŋ¹↓	¹juwv²gót+			

that	—	got	it	in	your	brain,	going	boom,	boom,
ðɛt	↑'gɔt̬ɪt	ɪn	jə	↑'bræǐn|	ˌgœ̈ɪn	'bʊm	'bʊm		
ðat+	²gótit+	in+	jə+	³bréjn¹|	¹gə̀win+	²búm+	búm+		

boom,†	all	the	time.
'bʊm|	'ǫ•ɫðə	ˌt͡sɑ̠•ɪm|	
búm|	³ówlðə+	²tájm¹↓	

D:
But	with	the	teddy	boys,	when	they	all
bət	'wɪð	ðə↑'tʰedɪˌbɔɪz|			wen'ðæǐ	'ǫ•ɫ	
²bət+	³wíð+	ðə³tédibòjz¹|			²wen³ðéj+	ówl+	

go	mad,	and	all	that,	all	that*	what	was
ˌgœŭ	↑'mæ•d|	ə'nǫ•ɫ	ˌðæʔ|	'ǫ•ɫ	'ðæʔ|	ˌwɔʔ	wəz	
gə̀w+	³mád¹|	²ə³nówl+	²ðát¹|	³ówl+	ðát+|	¹wòt+	wəz+	

† Boom, boom, boom is intonationless, being chanted on a monotone.

in the paper about them, rioting, I do not believe
ɪnðə'pæɪprə‚bɛ͟ə̆ʔm̩| 'rɑ·ɪ̆ətˢɪn| ɑ̆ɪ 'dœŭnt bə'li·v
inðə³péjprəbàwtəm²| ³rájətin¹| ²aj+ ³dɔ́wnt+ bəlíjv+

that — that is because the music got hold of them.
↑'ðæt ↑'ðæʔ ɪz bɪ‚kɔzðə↑'mjü·zɪk ‚gɔʔ ↑'hŏŏdɔvəm|
³ðát+ ³ðát+ iz+ bikòzðə³mjúwzik+ gòt+ ³hɔ́wldovəm¹↓

I believe it's because some peo — *the people who*
'ɑ̆ɪ bə'li·v ɪts bɪ‚kɔz ↑'sʌm ‚pi·| ðə'pi·pɫ u·
³áj+ bəlíjv+ its+ bikòz+ ³sə́m+ pìj| ²ðə³píjpəl+ uw+

have got the music in their mind, and that, who it
↑ᵛæv ‚gɔt ðə‚mjü·zɪk ɪnðeə̆ ‚mɑ·ɪ̆nd ən‚ðæt| u· ɪt
³áv+ gòt+ ðəmjùwzik+ inðeh+ màjnd+ ənðàt¹↑ ²uw+ it+

does really get a hold of — well, far and few
'dʌz ↑'rɪə̆li ‚geţə ‚hŏŏɫdɔv| ‚wĕš̆| 'fɑ· ən↑'fjü·
³dɔ́z+ ³ríhlij+ gètə+ hɔ́wldov¹↑ ¹wél¹↑ ³fáh+ ən³fjúw+

between, but — they've done it, they've got talked
bɪ↑'twi·n| bət 'ðeɪ̆v ‚dʌnɪt| ðeɪ̆v ‚gɔt ᵛtˢo̯·kt
bi³twíjn¹| ²bət+ ³ðéjv+ də́nit¹↑ ²ðejv+ gòt+ ³tówkt+

about, and it seems a natural thing now, that
ə‚bɛ͟ə̆ʔ| æn ɪt 'si·mz ə'nætʃrəɫ ↑ᵛθɪŋ ‚nɛŭ| ðət
əbàwt¹↑ ¹an+ it+ ²síjmz+ ənátʃrəl+ ³θíŋ+ nàw¹↑ ²ðət+

people want to do it, because they want to be
'pi·px ↑ᵛwont tʰə‚du·ɪt| bɪko̯·z 'ðæɪ̆ ‚wont tʰəbi
²píjpəl+ ³wónt+ tədùwit¹↑ ²bikowz+ ³ðéj+ wònt+ təbij+

talked about. I do not think it makes
'tʰo̯·ktə‚bɛ͟ə̆t| ɑ̆ɪ 'dœŭnt ‚θɪŋk| ɪt 'mɛɪ̆ks
tówktəbàwt¹↓ ²aj+ ³dɔ́wnt+ θìŋk²| ²it+ ³méjks+

you go like that, because — I know I liked it
jü‚gœŭ lɑ̆ɪk ‚ðæt| bɪkəz ɑ̆ɪ 'nœŭ ɑ̆ɪ 'lɑ̆ɪktɪʔ
juwgə̀w+ lajk+ ðàt¹| ²bikəz+ aj+ ³nə́w+ aj+ lájktit+

and	*all*	*that,*	*but*	*I —**	*it*	*do*	*not*	*make*	*me*
ə͵nǫ·ɫ	͵ðæ·ʔ‖	bət	'ɑ̤ǐ‖	ɪt	'dœŭm	͵mɛĭk	↑'mi·
ənówl+	ðàt¹↑	¹bət+	³ɑ́j‖	²it+	³də́wm+	mèjk+	³míj+

going	*like*	*that.*	*I*	*mean,*	*it*	*makes*	*me*	*tapping*
͵gö̈ən	lɑ̤ĭk	͵ðæʔ‖	ɑ̤ǐ͵mi·n	ɪʔ	'mɛĭks	mi	↑'tˢæpɪn
gə́wən+	lajk+	ðàt¹↑	²ajmìjn+	it+	³méjks+	mij+	³tápin+

my	*foot,*	*and*	*things*	*like*	*that.*	*I*	*think*	*that*	*is*
mɪ↑'fʊʔ	ņ	↑ᵛθɪŋz	lɑ̤ĭk	͵ðæʔ‖	ɑ̤ǐ	'θɪŋk	ðæts
mi³fút+	ən+	³θíŋz+	lajk+	ðàt¹↑	²aj+	³θíŋk+	ðats+

as	*far*	*as*	*it*	*goes.*
əz	↑'fɑ·	əzɪt	'gœŭz‖]
əz+	³fáh+	əzit+	³gə́wz²↓/

Index

1. GENERAL INDEX

2. INDEX OF SOUNDS

This is an index of syllable peaks and of consonants, as well as of a few phonetic segments of special interest. The phonemic segments appear in the same order as in 2.2.

3. INDEX OF WORDS

This index relates to phonological problems. Only those words are included (1) which either differ, or are said to differ, from RP in their phonological composition, (2) which are quoted in connection with a discussion of phonemic analysis, or (3) which are of special interest in other respects.

Thus, the index does not contain (1) groups of words (with a few exceptions), (2) words which are quoted as examples of allophonic variation, including syllable cut (for such problems, see Index of Sounds), and (3) words cited as examples of a phoneme distribution which is the same as in RP.

4. INDEX OF AUTHORS